WORLD WAR II
SACRAMENTO

WORLD WAR II SACRAMENTO

★

Special Collections of the Sacramento Public Library

The History Press

Published by The History Press
Charleston, SC
www.historypress.com

First published 2018

Manufactured in the United States

ISBN 9781467138086

Library of Congress Control Number: 2017963235

Notice: The information in this book is true and complete to the best of our knowledge. It is offered without guarantee on the part of the authors or The History Press. The authors and The History Press disclaim all liability in connection with the use of this book.

For Amanda's daughter, Amelia
For James's son, Liam
For Eric's father, Don, and his wife, Colette

CONTENTS

PROLOGUE

In the Sacramento County farming community of Florin, located some eight miles southeast of the state capitol building, sixteen-year-old Florence Nobuko didn't know what to make of it all. She and her siblings were leaving a late-morning service at the Florin Methodist Church when they heard that something terrible had just happened in Hawaii. It was during the drive back home that news crackled out over the car radio, at last confirming the Japanese attack on Pearl Harbor. They pulled into the driveway of the family's twelve-acre grape and berry farm on Florin Road and quickly entered their one-story home. Inside, Nobuko saw her parents staring across the living room as if they had both seen a ghost. Her mother told the group that, moments earlier, a

> *picture of the Palace of Versailles—which had hung above the piano ever since* [she] *could remember—fell and knocked the world globe to the floor. It was probably a coincidence but it was eerie that the picture, symbolizing the place where the peace treaty was signed after World War I, would crash at approximately the same time as peace was being shattered.*[1]

It surely didn't occur to the Nobukos in December 1941 that they were living out *the* defining event of the twentieth century and one that, over a three-and-a-half-year period, would claim the lives of over 400,000 Americans (including 477 Sacramentans), turn the United States into a superpower and transform the capital city in nearly every conceivable way.

In the following pages, we will attempt to tell the story of Sacramento during World War II. The idea of covering the "next war" was a natural progression from the Sacramento Public Library's previous work, *World War I and the Sacramento Valley*, published by The History Press in 2016. Much like that book, source materials for this title were almost all primary in nature, with most coming from the Special Collections of the Sacramento Public Library and the Central Library's third-floor periodicals collection. Ephemera, newspaper articles, government documents, oral histories and the rare monograph form the bibliographic backbone.

Coverage is demarcated on one end by Pearl Harbor and on the other by the first few years after the war. That said, for needed context, a smattering of topics prior to—and after—the war will be discussed in the introduction and conclusion. Rather than viewing this book as a unified narrative, we encourage the reader to regard each chapter as a unique essay dedicated to a specific portion of the area's World War II experience as opposed to following a sequential timeline. Geographically, the book's purview is Sacramento County. Events from outer counties may be used to buttress assertions and better explain themes, but considering the vast array of information on the war, it was essential that the book's focus be kept sharply on the county.

To avoid confusion with terminology, please note the following. McClellan Field, the Sacramento Air Depot and the Sacramento Air Service Command all refer to the same installation north of Sacramento proper. The Signal Depot at North Seventh and B Streets was a procurement and transport facility for signal equipment, while signalmen (e.g. radio operators, linemen) were trained at Camp Kohler, a completely separate spot, also located north of the central city. Lastly, the term Civilian Defense was predominant during World War II and will be used instead of the more familiar Civil Defense, which was adopted during the Cold War.

Also note that almost all content relating to the Signal Depot will be discussed within the war work chapter, "With One Purpose: Sacramento's War Work." This, in spite of the depot being firmly under military jurisdiction, will smooth out the war work narrative and eliminate any redundancy between chapters.

Finally, for fear of replicating recent scholarship, we have elected not to provide an in-depth chapter on the internment of the Sacramento area's Japanese American residents. Previous historians—in particular, Kevin Wildie with his excellent *Sacramento's Historic Japantown: Legacy of a Lost Neighborhood* (The History Press, 2013) and Wayne Maeda's classic *Changing Dreams and Treasured Memories: A Story of Japanese Americans in the Sacramento*

Region (Sacramento Japanese American Citizens League, 2000)—have told the story well and somewhat exhaustively. Instead, readers will find that meaningful content about the topic surfaces throughout the book.

The Nobuko family never returned to Florin. Amid the chaos of Japanese American internment, Florence's father sold the farm, which had been central to family life and labor since 1912, for a pittance of its actual worth. After confinement at Tule Lake, California, and Topaz, Utah, the clan fragmented, resettling in Colorado, Missouri and Illinois. Without the war, it's arguable that none of this would have happened, and yet the Nobukos were just one Sacramento County family among thousands, whether Japanese, Anglo, African or Mexican American, who had to make their own way through nearly 1,400 straight days of uncertainty. If the story of the Nobuko family offers a narrow window into wartime Sacramento, it's the authors' sincere hope that the following pages provide an even wider view of a city and county straining their way toward victory under the lofty demands of total war.

ACKNOWLEDGEMENTS

We gratefully acknowledge the contributions of the following individuals: Sacramento Public Library director Rivkah Sass, Central Library manager Jessica Jupitus, Central Library supervisor Stephanie Manansala, Arden-Dimick Library supervisor Kerri Moore, Central librarian Gerald Ward and library communications analyst Linda Beymer.

We also appreciate the passionate and dedicated assistance of our library and archives colleagues in providing many of the images used in this book. They include Rebecca Crowther, Alex Guilbert and Dylan McDonald of the Center for Sacramento History, Caroline Harker of the Sacramento City College Archives, Kathleen Correia of the California State Library's California History Section and our friends at the California State Archives and the Bancroft Library at the University of California–Berkeley. We also acknowledge the assistance of Kate Igoe of the Smithsonian National Air and Space Museum, Melissa Salrin of the Whitman College and Northwest Archives, Peter Detwiler of Troop One of the Sacramento Boy Scouts of America, Ray Meyer of the Aerospace Museum of California and film and radio historian Matías Bombal.

We are indebted to Mick and J.R. Voss for their very kind assistance in telling the story of their father, Jack Voss, and Patricia Woo in telling the story of her brother, Joe Wayne Fong. Linda Osuna and Todd Laney also graciously provided terrific images of their fathers for the book.

Finally, and perhaps most importantly, we are grateful for the day-to-day contributions of our patrons. It is through their passion and curiosity that we are inspired to be the very best that we can be. Together, we are an irrepressible force for illumination.

INTRODUCTION

By James C. Scott

By December 1941, Sacramento, like the rest of America, was beginning to experience a turn of fortune so longed for since the shock of the Great Depression sent the city's unemployment rate to a dizzying 27 percent in 1932. Curtis Park's Western Pacific shops laid off two-thirds of its workforce. Benevolent organizations like the Community Chest and Salvation Army were overrun by the needy. The Libby, McNeil and Libby cannery on Alhambra and Stockton Boulevards made regional headlines for giving its surplus fruits and vegetables to struggling families, and a veritable second city of Hoovervilles—many known by creative names like Skunk Hollow, Shooksville (named for founder and de facto "mayor" Samuel Shooks), Rotten Egg and Rattlesnake—grew along the B Street Levee, stretches of Gardenland and the southern banks of the American River near present-day Rancho Cordova, a spot immortalized by photographer Dorothea Lange. In total, the Sacramento area's Hoovervilles provided shelter to nearly three thousand indigent citizens.

With the approach of summer 1933, however, the National Industrial Recovery Act was beginning to make incremental gains in the region as part of President Franklin D. Roosevelt's New Deal legislation. $7 million of federal funding, powered by the Public Works Administration (PWA) and Works Progress Administration (WPA), put thousands to work building the Tower Bridge, Grant Union and C.K. McClatchy High Schools, the auditorium at Sacramento Junior College, three of the world's largest overhead water tanks, and an Art Deco–style fire

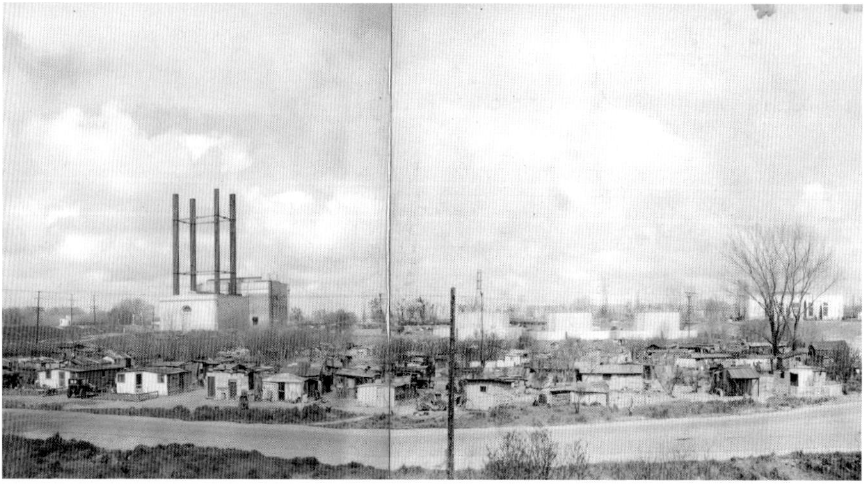

Sacramento's Jibboom Street Hooverville, 1935. The PG&E power station sits at left, while at right is the city's water filtration plant. *Bancroft Library, University of California–Berkeley.*

control station within Winn Park at Twenty-Eighth and P Streets. Even out-of-work librarians found meaningful employment through the PWA, creating a true masterwork with the 1900–39 index of the *Sacramento Bee* and *Union*. This doesn't include the countywide construction of nearly forty other public buildings and the laying of some 220 miles of fresh highway.[2]

At decade's end, the Sacramento economy had finally steadied, evidenced in part by substantial gains in sales tax collections between 1934 and 1937.[3] The recovery enabled the city's citizens to pivot from domestic concerns to new ones festering abroad. The city's Tuesday Clubhouse, located at Twenty-Eighth and L Streets, ran a weekly program called the Sacramento Community Forum, where scholars from Harvard University to Sacramento Junior College delivered lectures on various topics of the day prior to engaging in open discussion with attendees on those same topics. Programs from 1936 and 1937 covered "The Problem of War and Peace and Europe and Asia," "Our European Policy: Isolation or Cooperation" and "What's Happened in Austria Since 1936." But perhaps the greatest sign of the Capital City's changing priorities came with the acquisition of the Sacramento Air Depot in 1938 and the rehabilitation of Mather Field in 1940–41, both bases offering ample proof that Sacramento and the nation, far from looking for a fight, would be ready if one ever came looking for them.

Based on what we now know would be dark days to come, the mundane tenor of Sacramento on December 6, 1941, almost appears staged. One thousand Sacramento children packed the Roxie Theater at 914 Ninth Street to meet Santa Claus, a rush was being put on the construction of a $550,000 viaduct connecting Sacramento and North Sacramento and members of the Sacramento Safety Council were painting "Look Before You Cross" on downtown street corners—just in time for three thousand Shriners who were set to march from the Southern Pacific depot on Fourth and I Streets to Memorial Auditorium at Sixteenth and J Streets for the initiation of sixty new nobles.

The morning to follow—December 7—saw a penniless Private Bob Andrews stuck at a quiet Mather Field while most of his comrades were off-base, taking advantage of weekend leave in Sacramento. Andrews's Sunday had thus far consisted of strolling about the base, taking photographs of the flight line and a not-so-mighty air force of T-6 Texan trainers, and lounging around Jefferson Barracks waiting to hear the New York Philharmonic Orchestra's presentation of Brahms and Shostakovich on KROY, Sacramento's Columbia Broadcasting System affiliate at 1240 on the standard band. Programming had just started when John Daly suddenly cut in with these unforgettable words: "We interrupt this program to bring you a special news bulletin. The Japanese have attacked Pearl Harbor, Hawaii by air." In the chaos to follow, Andrews remembered being issued a World War I–era British-made Lee-Enfield rifle, five clips of ammunition and a bayonet. By 3:00 p.m., all of Mather's T-6s had been armed with 30-caliber machine guns—two behind the propeller and one in the rear of the canopy—and all personnel were called back from leave and guard duty doubled.

For a carrier task force to get within two hundred nautical miles of a major American military installation without detection and then go on to vanquish a formidable enemy was an extraordinary feat, one that had been accomplished only once before—a year earlier, in fact, when British carrier-borne planes successfully attacked Italy's *Regia Marina* at Taranto Bay. Suddenly, in the eyes of the world, what hadn't seemed conscionable just hours and days earlier now was. Accordingly, cities all along the West Coast sought to plan for any conceivable eventuality. In the Sacramento region, facilities and dams of the Central Valley Project and Pacific Gas and Electric were placed under heavy guard and forest-fire lookouts throughout the Sierra Nevada Mountains were put on high alert for fear of arson. Perhaps the most visible sign of change in Sacramento

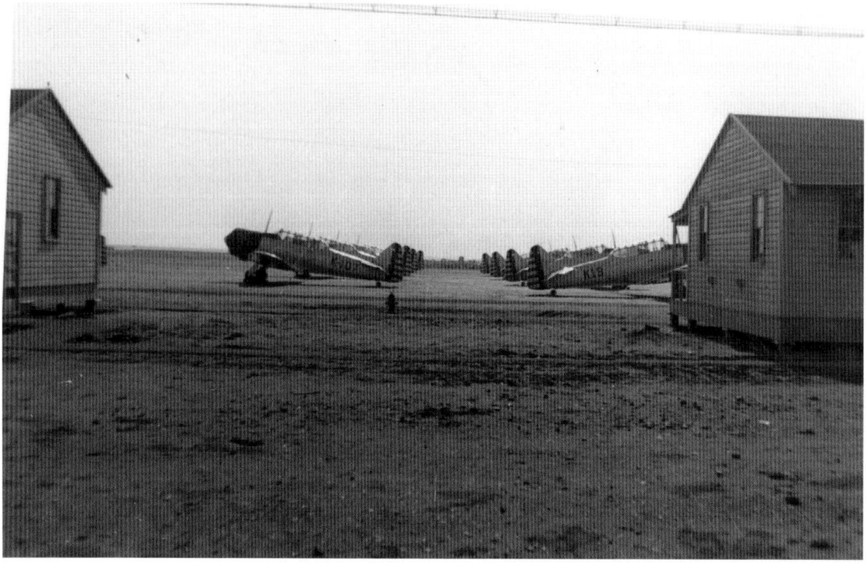

Pictured on the morning of December 7, 1941, are a few of Mather Field's T-6 Texans as photographed by Bob Andrews. *Center for Sacramento History*.

proper came with the blackout of the typically illuminated capitol dome. Beyond that, units of the California National Guard were on twenty-four-hour guard duty at the Tower and I Street bridges, the KROY radio transmitter and the city's water filtration plant. The Sacramento City Fire Department delivered sand—some twenty-five thousand pounds of it—to residents, businesses and schools throughout the city to extinguish flames in the event of an incendiary bomb attack. By 2:00 p.m. on December 7, hundreds of Sacramento Air Depot (SAD) employees were ordered back to work, and despite massive traffic jams inundating both Roseville Road and Watt Avenue en route to the airbase, several B-26s and P-40s were on their way to Alaska by midnight.[4] SAD pilots were also told to be on high alert for possible combat.

The aftermath of December 7 saw Capital City residents experience a broad spectrum of emotions. Some wanted to die. Maxine Parvin of 718 Tenth Street and Mattie Jones of North Sacramento both took poison to escape the dread that their husbands, both in the military, would be sent off to war zones. Though they went on to recover at the county hospital, Japanese American celery worker T. Okada, who, in his despondence over the attack on Pearl Harbor, hanged himself, was less fortunate. The native-born American and Lodi resident wrote in a parting note, "Everyone is so kind to me here. Let me die in the United States."[5]

Other Sacramentans just wanted to throw fists. Known bruiser Raymond Schneringer and an unnamed Japanese American duked it out over the declaration of war at a restaurant on the first floor of the Enterprise Hotel at 914 Second Street, and Schneringer was sent to the hospital with cuts and bruises.

And some just wanted to show how American they really were. On the afternoon of December 7—just hours after the announcement of the Pearl Harbor attack—seventeen-year-old Sacramento High School graduate and Sacramento Junior College (SJC) student Fumiko Yabe stood in the Sacramento Junior College auditorium to perform "Some Fine Day," an aria from *Madame Butterfly*. Before doing so, she announced, "I know that none of us feel up to a performance this evening given what happened this morning….Would you all join me in singing the 'Star-Spangled Banner'?" During a follow-up production on December 8, Yabe again performed the national anthem—a rendition the *Sacramento Bee* called a symbol of "the ideals of Christianity and of racial tolerance for which America stands."[6] Although written with the best of intentions, the story neglected to mention that while Yabe performed, FBI agents were arresting Rikitaro Sato, a resident of 410 N Street and president of the Sacramento Valley Japanese Association. Pictures of Yabe and Sato sat side-by-side in the *Sacramento Bee*'s December 8, 1941 issue, and President Roosevelt's Executive Order 9066, which called for the ordered evacuation of all residents of Japanese ancestry, sealed the fate of Yabe, Sato and thousands of other Americans for the duration of the war.

And yet amid the anxiety and uncertainty of a city revving up for war, *Sacramento Union* columnist Ada Weeks pleaded with citizens in a December 13, 1941 column to come to their senses and realize that "Life Goes On." "Why are people getting panicky and cancelling any number of prearranged affairs?" she asked. "Churches are afraid to have socials…[and] organizations are calling off pre-Christmas parties." Not a week into total war, Weeks's expectations were lofty, hoping that Americans could follow the stoicism of their English cousins. Excepting those Americans who were on the verge of internment, Weeks's point had merit in that social interaction, as she put it, "gives us contrast against dark thoughts and thoughts that might otherwise overtake us."[7] This spirit was perhaps best expressed through a children's Christmas show—boasting a cast of eight hundred boys and girls—that was performed to the delight of an audience of four thousand at Memorial

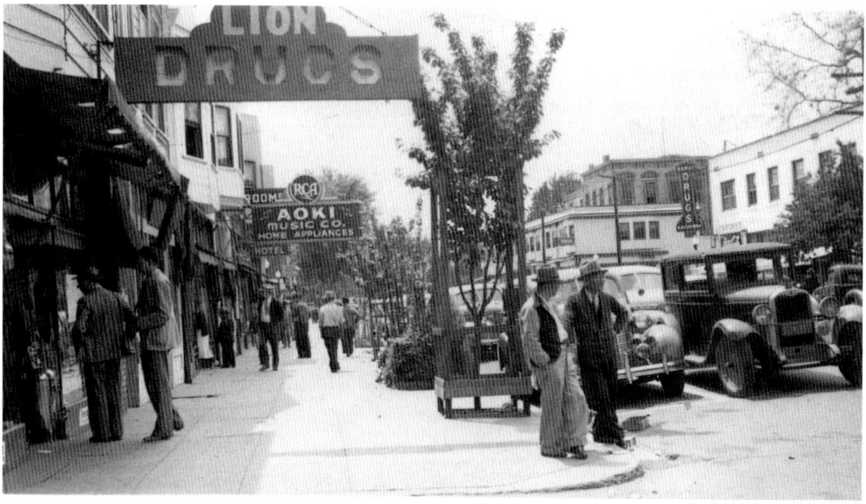

Pictured on May 9, 1942, is the corner of Fourth and L Streets, the heart of Sacramento's Japantown neighborhood. *Center for Sacramento History.*

Auditorium on December 12. The show went on despite heavy rain and a complete blackout of the city.

On the same day that Weeks's article ran, word appeared that Sacramento's first fatality of a war barely a week old was Ensign David Lester Cole of 2674 Franklin Boulevard. Cole, a graduate of both Sacramento High School and Sacramento Junior College, was known to be a good student who enjoyed botany, but his future was firmly focused on seeing the world with the U.S. Navy. He went on to serve as a Range Keeper Operator (RKO) for a series of batteries on the starboard side of the USS *Arizona*, set along Battleship Row, Pearl Harbor, Hawaii. Roughly a year after Cole received his commission on the deck of the USS *Illinois* in New York Harbor, Japanese "Kate" bombers, flying at an altitude of roughly ten thousand feet, dropped the bombs that hit one of the *Arizona*'s forward magazines. Seven seconds after impact, the resulting explosion—cataclysmic in size—tore the ship apart, ingesting so much oxygen that it put out fires on the nearby repair ship USS *Vestal*. Like so many of his *Arizona* shipmates, Cole's body was never recovered, making his Gold Star the first of hundreds to be given out to Sacramento County parents over the next three and a half years.

The outbreak of war predicated the emergence of the University of California's agricultural extension at Davis and its salient impact on local

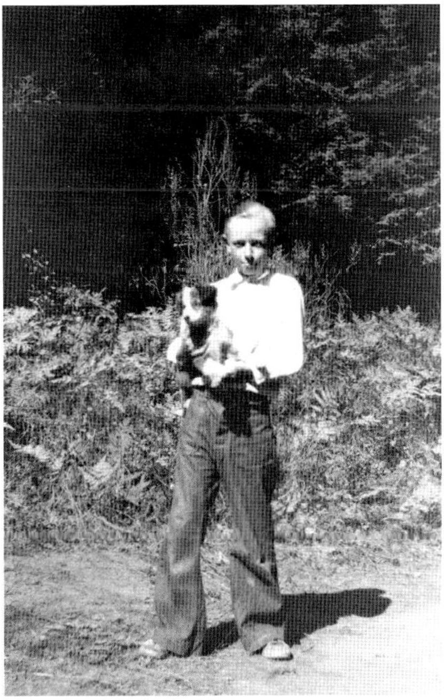

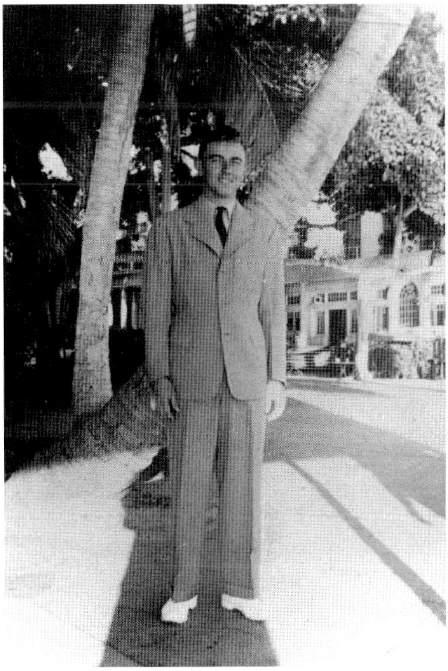

Left: With puppy in arm, David Lester Cole enjoys an idyllic childhood in 1930s Sacramento. *Center for Sacramento History*.

Right: Ensign David Lester Cole poses while on liberty at Waikiki Beach, Honolulu, Hawaii. *Center for Sacramento History*.

and national agricultural and food policy. Under the guidance of Elmer Stanley, the school's Sacramento County extension—one whose roots ran back to 1917 and World War I—came to ease the Depression-era plight of hundreds of farmers, including that of Leavitt Swalley, whose Natomas-based Swallow's Nest Farm was saved nearly 75 percent in costs by way of a streamlined irrigation system. The war demanded an acceleration of outreach efforts, and Davis dispatched a veritable army of agricultural experts to assist farmers while also coordinating the region's attack on labor shortages in the agricultural sector. Their successful efforts, most notably the ability to take classroom innovation and transform it into practical applications in the region's fields, ushered in an era of modern farming and vaulted the School of Agriculture to national, even global prominence.

Between the sad news of a fallen classmate and the inspirational magic of a child's Christmas, most Sacramentans embraced their new reality, partly out of patriotic duty and partly out of a simple desire to stay busy in the face of what had the makings of a long and costly conflict. Just as they had twenty-four years earlier during World War I, a small but eager industrial base, a determined military and civilian workforce, an aggressive plan for civilian defense, the reemergence of America's great tradition of citizen soldiery and a talent for courting military might all came together to set a brave pace for wartime Sacramento. The burdens of war also attracted the talents of countless Americans, diversified the cultural face of the region and showed the world that no nation, region or climate could match the agricultural innovation and production power of the Sacramento Valley. And yet, the old bugbear of what a democracy faces when its cherished civil liberties become juxtaposed with the imperatives of national security was never too far away. Although not always apparent at the time, the nation's inability to grasp right from wrong seems to have cast an immutable pall over those days that saw the Capital City almost entirely at its best and, for some measure, at its worst.

1

A CITIZENS' ARMY, READY FOR ACTION

BY AMANDA G. DEWILDE

On the night of December 8, 1941, Sacramento darkened its windows for the first blackout of the war after San Francisco reported that a large group of unidentified planes had approached the Golden Gate. At 7:34 p.m., local government officials received the first alert, which then spread by radio, telephone and word of mouth. Residents, shop owners and government offices turned off all lights, even those illuminating the capitol dome. Because this was Sacramento's first blackout, observance was spotty, even as tensions ran high. In addition to high-profile lighted bridges and water towers, Sacramento's billboards and streetlights remained lit because nobody could figure out how to switch them off. At 8:48 p.m., the blackout ended, and the following day, local police deemed it "not very successful."[8] This first blackout was one of many in the nights to follow as the region perfected its response. It signaled the first time that Sacramentans had to brace for an attack on home soil as the city entered into a total war.

While Sacramento had little to fear from the European war making its way to the region, the bombing of Pearl Harbor turned attention to the Pacific. World War II was the first global total war, in which civilians were now considered targets, and the West Coast stood on alert to respond to the threat of sabotage or bombing by Imperial Japan. In the era before the invention of the atomic bomb and intercontinental ballistic missiles, the city readied for threats of surprise aerial assault and the launch of rockets from submarines parked just off the coast. Sacramentans were concerned with fires, flying glass and gas rather than atomic blast and nuclear fallout.

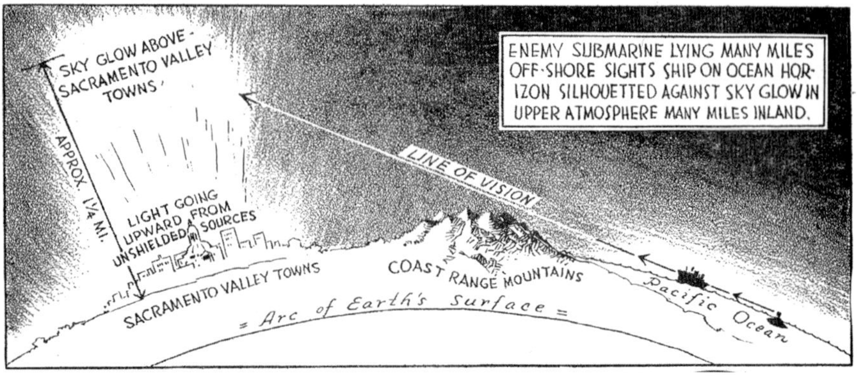

An illustration from the February 6, 1943 issue of *The Volunteer* shows how an enemy submarine might target an illuminated Sacramento. *Sacramento Public Library.*

Civilian Defense, composed of a corps of volunteers trained to defend their communities, was established prior to the war and came to the forefront after Pearl Harbor, with the fervor over preparedness building to a crescendo in 1942. Thousands of Sacramentans would be trained and equipped to respond to enemy attack by the war's end as members of the city's Civilian Defense Protective Services. Tens of thousands more would ration, salvage, guard war secrets and buy war bonds with help from the Civilian Defense Council.

Sacramento had been preparing for war on home soil for some time. In January 1940, the city took part in the most comprehensive war games ever held in the United States, a statewide drill conducted by the army and navy that involved more than fifteen thousand troops and thirty thousand sailors.[9] Army Chief of Staff George C. Marshall and H.H. Arnold, chief of the U.S. Army Air Corps, had visited Sacramento on January 17, and rumors circulated that the city was being targeted in the exercise. The massive pseudo-war reached Sacramento at 6:45 a.m. on January 18; sirens sounded the warning, and army planes took off from Municipal Airport northeast of the city to meet the "attackers." Though the drill tested the preparedness of Sacramento's military, it did not involve civilian defenders.

The first civilians to mobilize and drill in large numbers came from local American Legion posts, comprised mostly of World War I veterans who were devoted to promoting Americanism. The Legionnaires enthusiastically pledged hundreds of armed guards and volunteers, along with training and facilities, to assist in civilian defense. They also helped test Sacramento's defenses. In August 1941, Sacramento hosted the California American

Legion Convention, in which local posts kicked off the program with a realistic air-raid demonstration at Sacramento Stadium on the campus of Sacramento Junior College. The demonstration included a mass squadron of airplanes piloted by private fliers and California National Guardsmen that flew over the city at sunset to "create background for the show, giving the public an idea of how it feels to live under the nerve wracking tension of threat of destruction and invasion from the sky."[10] Once darkness fell, an air-raid siren sounded, and civilian defenders—from the Red Cross to the Sacramento Fire Department—went into action to protect a massive model of the city of Sacramento constructed in the stadium by the city's parks and recreation department. Soon after, the planes bombed the model city with fireworks and black-powder explosions to give a sense of the destruction Japan might inflict, and ground troops targeted parachutes dropped from the invading planes.

As Sacramento was exploring the possibility of its involvement in the war, civilian defense was taking shape at the state and national levels. President Franklin D. Roosevelt identified the need for an organized civilian defense corps just after war was declared in Europe. The United States entered an official state of emergency on September 8, 1939, for the "strengthening of the national defense within the limits of the peacetime authorizations."[11]

At the state level, Attorney General Earl Warren called for training more than 1,500 policemen to combat sabotage, subversion and espionage. In January and February 1941, Warren met with 125 law enforcement representatives gathered in Los Angeles to analyze, discuss and make recommendations regarding readiness for emergencies.[12] The group was stirred by five hours of testimony given by an eyewitness to the invasion of France, and participants took his advice on preparedness, along with repeated warnings to be mindful of spies and fifth columnists (subversive agents within the population). The gathering identified possible disasters that might befall the state during wartime, including sabotage, bombings by enemy aircraft, military invasions and gas attacks. In attendance from Sacramento were representatives from the FBI, Sacramento Police Department, McClatchy Broadcasting Company and Southern Pacific Railway. Sacramento County was selected as the hub of Region VI of the defense network, along with Butte, Colusa, Glenn, Sutter, Yolo and Yuba Counties. This meant that Sacramento County officials would call meetings and decide how to prepare for an attack anywhere in the Sacramento Valley. Sheriff Don Cox chaired the regional council, and Police Chief A.K. McAllister was delegated to call regional meetings. Law enforcement and fire protection formed the core of paid civilian defense work in Sacramento. In addition to supplying guards and responding to emergencies, the Sacramento County Sheriff's department contributed its Aero Squadron for a civilian airplane force that formed in the spring of 1941.

Soon, a formal civilian defense body was created at the national level. President Roosevelt established the national Office of Civilian Defense on May 20, 1941, to provide for better coordination of civilian participation in defense and to boost national morale. Roosevelt selected New York mayor Fiorello La Guardia to head the office, and La Guardia in turn appointed Eleanor Roosevelt as assistant director. California became a focal point for their work. The two flew to Los Angeles on December 10, 1941, just three days after Pearl Harbor was attacked. In a state of panic on the flight over, they were told that San Francisco had been bombed, but a telegraph soon corrected the error—a blackout had been issued for the entire coast after enemy planes were heard from army posts on the coast. Everyone was on high alert. La Guardia and Roosevelt traveled up and down the California coast to survey the state's preparedness and raise awareness about the necessity of civilian participation in national defense. They met the State Council of Defense in open session, and the group decided to open a central office in Sacramento. The office would be located at the state fairgrounds at Stockton Boulevard and Broadway, where other war agencies would soon set up shop.

In addition to preparing for a surprise attack, prior to Pearl Harbor, the Office of Civilian Defense was concerned with ferreting out subversive influences from Axis sympathizers. In an address to the nation during Civilian Defense Week, November 9–16, 1941, General George C. Marshall announced that fighting German sabotage would be "a vital purpose in completing our general organization for the security of America" and declared that such civilian defense work would "exert a strong influence in combating secret and destructive efforts to divide and confuse our people."[13] He warned of the risk from fifth columnists and the "wholesale sabotage" of industry and munitions plants in particular. In addition to determining loyalty, a national civilian defense corps would fight propaganda. Because it was thought that sabotage would come from Germany at that time, the Office of Civilian Defense directed its efforts toward protecting the Atlantic Seaboard. But after Pearl Harbor, many questioned the threat posed by Japanese Americans whose loyalty to the emperor, it was feared, might trump loyalty to the United States. On December 8, 1941, Governor Culbert L. Olson announced that plans for the possible segregation and surveillance of

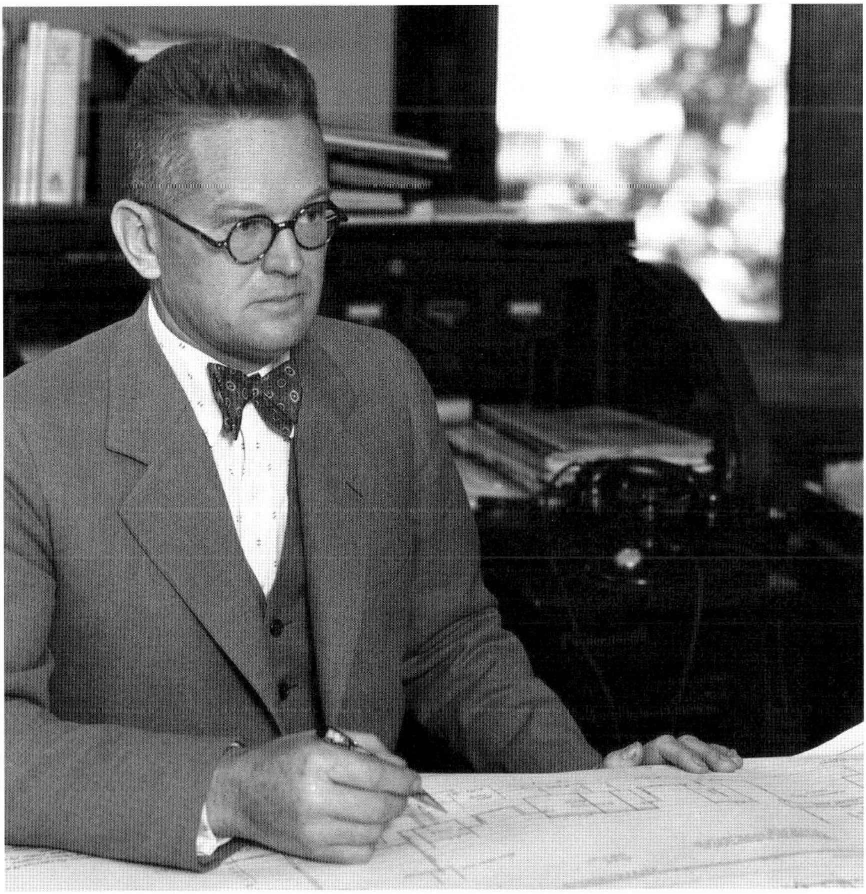

City Manager James S. Dean received orders from the State Council of Defense in early 1941 to form a local defense organization. *Center for Sacramento History.*

Japanese Americans would be discussed at the State Council of Defense's first meeting. In Sacramento, Police Chief Fritz Kaminsky put heavy police patrol on the Japanese section of the city.[14]

Although preventing sabotage became a significant concern for those living on the West Coast, the Civilian Defense Council dropped its training for fighting sabotage and turned the task over the FBI and naval intelligence. Immediately following Pearl Harbor, Japanese Americans in Sacramento were placed under surveillance, and some were taken into custody by the FBI, which rounded up 178 "enemy aliens" in Northern California—101 Japanese, 59 Germans and 18 Italians. Though civilians were not training on combating subversion or sabotage, participation in civilian defense activities became a measure of loyalty. Lieutenant Colonel Harry L. Perkins, intelligence officer with the Sacramento Air Depot Control Area Command, labeled those who didn't sign up with civilian defense as "unknown enemies of America and allies of our enemies."[15]

In June 1941, Sacramento received authorization from the city for its own Sacramento Civilian Defense Council. Because the nation was fighting a total war, local civilian defense councils were authorized as catch-all organizations for all things homefront. The Sacramento council was tasked with training and coordinating air-raid wardens; guarding military and production information; educating the public in the conservation of food, clothing, transportation and health; salvaging essential materials; and encouraging the purchase of war bonds and stamps. In essence, the council facilitated most volunteer war work in the community.

Sacramento opened the new Civilian Defense Council offices at city hall. When citizens were called into action for drills, the office was abuzz with activity and filled with officials from all levels of local government, along with representatives from the communications and transportation sectors. In the event of an attack, the central headquarters could call in Chairman and Mayor Thomas B. Monk; Executive Director and City Manager James S. Dean; Fire Chief Terrance Mulligan; Chief of Police Alec K. McAllister; Fred J. Jones, chief of Sacramento's Office of Civilian Defense; George F. Watrous, chief of the Disasters Division; and representatives from the Pacific Telephone and Telegraph and Pacific Gas and Electric companies.

The Civilian Defense Office broke down its functions into two departments: Civilian Protection and Civilian War Services. Homefront work—committees on salvage, transportation, nutrition, recreation, consumers, services for servicemen, health and medical, welfare and childcare, housing, education, war savings, agriculture, labor supply training and other war activities—fell under the heading of war services. Block leaders administered these functions down to the community level. On the side of protection landed disaster response and defense functions. This group's priority was to prepare Sacramento residents for emergency attack through air-raid drills.

The city gave orders to shield lights in a blackout ordinance adopted on December 12, 1941, and ensuing air-raid drills prepped the city for "imminent peril of attack from the sky."[16] The Sacramento Safety Council, with authorization from the Civilian Defense Council, authored an easy-to-understand pamphlet with detailed blackout and air-raid rules that was distributed door-to-door to all Sacramento homes by Boy Scouts. According to blackout instructions, upon hearing the air-raid siren sound, civilians were to turn off all lights in their homes and stay put. If practical, family members could carry on their activities in a central, windowless room. Business were to turn off their lighted signs, and traffic signals were to be shielded to prevent light from being directed upward. Drivers were to pull to the side of the road and shut off all lights.[17] In the first issue of *The Volunteer*, the Sacramento Civilian Defense Council's weekly newsletter, which began publication on August 26, 1942, a short article gave the reach of various lights: "In a blackout, a lighted match can be seen at ½ mile, a lantern can be seen at 1¼ miles, a blast furnace glow is visible 25 miles and a lighted window can be seen 12 miles." Other locations in the county issued their own instructions appropriate for their communities. In Folsom, the Defense Council instructed residents to prohibit their dogs from running loose at night, "Your A.R.W. [air-raid warden] must move fast to perform their duties during a blackout and most dogs will attack a running person in the dark."[18] When Christmas arrived two weeks after Pearl Harbor, Catholic churches canceled their traditional midnight masses.

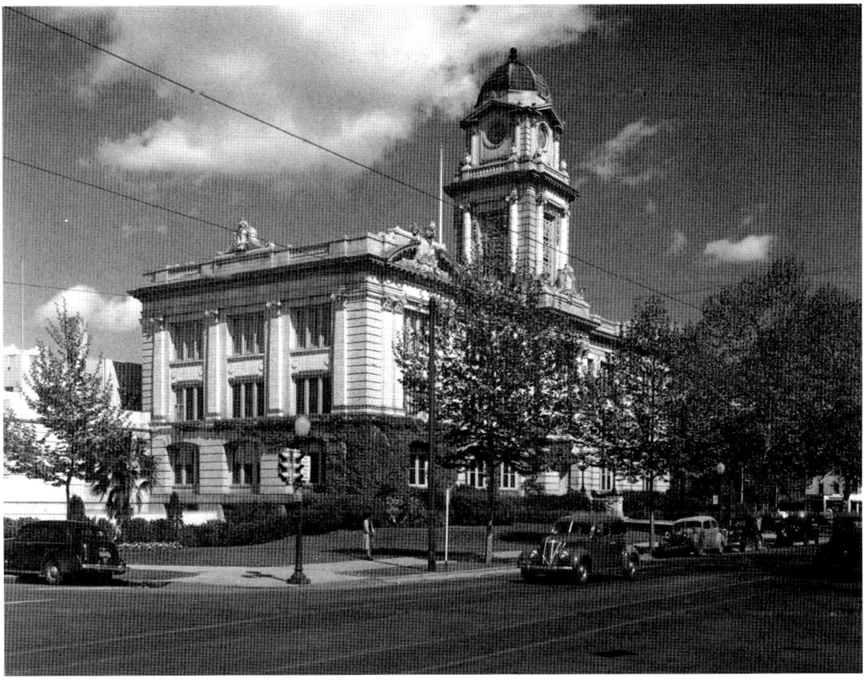

Sacramento City Hall, pictured here about 1941, housed the general headquarters of the Sacramento Civilian Defense Council. *California State Library.*

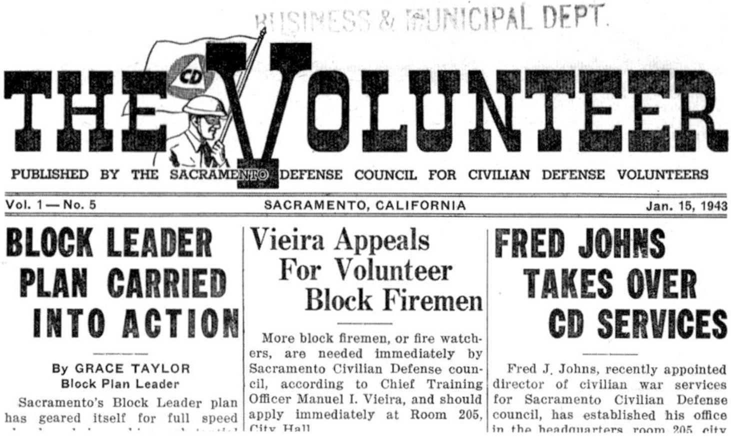

THE VOLUNTEER

PUBLISHED BY THE SACRAMENTO DEFENSE COUNCIL FOR CIVILIAN DEFENSE VOLUNTEERS

Vol. 1—No. 5 SACRAMENTO, CALIFORNIA Jan. 15, 1943

BLOCK LEADER PLAN CARRIED INTO ACTION

By GRACE TAYLOR
Block Plan Leader

Sacramento's Block Leader plan has geared itself for full speed

Vieira Appeals For Volunteer Block Firemen

More block firemen, or fire watchers, are needed immediately by Sacramento Civilian Defense council, according to Chief Training Officer Manuel I. Vieira, and should apply immediately at Room 205, City Hall

FRED JOHNS TAKES OVER CD SERVICES

Fred J. Johns, recently appointed director of civilian war services for Sacramento Civilian Defense council, has established his office in the headquarters room 205, city

The Volunteer kept civilian defense volunteers apprised of the latest from the Civilian Defense Council along with new training and volunteer opportunities. *Sacramento Public Library*.

Until Sacramento could be outfitted with sirens, the city's air-raid warning system alerted residents to the start of a drill with short blasts from whistles at industrial plants and railyards. Less than two weeks after Pearl Harbor, the city purchased massive Bullard sirens for air-raid warnings to reach all parts of the city, and in 1942, the city added two Federal Electric sirens. One went high atop the California Western States Life Insurance building at the corner of Tenth and J Streets, and the other was installed on the water tank at the state fairgrounds.[19] All sirens were controlled by a master switch at the police station. Were the air-raid sirens to sound, people were instructed to go immediately to the nearest four- or five-story concrete building and wait on the first-floor or basement levels, enabling them to be shielded from flying fragments or indirect blasts. Guards would then be dispatched to protect the levees, communications systems, utilities, dams and oil refineries. During weekly air-raid drills at local schools, children gathered on the first floor and lined up along hallway or classroom walls, away from windows.[20]

Additionally, Sacramentans were ready to respond if incendiary bombs landed on their property. The city provided every home with fifty-pound sacks of sand from public sand piles throughout the city. Residents were instructed to "[c]over bomb with sand to keep down heat, then scoop bomb onto flat shovel and place in a bucket containing about four inches of sand. Carry the bucket to the street or back yard and permit the bomb to burn itself out. After removing the bomb, apply water from a hose or bucket to any burning area in the home."[21]

Civilian defense training and preparedness peaked in 1942. Pearl Harbor remained relatively fresh in the minds of Americans, and attacks by Japanese submarines at Ellwood Oil Field in Santa Barbara and Fort Stevens in Oregon put the Pacific coast on alert. By the end of 1942, nearly twenty thousand Sacramentans were trained and prepared to enforce blackouts, heal injured citizens, safeguard property, put out fires and otherwise defend the city.[22] Only sixty out of every one thousand civilian defense volunteers were needed for the more active roles in command section, drivers corps, messengers, rescue squad, auxiliary police, auxiliary firemen, air-raid wardens, fire watchers, demolition and clearance units, road repair units, decontamination units, emergency welfare services, emergency medical units and nurses' aid corps. Volunteers in these roles trained at Sacramento Junior College, completing twelve weeks of intensive study taught by forty special instructors.

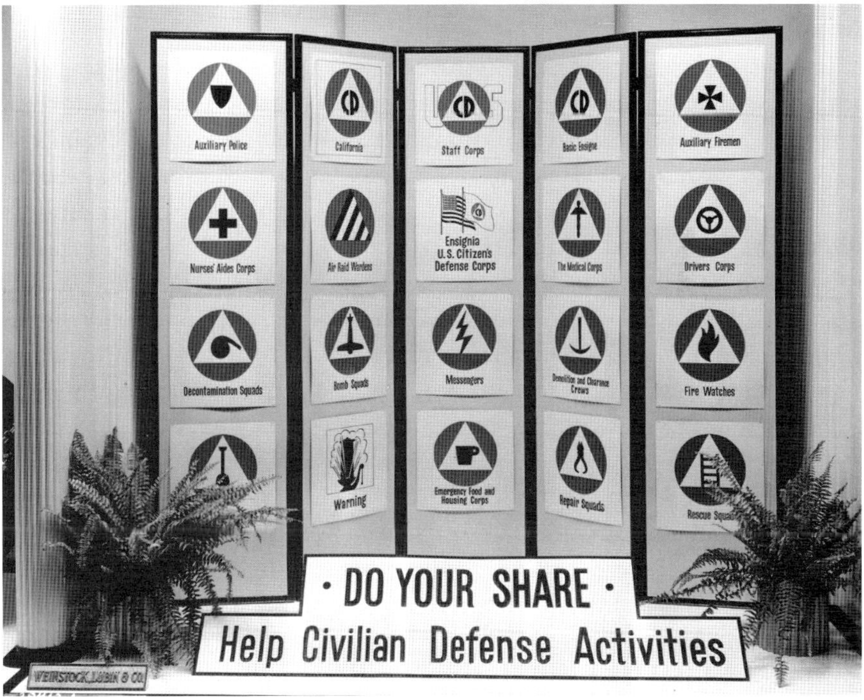

A window display at Weinstock, Lubin and Co. shows off the multitude of volunteer roles available through the Sacramento Civilian Defense Council. *Center for Sacramento History.*

One of the most in-demand civilian defense jobs was that of an air-raid warden. By August 1942, California had built up a corps of more than 150,000 wardens. A few were assigned to each sector of about 500 residents and given the responsibilities of getting to know the neighborhood and enforcing proper observance of blackouts. Many others signed up to spot fires and enemy aircraft. Fire protection was a key component of civilian defense because—as noted by the Sacramento Civilian Defense Council—a single enemy plane was capable of starting four hundred fires. A few hundred men in Sacramento between the ages of sixteen and sixty became fire watchers and were trained to spot fires from rooftops. Fire guards assigned to every residential block were trained to control small fires. They received training in fire defense, gas defense and first aid at Sutter Junior High and were outfitted with a fire extinguisher and gas mask.

Hundreds of Sacramentans served as airplane spotters, and Sacramento claimed its unique contribution to their training—local junior and senior high school students built 350 model planes for a national model aircraft project to assist with training civilian defense workers. The model craft ranged in wingspan from five and a half to twenty-five inches and represented fifty types of Axis and Allied warplanes.[23] Once spotters were trained, they set up in towers like the thirty-foot airplane observation tower constructed by the American Legion, which was furnished with radios, a phone and heat and was manned by air-raid wardens—women during the day and men at night. Spotters sent their reports to Sacramento's Aircraft Warning Filter Center, where about two hundred women evaluated reports of passing planes submitted by ground observers and submitted credible threats to Western Defense Command. Twenty-five women manned the filter center in four-hour shifts around the clock.[24]

Women often signed up for emergency medical work and took nursing courses at Grant Union High School through a program sponsored by the Red Cross. Volunteers prepared to staff six casualty stations and a one-hundred-bed emergency hospital located at the Scottish Rite Temple. The emergency facilities later moved to the bottom floor of the Sacramento County Hospital. Men also joined the auxiliary police, receiving instruction in the use of revolvers, shotguns and submachine guns. And hundreds of teens and young men became messengers, delivering critical messages door-to-door.[25]

As civil defense groups formed and volunteers signed up throughout the region, the concern over a possible invasion was getting a little too serious for some. Captain Cornelius N. Boyer, a ninety-five-year-old Civil War veteran and vice department commander of the Sacramento Grand Army of the

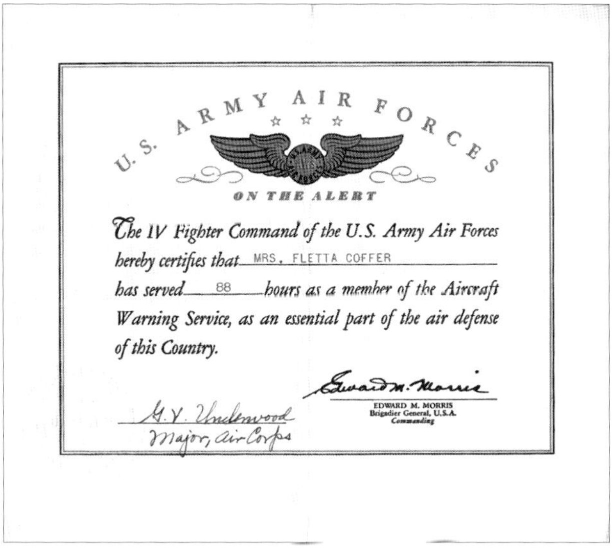

U.S. ARMY AIR FORCES

ON THE ALERT

The IV Fighter Command of the U.S. Army Air Forces hereby certifies that MRS. FLETTA COFFER *has served* 88 *hours as a member of the Aircraft Warning Service, as an essential part of the air defense of this Country.*

G.Y. Underwood
Major, Air Corps

Edward M. Morris
EDWARD M. MORRIS
Brigadier General, U.S.A.
Commanding

Ground observers like Fletta A. Coffer began monitoring plane activity over Sacramento in the summer of 1941. *Sacramento Public Library.*

Republic, gathered his own civilian defense army in early 1942, enlisting housewives in a "Rolling Pin Brigade" to repel any parachutists that dared invade the country.[26] The joke was meant to improve morale—paranoia bordering on hysteria was mounting at civilian defense meetings, and Boyer wanted to bring a little levity. So, he proposed a brigade of 10,000 loyal women armed with "a woman's weapon." Were Japan or Germany to invade, they would be met with Boyer's "mighty husky women." He first signed up 37, but word caught on across the country, and by the fall, more than 1,400 women from almost every state had registered. When Boyer died in February 1945, he was the second-to-last surviving Civil War veteran in the Sacramento area.

The fervor over civilian defense had waned by 1943. While Japan made early progress across the Pacific with victories in the Philippines, Singapore and New Guinea, the threat didn't seem so close after Japan's defeat at Midway. Civilian defense training classes moved to Sutter Junior High School, and enrollment dropped to its lowest since the outbreak of war. William K. Purves, a music instructor at Sacramento Junior College appointed to head up the civilian defense training program in 1942, warned that the region had acquired "a far too complacent attitude."[27] The threat of invasion was felt to be so remote that when the State of California Basic Plan for Evacuation was published in November by the State War Council, it was thought that invasion would "only follow stupendous military reverses or the loss of our fleet." The plan primarily addressed the threats of sporadic raids from carrier-based planes, shelling of coastal areas by hostile naval units, major acts of sabotage and riots or other local disorders on a major scale.

Despite declining interest in civilian defense, or perhaps because of it, Sacramento displayed its defense prowess through a massive citywide drill on April 19, 1943, with scenarios of ten incidents, including gas and bombing attacks involving 160 victims. More than 5,000 civilian defense volunteers were mobilized. Residents of the New Helvetia defense housing project responded to a mustard gas attack and high explosive bombs, assuming a dozen casualties in the project's destruction. The Civilian Defense Corps contributed volunteers in decontamination, demolition and clearance crews, along with auxiliary police and an ambulance corps. The largest raid occurred at the capitol, where 30 "victims" were trapped by fire and rubble following an explosion. Many residents flocked to the location to view dramatic aerial-ladder rescues from the roof.[28] In addition to this special demonstration, Civilian Defense made monthly air-raid drills more interesting by dropping red flares and paper cartons throughout the city to simulate bombs. Residents were to report the fallen cartons to their local air-raid wardens.

While thousands of Sacramentans organized for enemy attack with Civilian Protective Services, these roles only represented part of the civilian defense picture. Under the umbrella of Civilian War Services, the Defense Council directed all domestic energies toward the war effort. Most of these activities were coordinated by librarian Grace Taylor, who was temporarily relieved of her library duties to form the Sacramento Block Plan. The plan equipped homes to fully participate in the war effort, building tight-knit communities that would ration, plant victory gardens and collect scrap together. Every month, block plan leaders tackled a new project, from training in home nursing to victory gardening. More than one thousand leaders signed up to cover the city and were imparted with the value of homefront contributions by Grace Taylor: "This is not a man's war. It is not a woman's war. It is not a private war, for any group or class. This is a total war, in which you all must participate."[29] A native of Sacramento, Grace had been city librarian since April 1933. After she returned to her library duties full time in May 1943, Mrs. Fred J. Klaus took over as block plan leader. Grace Taylor later married James S. Dean, executive director of the Sacramento Council of Defense, in 1945.

Through the block plan and other Civilian War Services efforts, the Civilian Defense Council educated Sacramentans in rationing and in the conservation of food, clothing, transportation and health. World War II rationing brings to mind food conservation, but belt-tightening took place in

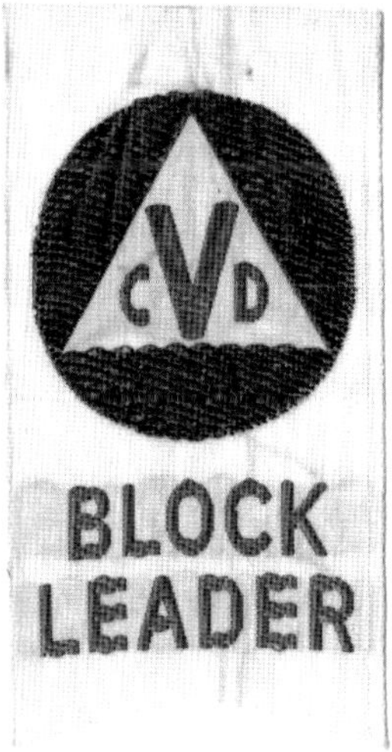

Block Leader insignia issued to Mary Ribzinski, who joined one thousand Sacramento women in equipping their neighborhoods for the homefront fight. *Sacramento Public Library*.

a multitude of areas. When the Japanese seized the Dutch East Indies, they cut off 90 percent of the American rubber supply, stripping rubber of all types from shoes, water bottles, bicycle tires and even rubber panties. These materials went into making bomber tires, pneumatic rafts and other military equipment. Tires not used on vehicles had to be sold or turned over to the government under the Idle Tire Purchase Plan, and tires underwent inspection annually. As a tread-saving measure, drivers were required to drive very slowly—a maximum of thirty-five miles per hour. Out of tire rationing was born the Americans Behind the Lines Conservos, an idea conceived by John M. Clark, commander of the Fourth Air Service in Sacramento.[30] The group recruited at gas stations and took a pledge to conserve gas, tires and autos. There was also a nationwide effort to send in scrap metal for use on guns, tanks, airplanes and other equipment. In addition to conservation, the numerous wartime bond drives also fell under civilian defense, and Sacramento block leaders posted signs with slogans like "Remember Pearl Harbor," "They Give Their Lives, You Lend Your Money" and "Let's All Back the Attack: Buy More New Bonds" to sell them.

Patriotic cards placed in the windows of businesses and homes were ubiquitous during World War II. They were also a valuable tool in civilian defense. One sign indicated that a location would serve as a block house—available as an air-raid shelter to children in the vicinity during a drill. Another sign, the V emblem, designated a home as having qualified for the five-point V-Home program. V homes agreed to

> *1. Follow the air raid warden's instructions to protect America's homes against air attack*
> *2. Conserve food, clothing, transportation and health*
> *3. Salvage essential materials, so that they may be converted for immediate war uses*
> *4. Guard military and production information carefully and kill rumors*
> *5. Buy war savings bonds and stamps regularly*[31]

Outside of formal volunteer roles, Sacramentans contributed their skills and resources to civilian defense projects. Local artists, in particular, found a multitude of creative uses for their talents. Some joined the Volunteer Artists for Victory (VAV), producing propaganda posters and training material for civilian defense. Theodore Baggleman, president of the VAV, put together a display for the Crocker Art Museum in February 1943 showing simulated bomb damage in Sacramento. The exhibit included one hundred photos from the Sierra Camera Club, along with one hundred paintings by eight American artists on the theme of "Soldiers of Production." And when the Civilian Defense Council designed a system of district tests to train volunteers, the VAV painted large posters to illustrate the damage from enemy bombs.[32] Students at Sacramento Junior College also found their art skills of use to civilian defense through courses in creating posters, camouflage, reconnaissance drawings, military industrial design, war illustrations, war cartoons and art for morale building.

With so much time and effort dedicated to defending Sacramento, how real was the threat of attack to the capital? There were a few false alarms, especially early in the war. On December 27, 1941, unidentified planes were spotted over Sacramento, and the city went into its fifth blackout of the war. It was the first alarm to originate in Sacramento and not the Bay Area. The city's greatest threat was kept secret until August 1945, when newspapers lifted their censorship of reports on Japanese balloon bombs, at which time local newspapers reported on all nearby bomb landings that had taken place over the previous year. Few came close to Sacramento. A balloon bomb was discovered at the Michigan-California Lumber Company near Placerville on October 16, 1945, one struck a powerline at Camp Beale in early 1945 and exploded and another landed in a duck pond dangerously near naval ships at Mare Island. There was also a sighting near Clarksburg in Yolo County, but no bomb was found.[33] Although the Japanese never came close to directly attacking Sacramento, the city felt a legitimate threat due to its large military presence and proximity to the Bay Area.

By the end of the war, tens of thousands of people had volunteered for Civilian Defense, more than would ever again volunteer for a single organization in Sacramento. Although most attention went to volunteers who readied for a surprise attack, the homefront work contributed by the Civilian Defense Council and administered by block leaders did far more to further the war effort. After the war, the State Civilian Defense Council was folded into the Disaster Council, and Sacramento's office closed for a few years. In 1950, Governor Earl Warren reactivated the civilian defense

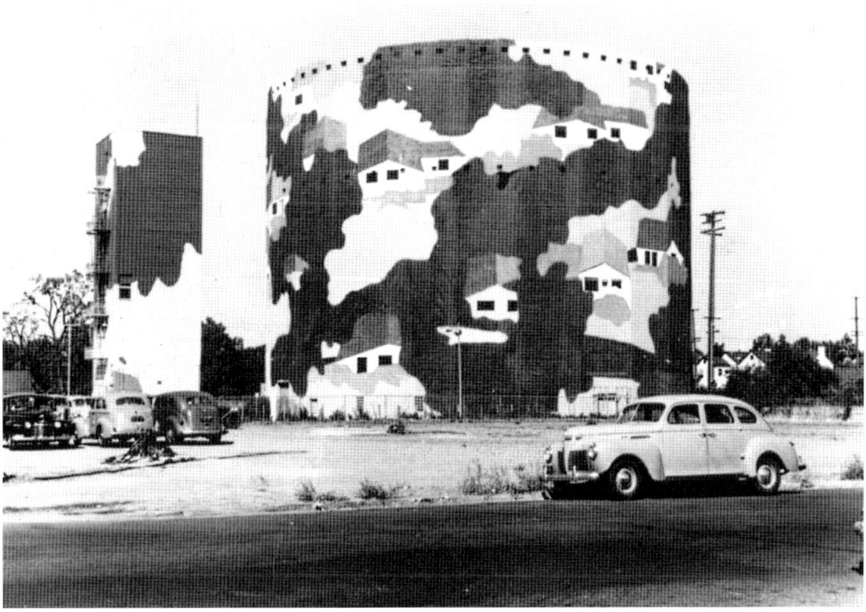

All of Sacramento's water tanks were camouflaged during the war years, including the tank at Alhambra and Twenty-First Streets, pictured here. *Sacramento Public Library.*

function of the State Disaster Council and announced plans for a statewide air-raid warning system. Interest peaked in 1951 during the Korean War and again during the Cuban Missile Crisis in 1961, as Sacramento's new civil defense entered the atomic era with drills, fallout shelters, modern warning systems and evacuation plans. But the city would never again train and equip so many civilian soldiers as it did during World War II. The origins and early work of the Sacramento Civilian Council of Defense demonstrate the city's commitment to the homefront battle in its first entry into total war.

2

THE HUB OF WEST COAST NATIONAL DEFENSE

By James C. Scott

The military presence in World War II–era Sacramento formed a crescent-like constellation, starting with Camp Kohler in the north, bending southwesterly to the Air Depot, dropping south to the Signal Depot near the confluence of American and Sacramento Rivers and then east again toward Mather Field. Few American cities could claim as much. But it was the Capital City's perch along a barge-friendly Sacramento River, longtime status as a rail and highway hub, fairest of flying conditions and relative safety of the inland Sacramento Valley that made it ideally suited to help spur a war effort that would place a historic premium on air power. And yet, it's possible that much of it wouldn't have happened without the efforts of a tall, bespectacled Wisconsinite.

****

It helped that Arthur S. Dudley's Chevrolet Deluxe came with plenty of room. Even so, he, an assistant and three very official passengers from Washington, D.C.—clad in the olive drab garrison hats and finely pressed uniforms of the U.S. Army Air Corps—had to reckon with the Sacramento Valley's late-September heat, which meant that all windows were rolled down as they sped eastward down Folsom Road. It had the makings of a heady day for Dudley and Sacramento. A local paper referred to the visit to a dormant Mather Field as a "mystery," and as Dudley would state later

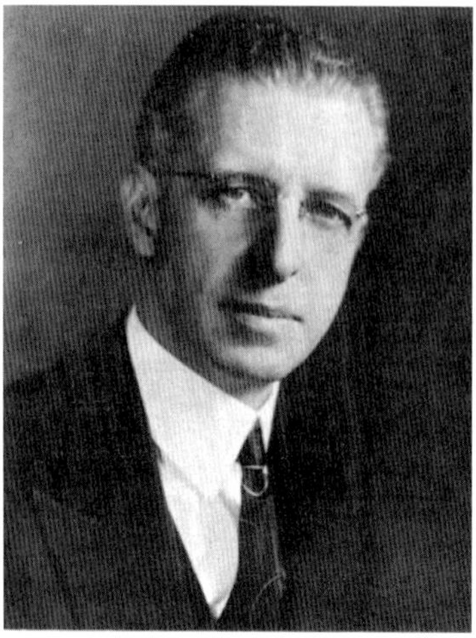

Arthur S. Dudley is regarded by many as the de facto father of the Sacramento Air Depot. *Sacramento Public Library*.

in the day, "If the project in mind [was] developed...it [would] be the only one of its kind in the United States."[34]

As secretary manager of Sacramento's chamber of commerce, Dudley was known to be a fellow who got things done. Just four years earlier, he had lobbied hard for and won a somewhat seamless transfer of airplane procurement and repair facilities from the antiquated Rockwell Field, in San Diego, to a 1,276-acre tract of wild oats and jackrabbits located seven miles northeast of Sacramento on the old Rancho del Paso land grant. Ground was broken there on September 8, 1936, as Governor Frank Merriam hit a dynamite plunger to set off a small, but still thrilling, explosion supplemented by a celebratory dinner at downtown Sacramento's exclusive Sutter Club for those involved in forming what would initially take on the somewhat prosaic moniker of "Sacramento Air Depot" (SAD) before officially changing in 1939 to McClellan Field. In truth, both terms (and various others) would be used interchangeably for decades to come to identify the same spot.[35]

By any name, the new post was a point of tremendous pride for Sacramento. It was Congressman Frank Buck, representing California's Third District, who gushed over the city's "public spirited citizens, newspapers, and civic bodies" who so tirelessly worked to bring the depot to the region.[36] Moreover, as a jewel to be admired from near and far, SAD was state-of-the-art, one of four of its kind in the nation and the only one on the West Coast. Washington, D.C.'s Smithsonian Institution proudly displayed a scale model of the complex during the spring of 1939, while Brigadier General George Marshall, speaking at a luncheon that April beneath the rafters of the massive Building 51 and over the airwaves on KFBK, declared the depot a symbol of hard-learned vigilance, stating, "In the last war we were not ready till the end. This time we are getting ready in advance."[37]

Marshall wasn't wrong (and he rarely was, for that matter). By April 1940, McClellan's shops were humming, having overhauled and repaired some 329 aircraft over the previous ten months. With the damage to facilities at Pearl Harbor and seizure of depots in the Philippines, the stakes grew exponentially higher for SAD, as it instantly became *the* spot for air logistics in the Pacific Theater of Operations (PTO).[38] Accordingly, over a three-week stretch following December 7, the depot welcomed nearly 2,800 new employees for twenty-four-hour, seven-day-a-week operations to accommodate the needs of its biggest client—the Thirteenth Air Force, also known as the "Jungle Air Force" due to its operation out of the triple canopy–shrouded airfields of the Pacific. With the Thirteenth and other units engaged in the Battles of the Coral Sea and Midway (May and June 1942, respectively) and the American invasion at Guadalcanal (August 1942), McClellan stood front and center for procurement, repair and engine overhauls.[39] Even after similar depots in Spokane, Ogden and San Bernardino were completed in late 1942, the PTO remained McClellan's primary focus for the balance of the war.

SAD's first major wartime task, however, fell under "Project X," an operation whereby thousands of stateside aircraft were to be ferried overseas for action. In fact, the first planes to arrive in Hawaii after the Pearl Harbor attack were several B-17E Flying Fortresses that had been

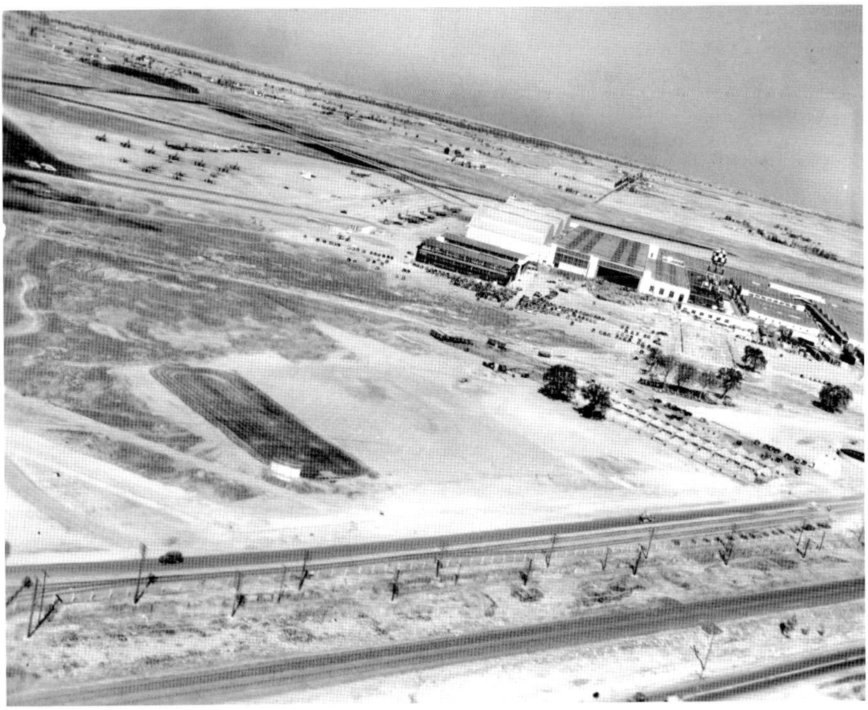

The Sacramento Air Depot, as seen from the south. Prominent is the arched roofing of Building 51. Roseville Road runs in the foreground. *Aerospace Museum of California.*

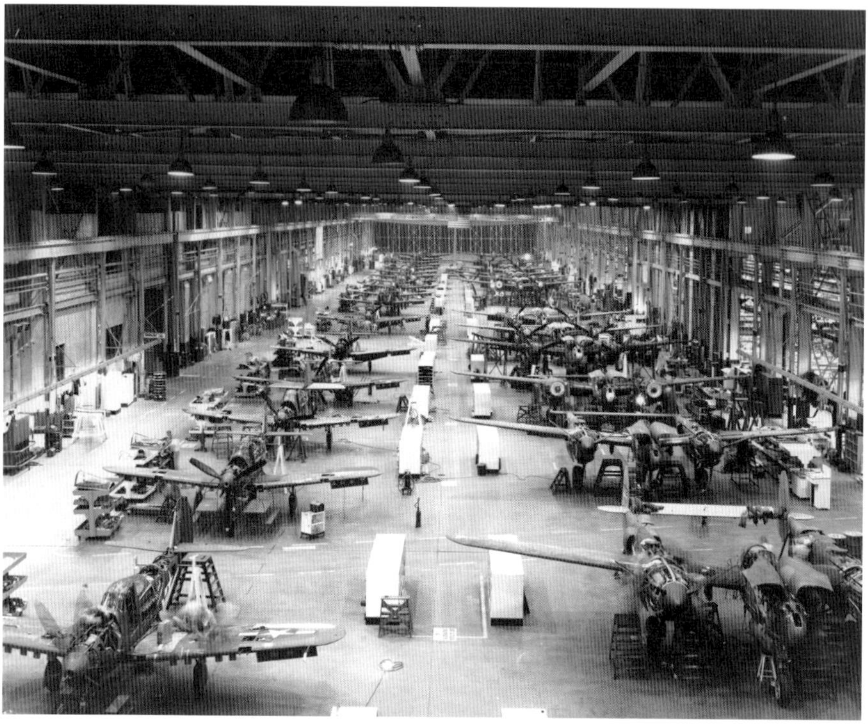

Shown are assembly lines at the Sacramento Air Depot, P-39 Airacobras to the left, P-38 Lightnings to the right. *Aerospace Museum of California.*

prepped by McClellan hands.[40] Beyond that, by October 1942, the depot had delivered a staggering 1,500 aircraft to Oakland and San Francisco facilities for shipment to the Pacific.[41] Transit to and from McClellan either came by air—via the base's three intersecting landing strips—or water, courtesy of a wharf that was built on the Sacramento River, ten miles west of the depot. Planes and sections of planes were moved over both the Garden Highway and a stretch of dedicated road, known in its early stages as the "Bell Avenue job," that ran east–west through open fields. Along with various other defense jobs in the Sacramento area, the WPA built the highway in late 1941 for $450,000.

Much of SAD's maintenance and repair magic took place in Building 51 (eventually renamed 251), the installation's undisputed centerpiece and hangar, measuring some six million cubic feet in size (or the equivalent of roughly thirteen acres) and composed of 5,530 tons of structural steel. A veritable beehive of action, 51—primarily designed to handle all versions of the B-17—could hold up to thirty aircraft at a single time and, in the context of city life at the time, shelter Memorial Auditorium, the municipal stadium (soon to be called Hughes Stadium), city hall and all three of Sacramento proper's water storage tanks.[42] It was also built, according to Brigadier General Christian F. Dreyer, constructing quartermaster at the time of McClellan's construction, to "allow for bigger aircraft than the B-17...looking forward to the day when there would be larger aircraft," yet a legendary list of smaller planes saw ample time in the wartime 51, including the P-47 Thunderbolt, P-38 Lightning, P-39 Airacobra, P-40 Warhawk and C-47 Skytrain.[43]

One of the depot's most secretive and certainly important procurement jobs came in March 1942 with the arrival of sixteen B-25 Mitchell medium bombers under the command of Lieutenant Colonel James Doolittle. Each plane's super-secretive Norden bomb sights, select blast plates and radio sets were removed, and three extra fuel tanks were added, modifications ordered by the bright and detail-oriented Doolittle in an effort to extend the group's operational reach. Curiosity must have smoldered away among depot employees, as outside of Doolittle and his crews, no one at the base knew that, within days of the visit, the group would be raiding five different Japanese cities in one of the more outrageously heroic missions of World War II.

While at the previous station, Eglin Field, Florida, each plane's carburetor had been set to a special lean fuel mixture in order to maximize distance for bombing Japan and then flying on to friendly airfields in China. McClellan mechanics, however, ordered to perform standard inspections, placed carburetor settings back to standard, assuming it the elementary thing to do. The adjustments caused a series of telltale backfires that sent the diminutive Doolittle into a rage. With there being no way to reset the carburetors to the lean mixture, Doolittle ordered the raiders to leave for the Naval Air Station at Alameda, but not before scrawling a single word across the depot's performance review—"Lousy."

The "fog of war"—even this early in the conflict—had clearly settled in and around the hangars and flight lines of McClellan. In truth, the strict secrecy permeating the mission meant that there would be greater chances for miscommunication. Still, it's not likely that SAD's carburetor modifications altered the outcome of the April 18 operation. The carrier transporting the raiders, the USS *Hornet*, was discovered by Japanese patrol boats some 170 nautical miles short of the designated launch point, meaning that the planes had to fly well beyond their originally gauged distance anyway. Most of the

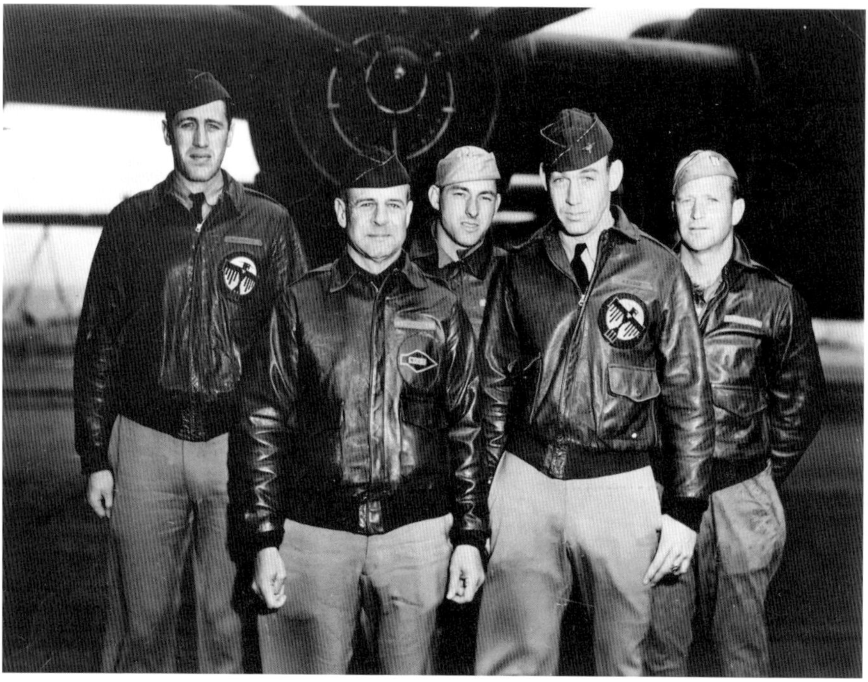

Lieutenant Colonel James Doolittle (*second from left*) and crew, spring 1942. They stopped at McClellan before their raid on Japan. *National Archives.*

B-25s were still able to crash-land in China, and of the eighty American airmen who participated in the raid, eight died, including three who were executed while in captivity. A year later, on April 23, 1943, the front page of the *Sacramento Air Depot News* reported the executions "for the sober consideration of every officer and man and every civilian at McClellan Field."[44] The news devastated the depot, but history would go on to view the raid as a sorely needed boost to the nation's morale and an action that turned Doolittle and his men into legends.

An additional McClellan brush with greatness came with the arrival of "Suzy-Q," a B-17E originally prepped at McClellan in January 1942, returning to the depot in April/May 1943 for both repair and overhaul. "Suzy-Q"'s wartime record was fabled. The plane participated in the Battle of the Coral Sea with engagements at Java, New Guinea and the Solomon Islands, along the way claiming twenty-six Japanese planes shot down, a tally that extended over one hundred combat missions. During her stay, the depot patched up bullet holes, overhauled stressed Wright Cyclone engines and touched up the ship's olive drab coat and distinctive nose art of a Native

American warrior. With its departure from the depot on Monday, April 26, all work in Building 51 ceased as maintenance crews gathered to watch the fruits of their labor taxi westward for takeoff. Once aloft, "Suzy-Q"'s pilot, Lieutenant Colonel Felix Hardison (the plane's name was inspired by his wife's middle name, Suzanne) guided the ship back over the field in a gesture of thanks that must have electrified personnel. Hardison then banked to the north and took a moment to radio the control tower with the following message: "I want to express my appreciation to the Sacramento Air Depot personnel, both military and civilian, for all you have done for us."[45]

Concurrent with "Suzy-Q"'s visit, the depot reached its highest employment level of the war with twenty-two thousand military and civilian jobs. Laundromats, hotels, restaurants, movie theaters, and taxi companies from Roseville to Elk Grove all stood to benefit. A run through the base paper, the *Sacramento Army Depot News* (or *S.A.D. News*), reveals a series of ads that catered to the specific needs of those attached to the base. The Eastern budget store at 1112 J Street claimed a "Scoop! Furniture Scaled Exactly

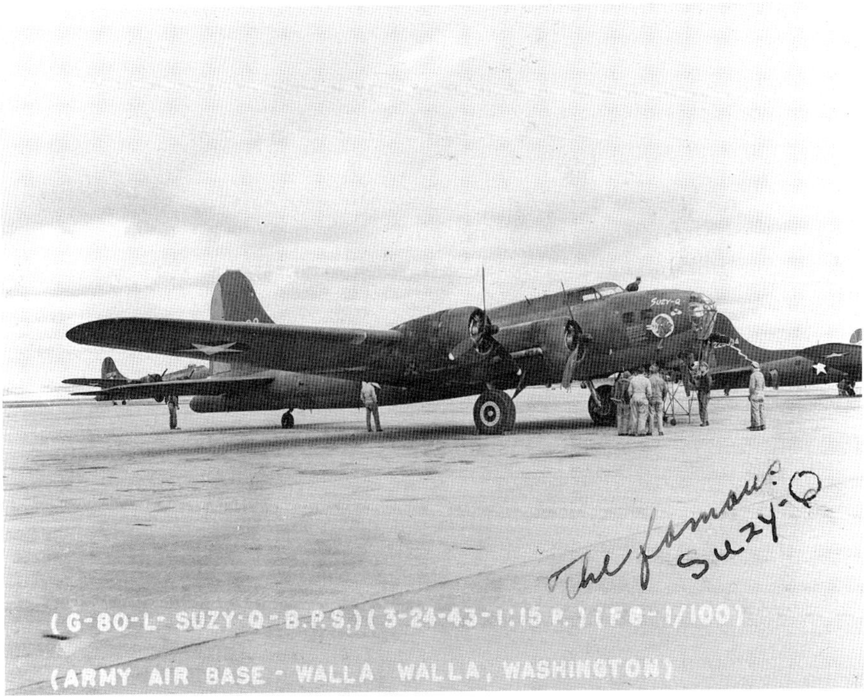

"Suzy-Q," one of the most famous planes to transit McClellan during the war, 1943. *Whitman College Archives.*

for a Defense Worker's Home—3 rooms for only $179,"[46] whereas Del Paso Heights contractor E.L. Schutt made a compelling argument by simply stating that "when tires get bad and they ration gasoline, a home within easy walking distance of the Depot will be pretty swell."[47]

With gasoline rationing a foregone reality, auto travel to, from and around the base caused a new set of challenges. The Public Roads Administration saw the "forced retirement of passenger vehicles" to be a legitimate threat to worker transportation and the "war production effort."[48] To combat this, the depot took a variety of steps, including carpooling, which was powered by the mandatory registration of automobiles in an effort to connect those who drove with those who needed rides. The so-called "Share Your Ride" program was viewed as a success, as it kept workers on the clock while also cutting traffic rates on the approaches to the base by a reported 45 percent. Gibson Stage Lines also started operating a bus service between SAD and Sacramento via Fair Oaks Boulevard and the Arcade District. One of the many base couples, Jay and Dorothy Garner, were so committed to rationing and work ethic that they rode a single bike—Jay in the seat, Dorothy on his lap—to the depot and back from their Del Paso Heights home every day, averaging roughly 200 miles of travel a month. With over 1,200 acres of base to cover, transportation within SAD was also considered a challenge, with most personnel relying on bicycles and brisk walking. One novel form of transport came courtesy of the so-called "Elephant Trains," originally used to get visitors around the Golden Gate International Exposition of 1939–40 at Treasure Island, San Francisco. Without their original trunks, tusks and floppy ears, the repurposed people movers made regular runs on two routes around SAD.

As the facility operated under the stresses of war production and the many deadlines that came with it, the health of base morale was a constant concern. Moods were lightened, however, by a wide range of healthy distractions ranging from comics in the base newspaper to depot athletes going up against those from Mather and Beale. One of the two Japanese miniature submarines captured at Pearl Harbor was even placed on display in October 1942 as a way to both lift spirits and fill war bond coffers. Although the best was yet to come, as a month later, beloved comedian Bob Hope made a visit to SAD. After wisecracking his way through eighteen holes at the Del Paso Country Club, he gave a two-hour show inside the base's Hangar 5, using a massive crash truck as his stage.

Beyond what the occasional Hollywood icon could offer, SAD was blessed with its own brand of talent that came in the form of one the nation's best-

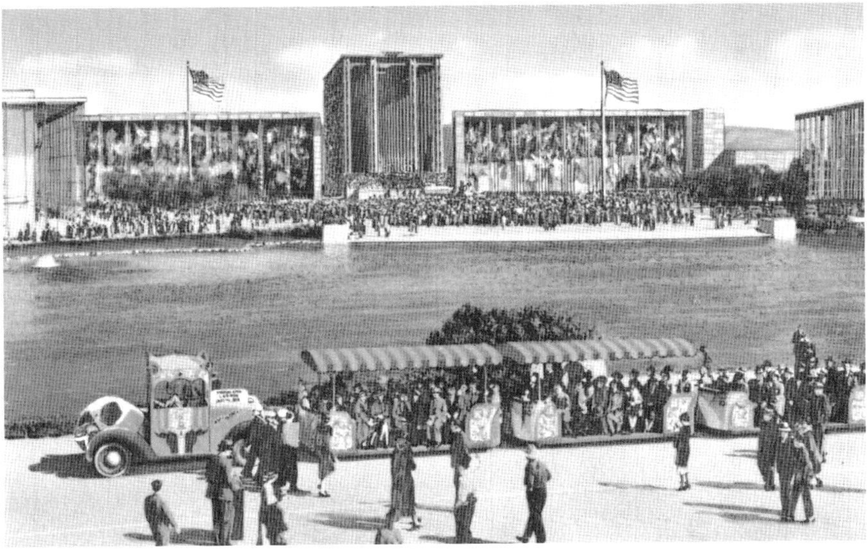

Pictured at San Francisco's 1939–40 Golden Gate International Exposition is an "elephant train." Many were repurposed to McClellan for on-base transportation. *Sacramento Public Library.*

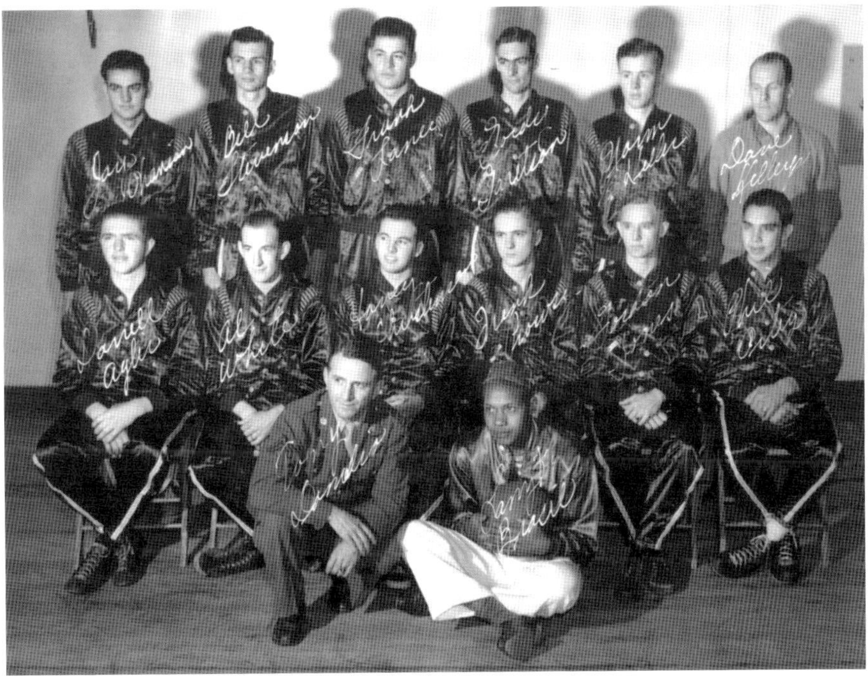

The McClellan basketball "Commanders" in 1945. Standing third from the left is Frank Laney, future Santa Clara University Athletic Hall of Famer. *Todd Laney.*

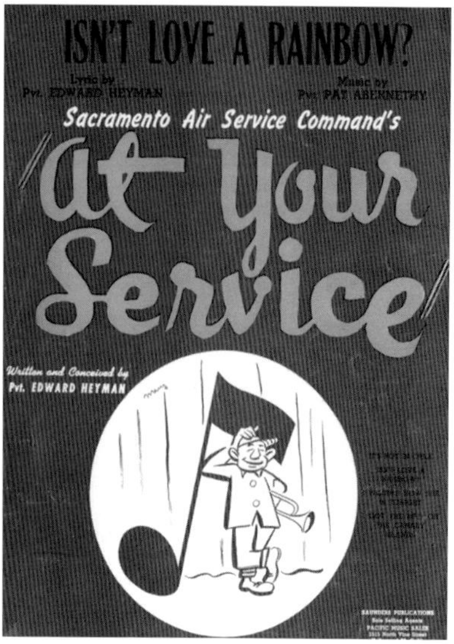

The cover of sheet music for McClellan's *At Your Service* presentation of "Isn't Love a Rainbow?" *Sacramento Public Library*.

regarded musical variety shows—*At Your Service*. Comprising 75 depot soldiers, it debuted on October 15, 1943, at the Sacramento High School auditorium under the leadership of Lieutenant Larry Cotton, a nationally recognized radio personality, and Master Sergeant Ezra Stone, also a well-known actor and director. Beyond artistic diversion, the vaudevillian production sought to raise money for McClellan's recreational and entertainment programs while educating the public on SAD's tasks and accomplishments. *At Your Service* appeared five more times in Sacramento before heading out to other spots in California, including the lengthy archipelago of sub-depots that operated in the state. The *Sacramento Bee* called the show "crowded with comedy acts and dance, all spiced up with agreeable music…[and]…it opens and closes with pageants to show the importance of the Air Service Command, and in between takes a satirical fling at almost everything in the army, to the great edification of the audience."[49] Notable were a comedy skit presenting four Guadalcanal GIs lying on a beach—sharing with one another the most effective way to knife enemy soldiers—and a rousing closing rendition of SAD's official fight song, "The Spirit of SAD," written by McClellan airplane crating worker Kyle Moore:

> *We pledge allegiance to the USA, and we'll work with all our might*
> *We're men and women working side by side, and we're bound to win this fight*
> *We're glad to have a chance to do our bit for this land of liberty*
> *We'll "Keep 'Em Flying" on to Victory*
> *In SAD.*

As conflict droned on and workloads increased, McClellan's production methods matured in kind, due in no small part to the July 1943 arrival of new base commander Brigadier General Clinton W. Howard, reputed to have one of the most adroit technical minds in the U.S. Army Air Forces.[50] Along with the input of several depot employees, Howard instituted a clever series of workflow modifications that increased efficiency by 25 percent between December 1943 and June 1945, all done with 35 percent fewer civilian employees than existed in June 1943.[51]

As the war wound its way down, SAD's regional impact had been undeniable. According to historian Joseph McGowan, $28 million of federal spending made its way through McClellan, which stood as just one installation of many in a state ranked first in the nation for the amount of federal funds spent for aviation—an unqualified success that boosted the local economy, made a meaningful contribution to the war effort and gratified Dudley who, all along, knew that SAD was *the* prize, but far from the last of his defense-centered acquisitions.[52]

****

AND HERE WAS THE secretary manager again, stumping for his beloved Sacramento. After pulling up to a dust-covered Mather, Lieutenant Colonel H.M. Hesky, Major W.C. Lee and Captain Reuben Kyle slammed doors, rolled up sleeves and took a collective breath as they looked out over the expanse devoid of modern runway, radio tower, barracks or paved roads. The somewhat bleak panorama made a professionally trained photographer like Dudley wince while also marveling at how quickly things had changed since Charles Lindbergh landed there in 1927 to the adoration of thousands. And still, Dudley had ample reason for optimism.

In the mid-1930s, the Chief of the Air Corps and Major General Oscar Westover gave Dudley a simple choice: he could have the Rockwell facility moved to Sacramento *or* he could have Mather Field reactivated. As the reader already knows, Dudley chose the former, reasoning that with America's entry into the war, Mather's rehabilitation would happen anyway. Located eleven miles east of Sacramento, Mather had roots as an aviation training school that ran all the way back to the Great War. Although decommissioned after the 1918 armistice, it was reopened for the wildly successful April 1930 U.S. Army Air Corps maneuvers, pitched by Dudley's chamber of commerce as the Battle of California. The air resources of the Blue Army were to repel those of an invading Red Army, with seventy-five airplanes for each side. Participants included a who's who of aviation aristocracy, such as Henry "Hap" Arnold, Frank Andrews, Carl Spaatz and Roy Kirtland. Later that same year, Mather reopened to Colonel Clarence L. Tinker's Twentieth Pursuit Squadron, but the budgetary shock waves of the Great Depression were enough to again close the field in 1932.[53]

But it was now 1940, and the world had changed from what it was just eight years earlier. The Japanese Empire's Greater East Asia Co-Prosperity Sphere was encroaching west, and in Europe, France had fallen and the first stage of Germany's planned invasion of the British Isles was well underway. It was just before Halloween 1940 when Dudley received the call he had been hoping for—and no doubt expecting—as he sat at the chamber office at 917 Seventh Street. Brigadier General Henry W. Harms informed him that "Mather [had] been allocated to the West Coast Air Corps Training Center for a bombardment pilot and bombardier training site which [meant] an advanced training school for pilots of two engine ships and bombardiers."[54]

Rehabilitation began in earnest on May 1, 1941, as 1,700 workers representing some twenty different contractors (thirteen from Sacramento) were tasked with a job that would eventually cost Uncle Sam $4 million. Notable local contributors were A. Teichert and Sons, which surfaced streets, and the Lawrence Construction Company, which built a 70-foot-high control tower and the base's only hangar. In three months' time, laborers assembled two hundred buildings comprising 8,430,000 board feet of lumber and laid base roads with enough concrete to construct a 32-mile-long highway within the 5,200-acre installation.[55] By March 1942, with the nation now firmly at war, Mather resembled nothing of its Great War self, expanding by nearly 500 percent, highlighted with the addition of a Teichert-built runway. Coming in with a price tag of $835,000 and shaped by 21,000 linear feet of concrete, the warm-up apron, ramp and crossing strips resembled a massive spider web reaching southward from the base and into the area's ancient array of vernal pools.[56]

Mather's first trainers—a total of nine T-6 Texans—arrived on May 14 1941, having been flown up from the North American aviation factory in Inglewood, California, with the first twin-engine AT-7 Beechcraft Navigator trainers landing in July. Mather was fully reconstituted by October 1941. By October 29, the 3031st Army Air Force Base Unit had already graduated its third class of flying students, a total of 124 representing some sixteen states. The navigation school welcomed its first cadets in early August, and all 16 graduated in mid-November. In time, Mather would become the largest navigation school in the West and just one of three in the nation. At any given point during the war, Mather had between 575 and 600 navigators in training, learning from a group of

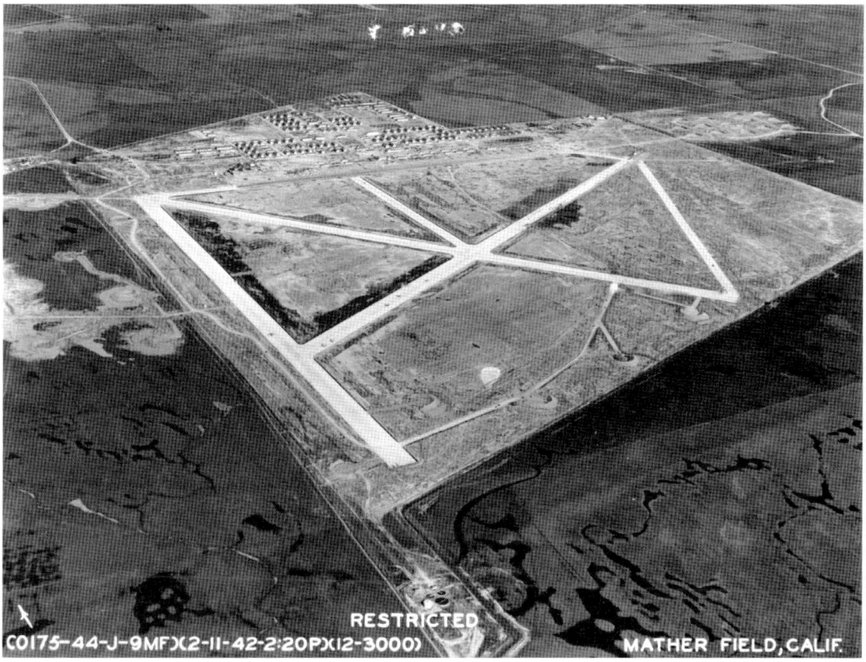

This spring 1942 image captures a reconstituted Mather Field and its A. Teichert and Sons–built runway as viewed from the southwest. *Center for Sacramento History*.

twelve AT-7s. Without any formal service academy for military aviators until 1954, Mather was fond of its well-earned nickname "West Point of the Air," presciently used in a *Popular Mechanics* article to describe the base during the April 1930 Air Corps maneuvers.[57]

Much like SAD, Mather grew into its own city. Roughly three thousand personnel ate at three different mess halls producing some ten thousand meals a day; drew their energy from public utilities; took in first-run moving pictures at the base theater; and received haircuts at the base's post exchange, or PX, which boasted a twelve-chair barbershop, a cobbler, a café, a tailor and a jeweler. There was even a portable canteen, quaintly called the "Check Inn." Operated by Mather officers' wives and later the Red Cross of Sacramento, it moved about the flight line, serving as an ideal spot for Mather personnel or transiting crews to catch a quick hit of doughnuts, coffee and friendly conversation. Mather also accommodated the religious needs of its Christian personnel with a four-hundred-seat chapel. The décor of the structure was portable and could be configured for either Catholic or Protestant services. Jewish service members were allowed passes to attend services and observe holy days at Sacramento's Mosaic Law or Temple B'nai Israel synagogues.

SAD may have had Bob Hope, but Mather had Jimmy Stewart. And unlike Hope, Stewart came to Mather as a soldier after having been commissioned in January 1942 as a second lieutenant and then sent to Sacramento in spring–summer 1942 for training to become an instructor in the piloting of twin-engine planes. The area's interest in the everyman actor was predictable. He was invited by theaters both city- and countywide to attend premieres, and when Sacramento Junior College held its Pioneer Dance in April 1942, Stewart was given the honor of selecting the "Pioneer Queen" by looking through the photographs of nineteen entrants. The lucky winner was Betty McBain, a sophomore majoring in music and curiously declared by the *Sacramento Bee* to be the "first dark haired girl selected for the Pioneer day honor."[58] By August, Stewart had been transferred to Kirtland Field in Albuquerque, New Mexico, to pilot bombardier-training planes. McBain went on to Oakland's Mills College, but before leaving Sacramento, she fell

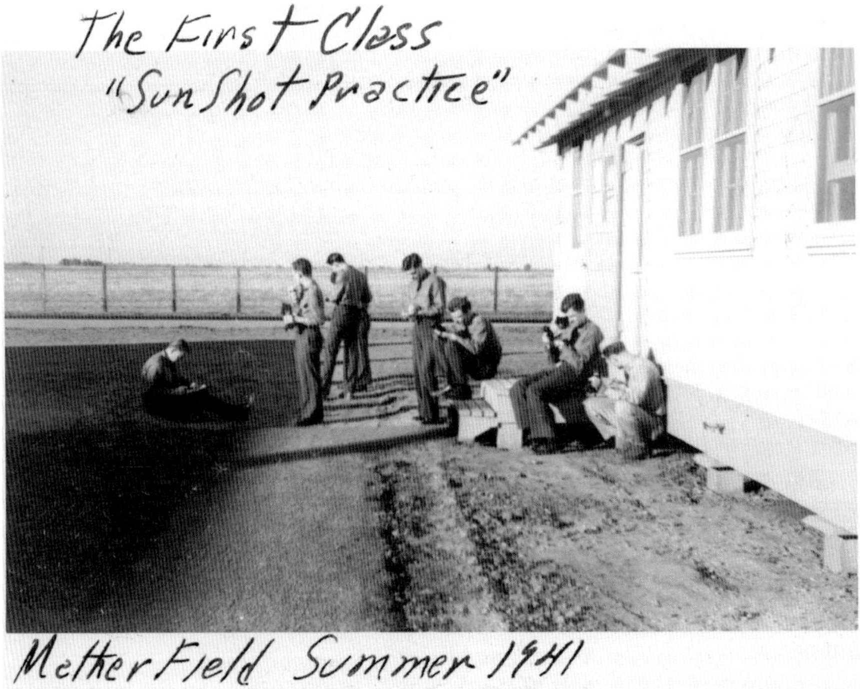

In this 1941 image, Mather's first class of navigator cadets "shoot the sun" with their newly acquired sextants. *Center for Sacramento History*.

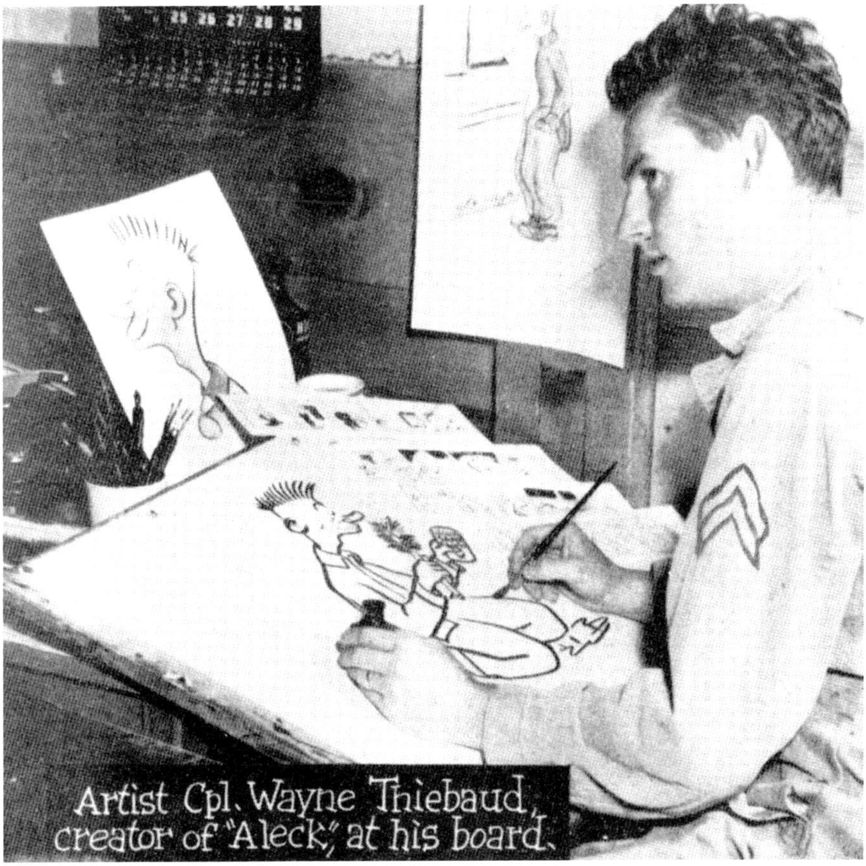

Wayne Thiebaud, shown working at Mather Field, went on to become one of the nation's premier Realist painters and printmakers. *Sacramento Public Library.*

in love with Mather graduate and native Texan Captain James Beck Jr. They were married in September 1943.

Although few knew it at the time, an additional talent who would make his way through Mather was artistic tour de force Wayne Thiebaud. After a prewar stint at Walt Disney Studios, Thiebaud enlisted with his sights firmly set on becoming a pilot and, in 1942, was sent to Mather. However, during an early morning flight inspection, Thiebaud stumbled across a Quonset hut full of soldiers working at drawing tables. By day's end, he was transferred to the base's Special Services Department. The next two years would see him design promotional posters, paint murals, teach art classes and provide art and cartoons—*Aleck* being his best known—for the base newspaper, *Wing*

Tips. In late 1944, with Allied troops finally on European soil, Thiebaud's unit was to be shipped to Europe for the big push through Belgium and eastern France. However, on the day he was slated to leave, an officer approached Thiebaud with a photograph of his wife, asking the artist if he could paint a picture of her. In compensation, the superior assured Thiebaud that he would be taken off "that duty."[59] The artist obliged and stayed at Mather until August 1945, effectively avoiding Nazi Panzers at the Battle of the Bulge. At the end of the war, Thiebaud headed to Los Angeles to work as a cartoon and layout designer for Rexall Drugs. By 1950, however, the allure of Sacramento was too much. He was back in the place he said he "loved… when [he] was there with the Army Air Force," with "the trees, the light, the weather."[60] Thiebaud stands as just one of thousands of talented young men and women who, drawn by the military to Sacramento, would end up staying in the area, thereby making their talents Sacramento's talents.

On October 1, 1944, with the war's end well in sight, all of Mather's flight-training schools were terminated with the base's abrupt transference to the Air Transport Command. Nearly overnight, Mather went from the "West Point of the Air" to the "Gateway to the Pacific," effecting a full pivot to combat mobilization. The first westbound B-29 landed on October 6, with the base's most hectic stretch coming in June 1945, when it launched 234 B-29s and 200 other craft in support of concentrated attacks against the Japanese mainland.

Mather's most momentous, if not anxious, send off came on July 28, 1945, after the arrival of a B-29 called the "Laggin' Dragon." Piloted by Air Commander Edward M. Costello and copilot Harry B. Davis, it was the last of fifteen custom-built "Silverplate" B-29s designed to carry only the most robust of ordnance loads. The "Laggin' Dragon" sat on Mather's flight line under the veil of high security and an added crew of

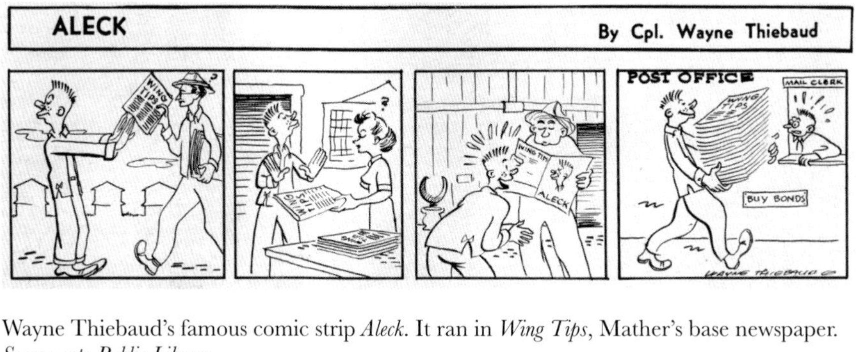

Wayne Thiebaud's famous comic strip *Aleck*. It ran in *Wing Tips*, Mather's base newspaper. *Sacramento Public Library.*

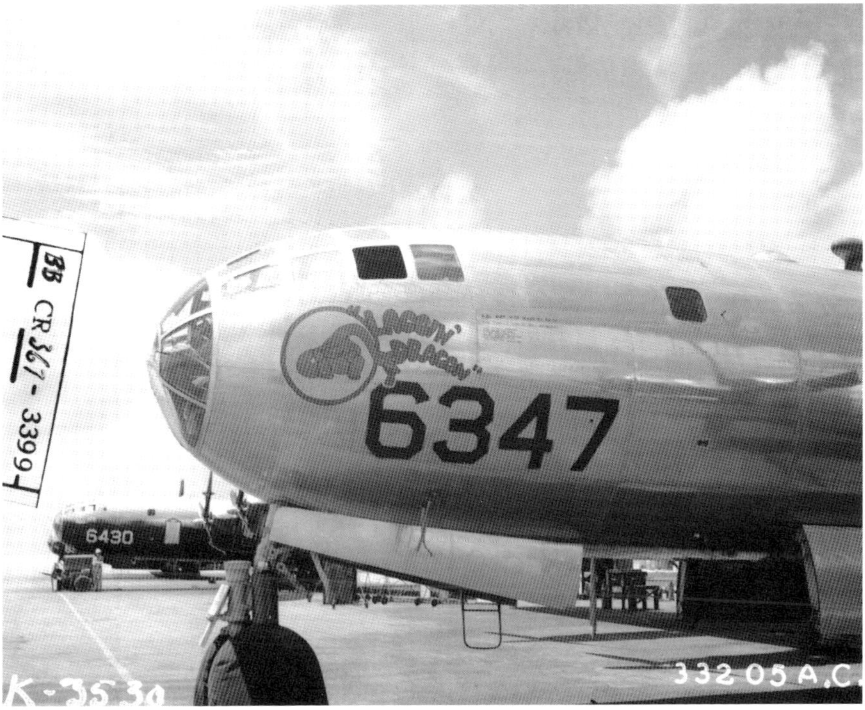

The "Laggin' Dragon" sits safely on Tinian just days after nearly flying its way into disaster at Mather Field. *Smithsonian National Air and Space Museum.*

odd handlers who wore olive-drab uniforms without insignia. Much to the vexation of Mather's ground crews, who insisted on a standard multipoint inspection for every plane prior to takeoff, the strangers demanded haste. The "Laggin' Dragon" was only fifty feet up when a powerful airstream pushed open a hatch holding the plane's life raft, which then wrapped itself around the right control elevator on the plane's tail. Costello and Davis immediately fought to stabilize the ship as its nose abruptly dropped. At three hundred feet, the pilots finally wriggled the raft loose, but "large areas of the elevator fabric had been torn off, and more pieces were being furled off into the wind."[61] It was at this point that a laser-focused Costello contemplated either crash-landing or seeking enough altitude for a chance bailout of the crew. He also knew that whatever the plane carried was important enough to avoid crashing. Even so, the rest of the crew assumed the crash posture. At the last moment, however, and to the shock of a control tower crew who had all but convinced themselves that crash landing was imminent, Costello conjured a moment of brilliance and brought the B-29

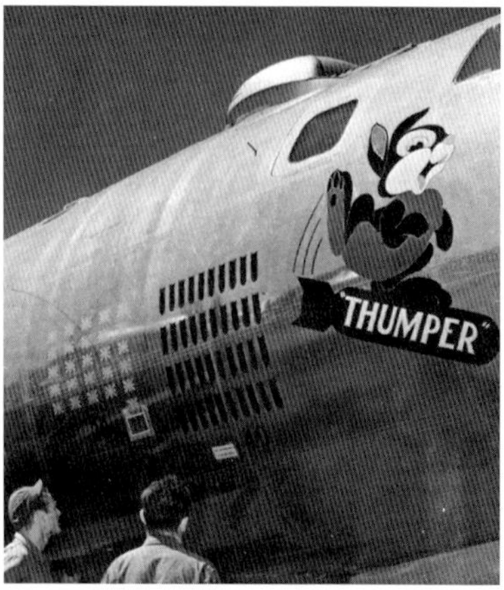

Pictured in 1945 at Mather Field is "Thumper," one of the more accomplished B-29s of the Pacific war. *Sacramento Public Library.*

down for a perfect landing. Muscle, guile and training may have won the day, but the crew also benefitted from the plane's new reversible propellers, which helped steady it upon landing. As nerves settled, Mather crews replaced the shredded elevator with that of another B-29, and the "Laggin' Dragon" flew off to its final destination, Tinian. Barely known to the plane's crew and not at all to any of Mather's personnel was that the "Laggin' Dragon" carried the disassembled and coreless "Little Boy," the atomic bomb that, in ten short days, would be dropped on Hiroshima.

By war's end, Mather's mission was again shifted, this time to what was officially referred to as an Aerial Port of Embarkation and unofficially as the "Sunset Project." All told, the base was responsible for repatriating some 1,266 planes and 17,534 crews and passengers, all of whom passed through Mather's building 4474 and beneath a large banner that read "Welcome Home—Well Done." Not without a touch of irony, one of the more notable passengers to be transited back through Mather and 4474 was none other than General James Doolittle who, as the reader will remember, started the war as a lieutenant colonel and in a huff at SAD.

The first wave of returning B-29s arrived from Saipan on September 27, including a B-29 called "Thumper" that had flown forty missions (including five raids over Tokyo), shot down twenty-six enemy planes, and participated in the first island-based mission against the Japanese mainland. The "Enola Gay," the "Silverplate" B-29 that became famous for its history-altering sortie over Hiroshima, arrived in November. Soon after, the "Great Artiste," which operated as an observer during the atomic bombing of Nagasaki, touched down after a long trip from the Marianas. When the plane landed, *Sacramento Bee* reporter Richard Rodda didn't miss a chance to ask blister gunner Raymond Gallagher if atomic technology should be kept a secret. In a surprisingly candid response, the Chicagoan said, "[I]t should be kept to ourselves because I don't ever want to see another one go off."[62]

****

With no feats of aviation greatness to speak of and a shorter than usual lifespan, Camp Kohler is arguably the most obscure of World War II Sacramento's military installations.[63] The camp sat twelve miles northeast of Sacramento, nestled within a grove of ancient oaks near the hardpan expanse of Walerga—so named for a flag station along the Southern Pacific line. It was Kohler's manifold mission to serve as a training center for the U.S. Army Signal Corps, a camp for prisoners of war, an overseas replacement depot for the U.S. Army Air Forces, a port of embarkation and home to the Walerga Engineer Depot.[64] However, the very origins of the installation had much more to do with detaining Americans—both native-born and naturalized—than figuring out how to beat fascists.

The headline accompanying a photographic montage of goings-on at Tule Lake Segregation Center in the July 18, 1942 *Sacramento Bee*, read, "Life Goes On as Usual in Relocation Camp."[65] Smiling children, a happy carpenter and a newborn stand bitterly juxtaposed to what, in the words of late historian Joseph McGowan, was "one of the most tragic, unnecessary, and unjust actions in the state's history" and far from an extension of usual life.[66]

Just prior to the war, Sacramento was home to the fourth-largest concentration of Japanese Americans in California. Given a total of two days to muster for relocation, all of them—nearly 3,800—were transferred to the so-called Walerga Assembly Center via buses boarded at Memorial Auditorium. Sachiko Louie, who was six years old and living in the Southside Park neighborhood of Sacramento, remembered in a conversation with the *Sacramento Bee* "the day my older sister came to pick me up from Kindergarten at Fourth and T streets, the FBI came to our home and the next thing I know we are in Walerga."[67]

It's likely that few Sacramentans knew where Walerga was when it was declared an assembly center. From there, most would be shipped to the Tule Lake Segregation Center, located amid the harsh aridity of northeastern Siskiyou County. The Work Projects Administration was charged with building the Walerga facility, which was started in March and completed in May 1942. It took up a 160-acre tract that consisted of two hundred tarpaper frame buildings, with each living structure designed to accommodate ten to twelve people. Constructed on the cheap and meant to be ephemeral, the center existed for a mere fifty-two days—still enough time for the trappings of community to develop, including a camp newspaper called the *Walerga Wasp*.

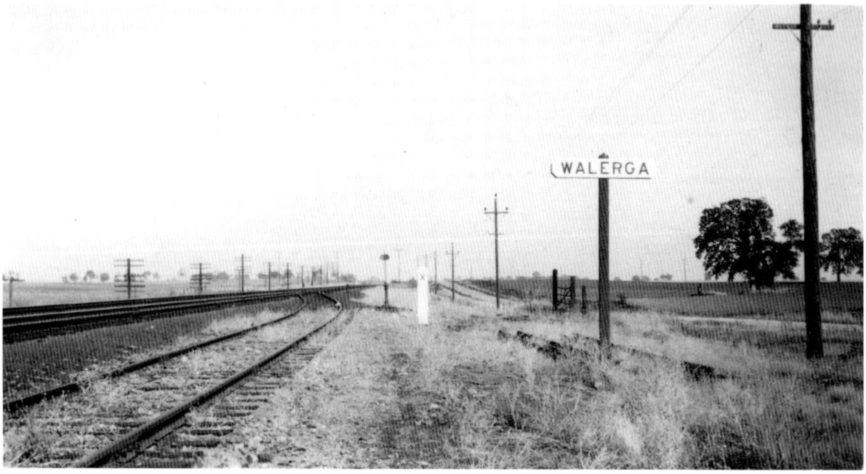

The flag station for Walerga, the eventual namesake of the Walerga Assembly Center. *Center for Sacramento History*.

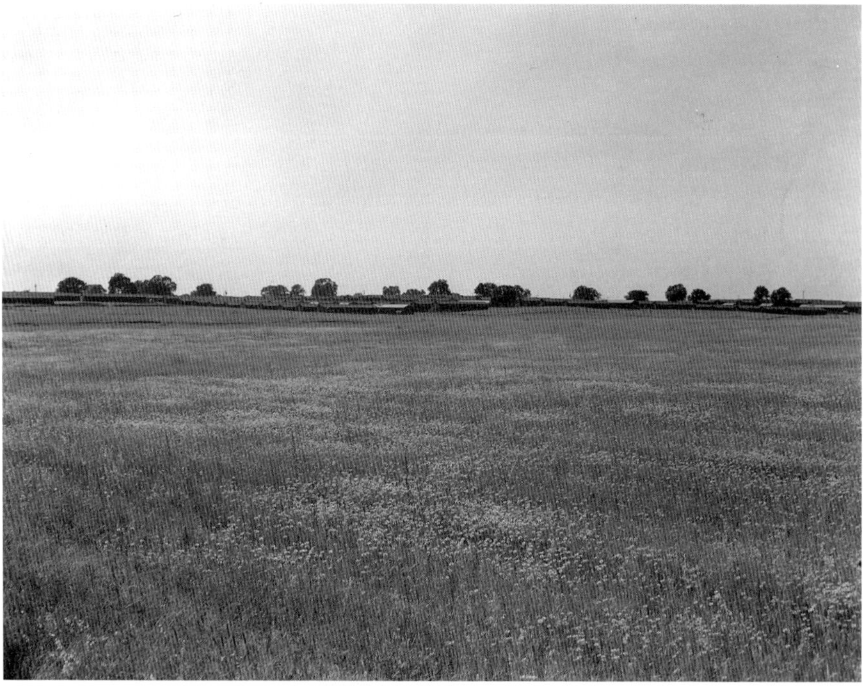

Pictured in spring 1942 is the hardpan expanse occupied by the Walerga Assembly Center. It would soon become Camp Kohler. *National Archives*.

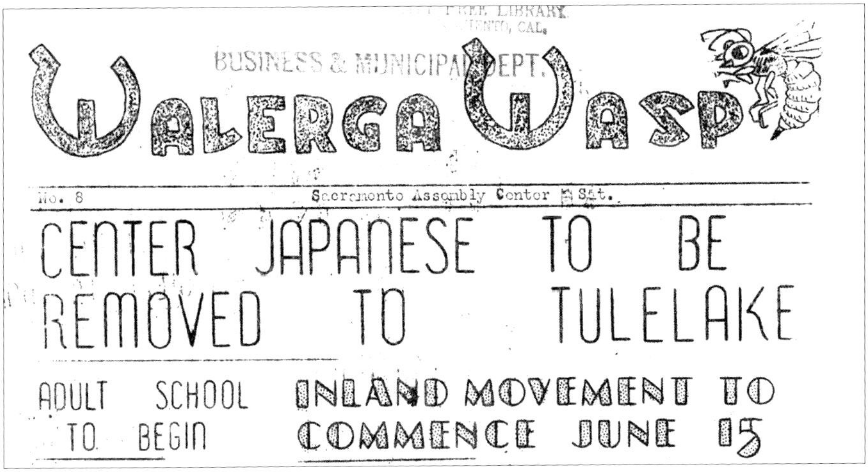

WALERGA WASP

No. 8 Sacramento Assembly Center Sat.

CENTER JAPANESE TO BE REMOVED TO TULELAKE

ADULT SCHOOL TO BEGIN

INLAND MOVEMENT TO COMMENCE JUNE 15

The masthead of the short-lived *Walerga Wasp*, the official newspaper of the equally short-lived Walerga Assembly Center. *Sacramento Public Library*.

It's through the *Wasp*, edited by George "Jobo" Nakamura, that we know about the center's library and post office. The paper also chronicled "Jam at the Wham," the big swing dance at the center's reception hall. "Song Fest," held in the central courtyard, saw 1,500 evacuees sing the Sacramento High School fight song "Fight Dragons Fight" and "It's Lincoln Junior High," among many others. We know about the marriage of Shizuye Nishimura, who had been working at the M Street Laundry, to Hiroshi Takahashi, a downtown carpenter. We know that Kenneth Nakayama was the first baby born at Walerga, on May 25, 1942, and that Dr. George Iki, the physician who delivered Kenneth, was disappointed—in jest, no doubt—that his mother didn't name him Walerga. We also know that the camp's Boy Scout troop observed Memorial Day by standing at attention for "Taps," followed by center residents singing "The Star-Spangled Banner." The last issue of the *Wasp*—an extraordinary documentation of American life during World War II—ran on June 14, and the last camp residents left for Tule Lake on June 23.

Walerga stood idle for a short period of time, as by mid-summer 1942, it was becoming clear that Signal Corps training centers at Fort Monmouth, New Jersey, and Fort Crowder, Missouri, were without the capacity to train the 70,000 signalmen that the army demanded. With the War Department already leasing Walerga, the choice was a relatively simple one. Basic training would be provided for 2,000 men. The most fundamental instruction in signal work would be given to the first group of trainees—481 in total—arriving in September 1942. Within the next six months, Kohler grew, eventually topping out at 3,800 acres with a 330-bed hospital, a massive laundry and a network of roads that would take on names like Midway, Bataan, Dutch Harbor, Corregidor and Avenue of the United Nations.

Of the thousands of men who passed through Kohler, the most famous—and perhaps the most miserable while there—was Pulitzer Prize–winning writer and playwright William Saroyan, who spent six weeks in November–December 1942 going through basic training while his actress wife, Carol Grace, and friend and silky socialite Oona O'Neill waited for him amid the comfort of Sacramento's Senator Hotel at Twelfth and L Streets. According to biographer John Leggett, Saroyan was surprised that he had to wait two weeks for leave and recalled the grief brought on by calisthenics in the morning darkness, the making and remaking of his bunk and, on the firing range, "the reverence with which the instructors handled a rifle and how they called it 'the piece.'"[68] After completing his basic training, Saroyan was transferred to the Signal Corps Photographic Laboratory in Queens, New York, and would, in time, refer to his Kohler days as "the most painful experience of his life."[69]

Although growing competent signalmen through firing range, infiltration course and classroom instruction was standard, there were a few more unusual avenues for Kohler instruction. One was the base's simulated French village. Although the nation was more than nine months off from the invasion of Normandy, base leadership saw a need to conjure real-life scenarios to acquaint soldiers with hand-to-hand combat, house-to-house fighting and the Nazi penchant for planting booby traps. Located near the western end of Kohler, the village was made up of four two-story structures complete with furniture, French-language signage, defenders and booby traps in "books, pictures, maps…on tables and the floor or hanging on the walls."[70] Months after being placed into action, eleven of the village's booby traps, each capable of firing a .30-caliber shell, were stolen, it is believed, by local children and never found.

Kohler also made use of the Tahoe National Forest to conduct signal exercises under simulated battle conditions. The trials took place over a five-day period near Downieville and Sierra City, where it was typical for up to 250 men at a time to participate in spring–summer maneuvers throughout up to twenty square miles of Sierra Nevada pine, granite and river rapids. Kohler's director of training, Lieutenant Colonel Fred Hover, admonished area hunters to "exercise extreme caution" lest one of his signalmen be

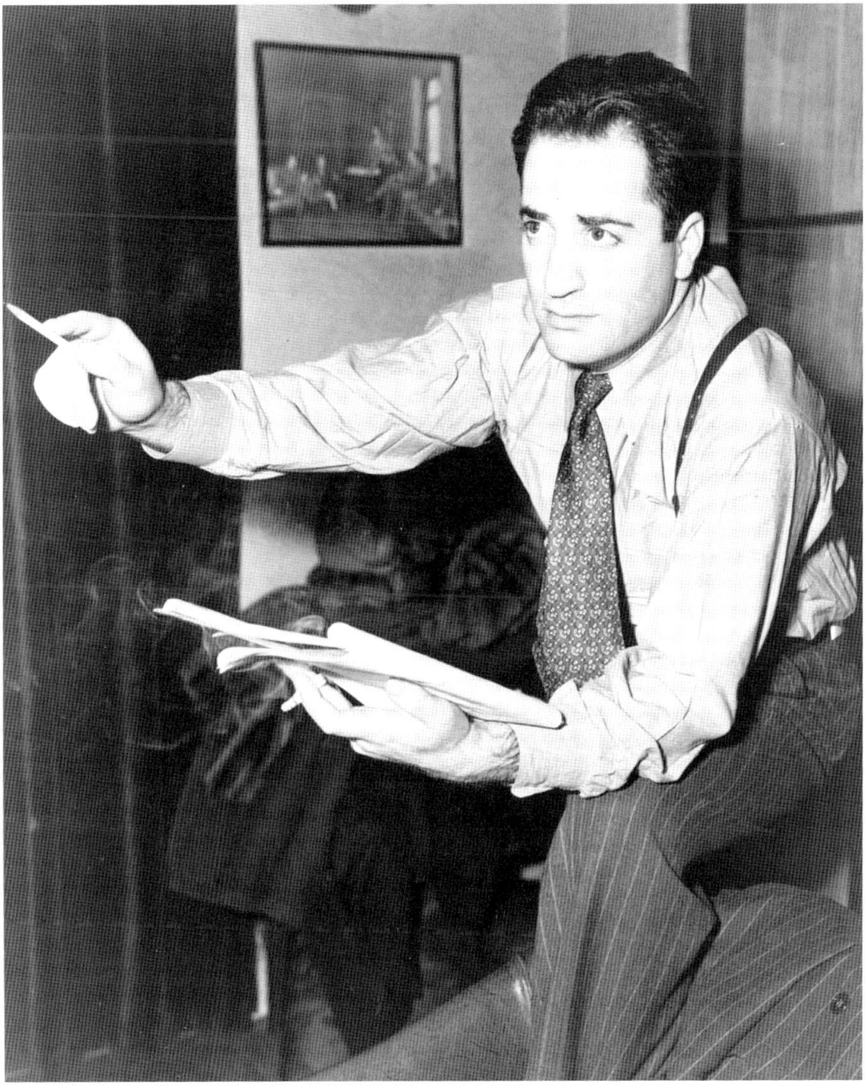

Playwright William Saroyan disliked basic training at Camp Kohler in 1942, but he was sipping drinks at London's Ritz by war's end. *Library of Congress.*

mistaken for wild game. Along the way, trainees under the 274th Signal Construction Company laid telephone lines for the U.S. Forestry Service and helped to enhance fire protection and communications in the Tahoe National Forest.[71] During the winter months, exercises were moved from the mountains to the milder climes of the Hunter Liggett Military Reservation, located some 150 miles south of San Francisco.

In 1943, with expansion as the guiding motivation, Kohler commandeered classrooms, dormitories and cafeterias at the University of California's College of Agriculture at Davis. It was at the so-called Western Signal Corps School that training for high- and low-speed radio operation and radio repair for both ground and airborne equipment was conducted. Wire training covered teletype installation and repair and instruction for "repeater men." Under Kohler command, the Davis campus and the Signal Corps Replacement Training Center at Walerga became known as the Western Signal Corps Training Center.

With the war winding down and the installation nearing the end of its military usefulness, questions arose about repurposing. One suggestion was to use Kohler as a temporary housing center for returning Japanese Americans. Dudley, who made Sacramento proud by winning McClellan and Mather, wouldn't have any of it. The Sacramento Chamber of Commerce, along with the American Legion and Veterans of Foreign Wars, told the War Relocation Authority (WRA) that returning veterans and their families deserved priority over, as Dudley put it, "the Japanese." In response, Northern California supervisor of the WRA Charles F. Miller was indignant, expressing as much in a formal letter to the chamber of commerce:

> *Let's not forget that these people coming into Kohler were uprooted bodily from their homes some three and one half years ago and placed in relocation centers. They weren't uprooted because they were charged with or convicted of any crime other than the accident of birth.*
>
> *Let's not beat around the bush Mr. Dudley. You're not nearly as much concerned with housing for returning veterans—Caucasians, of course—as you are with keeping out these returning people because they happen to be of Japanese ancestry.*
>
> *Incidentally, I think it's about time we stop calling these people "Japanese"... and thus confusing them...with our defeated enemies. The great majority of those returning were born in the United States.*[72]

In the end, the WRA got its way, and Kohler was opened to a trickle of former internees, holding no more than 125 at a time. The last group—a total of 100—was out by March 1946. Concurrent to Kohler's resettlement charge was its use by the San Francisco Port of Embarkation as a processing point for personnel returning home, accounting for a total of 35,893 servicemen, all of them shuttled east via rail or air by way of the airfield at McClellan. One of the few features to remain operable was the massive laundry (covering five acres) that provided cleaning for all military personnel in the Sacramento area. Of those who would turn out the lights at Kohler for the final time were the last of the area's German prisoners of war, who operated the laundry until it was turned over to McClellan.

Mather closed out the war by graduating its last navigator cadet on June 19, 1946, effectively making Lieutenant Oliver Dan Horton Jr. the nation's 50,000th navigator graduate since the start of the war. Crosstown, at the Air Depot, the rapturous news of V-J day meant that all civilian employees were given a two-day holiday starting with the close of the swing shift at midnight on August 15. Both Mather and McClellan would step from one conflict to another as instruments of Cold War deterrence doctrine, but not so for Kohler. Piecemeal liquidation, indecision regarding any significant postwar purpose and a sobering revelation that even the greatest promoter of twentieth-century Sacramento had his own moral blind spot characterized a slow, plodding dirge that ended with the reservation's effective closure in early 1946.

3

WITH ONE PURPOSE: SACRAMENTO'S WAR WORK

By Amanda G. DeWilde

World War II was a battle of mechanization, and from the aircraft carrier to the atomic bomb, the United States was at the forefront of designing and manufacturing more destructive and depersonalized tools of war. Tens of millions of American war workers joined the fight by going to the factory rather than the battlefield. With a unified purpose, they moved to urban centers and closer to military bases for plentiful jobs in wartime industry and support professions, driving unemployment to near zero. Sacramento trained and retooled for this new war work, with locals taking on jobs ranging from ship mechanics to counterfeiters of Japanese currency. While the largest airplane factories were located in Southern California and shipbuilding operations centered in the Bay Area, Sacramento was home to the largest Army Air Depot in the West. The city's workforce increased by tens of thousands, and its embrace of war workers of all backgrounds set it apart, priming the city for a postwar boom.

Throughout the war years, Sacramentans found work in areas classified as "essential industry" by the War Manpower Commission of the U.S. Employment Service. Applicants found and applied for a vast array of defense work and training through the U.S. Employment Service offices at 1106 Second Street and 1400 I Street—jobs at McClellan Air Force Base, at big manufacturing concerns like the Southern Pacific Shops and in smaller firms throughout the region. In jobs directly vital to the war effort, they qualified for occupational deferment from the draft. Ads for such work littered the classified sections of local newspapers. Other job postings contained a warning: Once employed in a "war essential" job, a worker was prohibited from applying for nonessential work.

Sacramento had a growing military presence at the time, and many civilian jobs opened up at area installations. At Mather Field, around 1,000 civilians were working in support roles alongside soldiers by 1943, and many more were spread across other locations like the Western Signal Corps Training Center at Camp Kohler northeast of the city and the Sacramento Signal Depot at Seventh and B Streets. But the biggest wartime employer of civilians in the region was the new Sacramento Air Depot, McClellan Field, the West Coast hub of air logistical support. McClellan boasted 18,439 civilians employed in radio repair, aircraft repair and dispatching supplies to combat units at its peak in March 1943.[73]

With about 4,000 employees, McClellan was already a sizeable installation prior to Pearl Harbor, and the bulk of its employees were civilians. Motivated by the rearmament of Germany and the nation's aggression toward its European neighbors, the depot steadily hired more workers and expanded into sub-depots at Mather Field and in Stockton, Mountain View, Taft and Bakersfield. By September 1941, McClellan employed 1,285 military personnel and 4,109 civilian workers.[74] A busy 24/7 production schedule began in November of that year—work was staffed in three shifts per day, seven days per week. McClellan was active around the clock and working diligently and efficiently for Uncle Sam.

Immediately after Pearl Harbor, McClellan came under the jurisdiction of Western Defense Command, which cut all red tape to funding, and the depot opened even more recruitment. The depot hired about 2,500 workers in the twenty-day period following December 7 and worked tirelessly to recruit for a wide range of jobs in nearly every department. In a wartime publicity booklet titled "A Camera Trip Through McClellan Field," a diverse civilian workforce was on display, working shoulder-to-shoulder for victory with the base's soldiers:

> *These soldiers and civilian workers are of all colors, creeds and classes. Mechanics and shopkeepers, farmers and laborers, lawyers and salesmen and men and women from scores of other occupations work together in close harmony with but one thought, one purpose, that men shall once more live in a world free from want and free from fear.*[75]

McClellan hired stenographers, clerks, storekeepers, tabulators, sorters and typists. Civilians also were needed to clean engine parts, drive trucks and

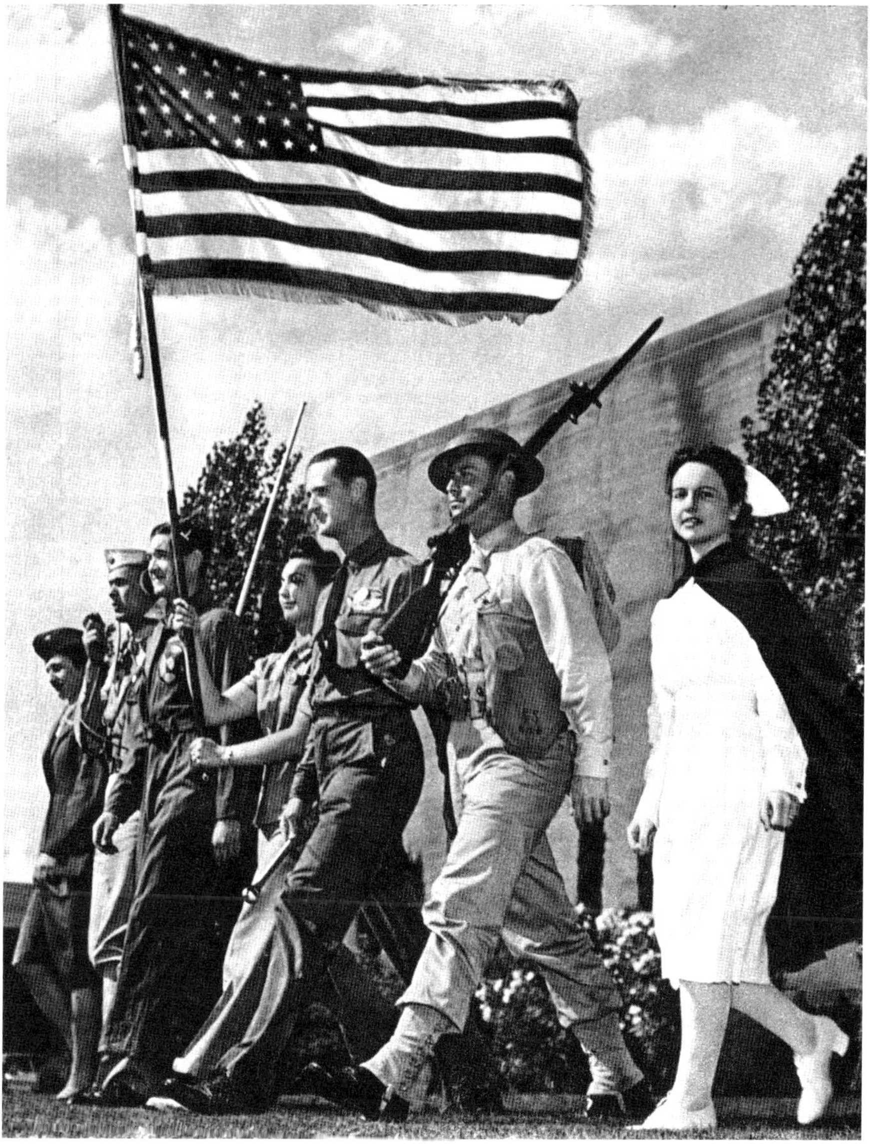

Civilians and soldiers march shoulder to shoulder in war work as pictured in the promotional booklet "A Camera Trip through McClellan Field." *Sacramento Public Library*.

make automotive repairs. Both men and women were hired for patrol work and firefighting. And McClellan hired civilian aircraft mechanics—coveted work that required additional training. The pace of training quickened along with recruitment. Tens of thousands were granted passes to visit the installation and apply for work, and women were recruited at the outset. Applicants were encouraged to take exams in mechanical work if they had any previous experience at all—aircraft-specific work was not required. Lois Moore from Roseville, who had done a bit of truck driving and mechanical repair, signed up with the first wave. In addition to some on-the-job training, courses were offered in aircraft repair at high schools, trade schools and colleges. Those who desired more training could take a mechanical aptitude test and enroll in a three-month course at Sacramento Junior College, getting paid while they trained.[76] Sacramento's mechanic learner course was incredibly popular. When the course was inaugurated on a statewide basis in February 1942, there were twenty thousand applicants.

Patriotic duty was a key component of the civilian orientation. In the 1942 base publication "How Can I Be a Good American Here?," issued to all civilian employees at McClellan, the answers were

1. *Show respect for military leaders.*
2. *Buy war bonds.*
3. *Safeguard military information.*
4. *Stay on the job and do the work you are requested to do.*

War workers at McClellan had a clear and common mission: "You are here to work with all your force, with efficiency, with alertness and carefulness, to keep American's planes in the air." And workers were reminded of the value of their efforts: "We have in our hands the moulding [*sic*] of our own futures. By working for the War Department we become part of the great effort to make our country strong, strong enough to do the job it must do if we are to remain free."[77]

The day after Christmas 1942, the War Department expanded civilian work hours to a forty-eight-hour, six-day week. The work intensity and workforce size remained high until new depots in Ogden, Spokane and San Bernardino became operational in 1943. Though the number of workers soon began to decline as the country suffered from labor shortages, productivity increased.[78]

Civilian war workers were eventually recognized alongside their military colleagues. In October 1943, U.S. Secretary of War Henry L. Stimson asked that service awards be conferred on civilian workers. In December, civilians at the Sacramento military installations were feted for their wartime contributions with substantial cash rewards and colorful lapel ribbons for both service length and meritorious service. A ceremony at McClellan was recorded by a newsreel crew, as 10,500 men and women received awards for working at the air depot for six months or more.[79] Cash awards also went to workers who contributed creative ideas and inventions for improving war production efficiency. Similar ceremonies were held at other locations. Mather Field's civilian workers received cash prizes for thinking up "Victory Ideas."

In contrast to the recognition afforded civilians at other local military installations, civilians at the Sacramento Signal Depot operated under the radar at the Bercut-Richards packing plant. Although the depot was activated in 1943, few knew about its existence or its operations until 1944, despite the fact that it employed more than 1,000 civilians. (The number would peak at more than 1,800 in July 1945.) First established on the state fairgrounds as a communications unit for Western Defense Command, the depot's role was to supply communications and electronics equipment to the army. The installation used warehouse space at numerous locations spread throughout the city.[80]

In private industry, many Sacramentans found defense work in small- and large-scale manufacturing operations. At the beginning of the war, thousands of Sacramento workers left the city for war work in the Bay Area and elsewhere at industrial firms that were scoring big government contracts. In response, War Industries Inc. was formed from thirty small manufacturers and machine shop owners on June 4, 1942.[81] W.G. Stone of the Sacramento Chamber of Commerce helped create the industrial pool to obtain war contracts for businesses that had a hard time competing with large scale industry. Because so many Sacramento firms were too small to obtain war contracts, War Industries Inc. offered organization and cooperation. By 1943, the company had expanded to forty-two businesses and brought in $5 million in defense contracts related to shipbuilding, ship-fitting and frozen goods. Many of the items produced were quite specialized, and the outfits retooled their operations to be more relevant to war industry. Christy Gun Works and Dosch Sign Company turned to producing wooden pulley blocks. Holland Building and Machine Works worked on tail shafts for Liberty cargo ships. The Earl E. Markwart Company, which once made service station machinery, switched over to producing special oil storage tanks. Other businesses that signed up with War Industries Inc. included the *Sacramento Bee*, Capital Lumber Company and Sacramento Shipbuilding Company.[82]

The largest single contract obtained by the group was a $300,000 naval contract awarded to N.M. Alling Iron Works & Shipbuilding company,

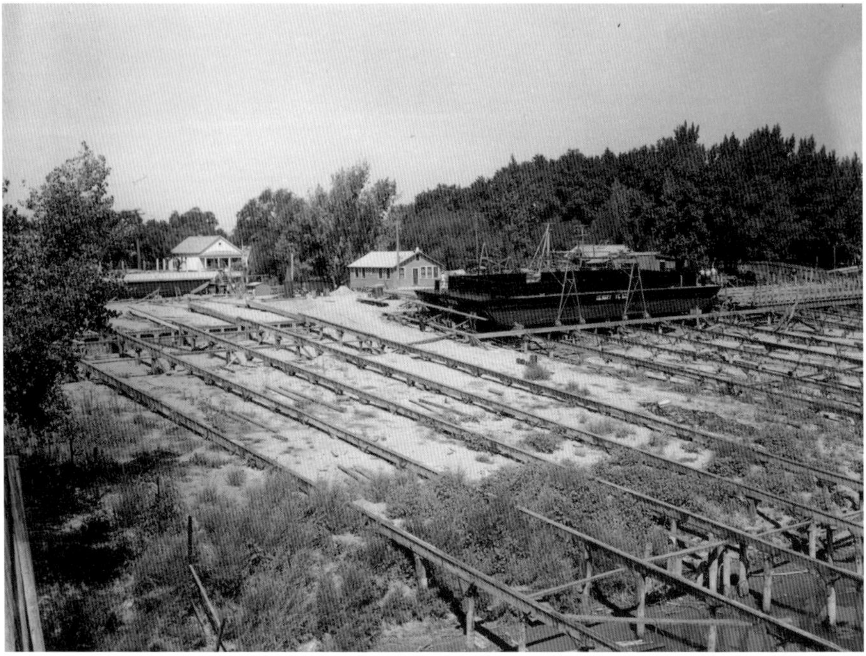

A barge sits under construction at the Sacramento Shipbuilding Company located at Second and F Streets in Broderick (now West Sacramento). *California State Library*.

located at 2415 Fifth Street, which built a couple dozen target sleds to be towed by ships for gunnery practice. The contract meant fifty new jobs for carpenters, steelworkers and the like and additional work for Thys & Miller Steel Foundry. The foundry, located on Folsom Boulevard, was Sacramento's first commercial steel foundry. Established in 1940 by Edouard Thys, a Belgian aristocrat and electrical engineer, and his wife, Pinky, Thys & Miller made steel casings during the war. Smaller-scale shipbuilding operations took shape on both sides of the Sacramento River. Because of a shortage of steel, many contracts called for the construction of wooden vessels with steel components. Alling also owned Sacramento Shipbuilding Company at Second and F Streets in Broderick, which offered shipyard work for local woodworkers. The company constructed wooden cargo barges for the navy and launched a vessel every two weeks. Also on the Yolo County side of the Sacramento River, the Otto Steinbrenner shipyards built 110-foot cargo vessels for the army, launching one per week.

The War Industries Inc. industrial pool was so successful at winning contracts that it earned an "E" Award for high achievement in production from the army and navy. Individual firms were recognized, too. Sacramento Engineering and Machine Works, which built high-precision supplies and equipment, became the only firm in Northern California outside of the Bay Area to win the E Award. Even Governor Earl Warren recognized Sacramento War Industries Inc. as adding "luster to the shining example of many California businesses."[83]

Sacramento's largest employer was the State of California, which put some operations on hold to take on a variety of war projects. In more creative work, the state contributed to projects such as Operation Toy Horse, which was run by the State Printing Office under contract with the federal government. Workers made counterfeit Japanese invasion money in an attempt to flood invaded territories with currency and disrupt the Japanese economy. Beginning in the fall of 1944, scores of temporary workers received shipments of scrip from the Stecher-Traung Lithograph Company of San Francisco, which they then examined, numbered, cut and bundled at Governors' Hall at the state fairgrounds. The operation shipped hundreds of millions of notes for use by the U.S. Navy and War Department. Clark R. Long, assistant director of the U.S. Treasury Department's Bureau of Engraving and Printing, praised the State Printing Office for its "fine spirit of cooperation and patriotism" in carrying out the contract.[84]

The California State Department of Public Works, which included the Division of Highways, Division of Architecture and Division of Water Resources, paused most work during the war, and local and federal public works projects were put on hold as well. An exception was made for those projects already underway and of wartime value, like the construction of Shasta Dam, which employed 1,900 people by 1940. Restrictions were eased by 1943. In the spring of that year, Governor Earl Warren won approval for expansion of the Central Valley Project, which had been restricted by the War Production Board to just include work on Shasta Dam and other power facilities. Governor Warren pushed for postwar plans toward the end of the war, both in building construction and highway expansion, and California reported 116 shovel-ready projects in early 1945.[85] Among them were local projects like the construction of Folsom Dam.

Federal agencies with offices in Sacramento did their part, too. The Sacramento office of the U.S. Geological Survey, located at 600 J Street, was tasked with producing maps from aerial photographs of the region of France from the Cherbourg Peninsula to Le Havre for the D-day invasion.[86] And many federal agencies that had focused on public works projects before the war, like the Works Progress Administration, helped

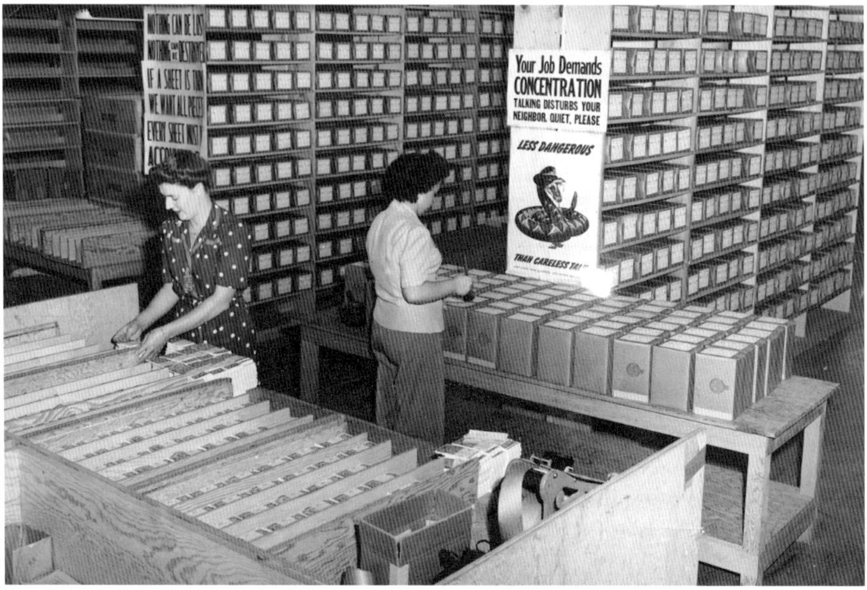

Workers sort notes and label boxes as part of the Operation Toy Horse counterfeiting effort at the fairgrounds. *California State Library.*

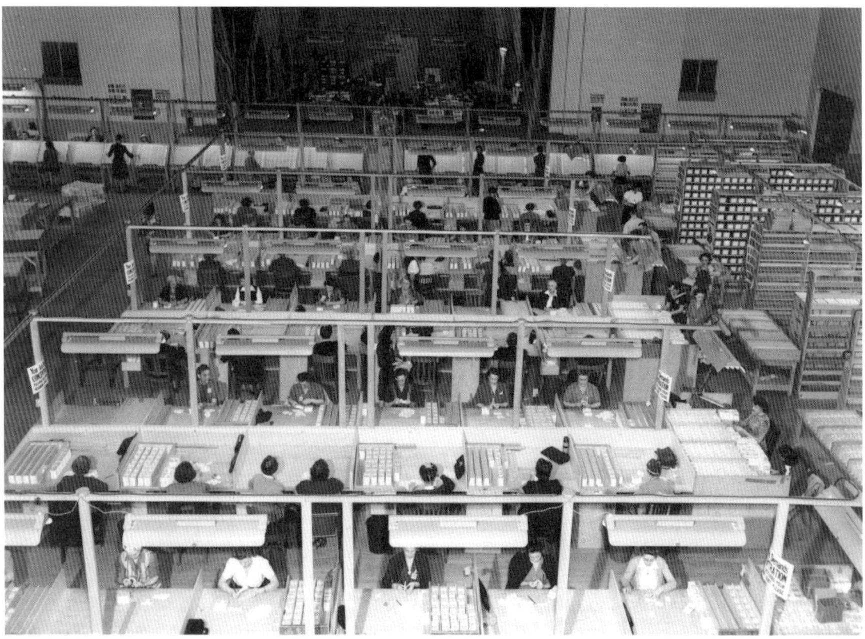

An elevated view of workers examining and sorting currency for Operation Toy Horse inside Governors' Hall at the California State Fair grounds. *California State Library.*

out with war work prior to their dissolution. The WPA took an active role in scrap-metal drives in Sacramento, removing abandoned streetcar rails to reclaim for conversion into war materials—amounting to as much as nine hundred tons of steel in 1942. The city's civilian defense work was funded in part by money from these scrap-metal salvage drives. The WPA also stepped in to assist the USO in providing recreational activities for personnel at McClellan and Mather Fields.

As Sacramento's defense industry hummed along during the war years, government and private employers overcame the challenges of finding housing for workers, training them for war work and incorporating new labor into the workforce.

Thousands of new workers were streaming into the Sacramento area by early 1942, and housing was in short supply. Even prior to December 1941, the commander at McClellan knew that housing would be a challenge for the many thousands of new residents scheduled to work at the base: "Neighborly goodwill, farsighted planning and vigorous pushing of necessary building work will make it possible to welcome our new fellow citizens and protect them from the chiseler and the profiteer."[87] In January 1942, the city building inspector

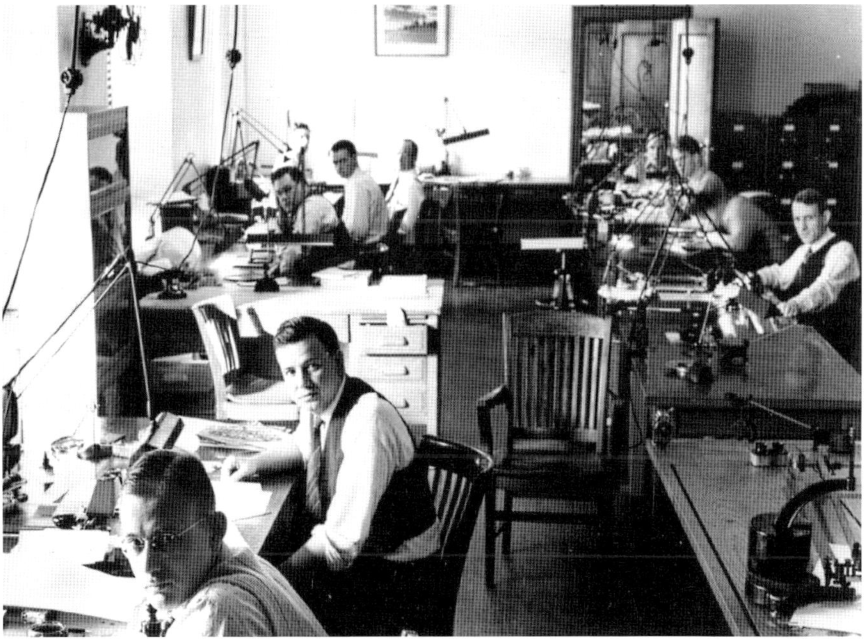

The Sacramento office of the U.S. Geographical Survey drew maps for the D-day invasion. *Sacramento Public Library.*

gave a green light to the city's first two defense housing projects—thirty modest homes located at Coloma Terrace, north of D Street between Forty-Sixth and Forty-Ninth Streets in East Sacramento, and in the H Street Tract No. 3 on El Dorado Way and on Fifty-Third Street. The five-room homes were built for around $4,000 each and financed with the application of Title Six of the FHA, which covered defense housing. By May, eighty-two homes were going in at Coloma Terrace at the rate of one a day.

Because few new homes were being built due to wartime restrictions on construction, public housing projects already underway were taken over by war workers. The New Helvetia apartments (today part of the Alder Grove housing project facing demolition) was the largest such project, located south of Broadway between Sixth Street and Muir Way. Though it started as low-income housing in May 1941, as it neared completion, the $1 million project was redesignated by the Sacramento Housing Authority as housing for war industry families. Most of the 310 units located in 62 buildings housed war workers. War workers also moved into the 168 units at the Dos Rios low-cost housing project located on North Twelfth Street near North B Street. The rules there required that the head of household be a citizen of the United States and that only single families apply. The homes there were still rented based on income, with those earning over $2,100 per year barred from the apartments.[88]

At McClellan, dormitories for 528 civilian women employees were constructed in March 1943. Despite this array of housing options, there was still a dearth of rooms for war workers. The Sacramento Defense Housing Bureau remained on the hunt for housing and solicited residents for space in their homes. The bureau created a special directory of rentals for black war workers and their families. In another attempt to free up affordable housing during the war years, rent freezes were instituted at the national level. In Sacramento, landlords registered at twenty offices spread throughout the city, verifying that they had frozen rents at March 1, 1942 rates.

Many of Sacramento's defense jobs required specialized training. While some applicants had expertise in mechanical and machine work that was readily adaptable to wartime needs, many job seekers required additional training. Sacramento Junior College was a center of the area's defense training and provided instruction day and night. Grant Union High School, which was located just north of the city, had opened just a few years before the war. Strategically situated near McClellan, Grant also became a hub for civilian training—much of it for younger workers. Even prior to Pearl Harbor, the National Youth Administration (a New Deal agency that later

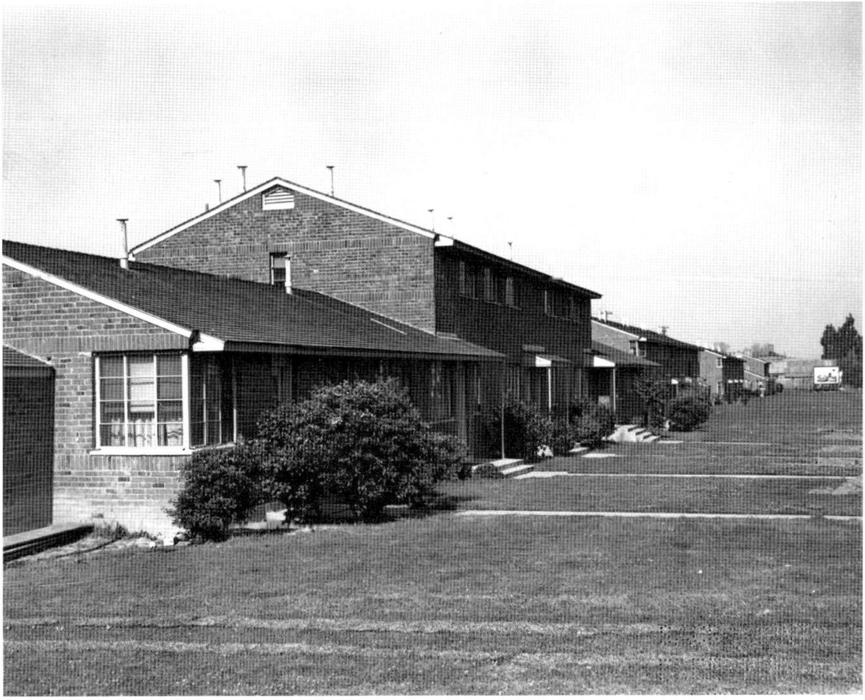

The New Helvetia housing project, pictured here in 1943, housed hundreds of defense workers and their families. *Sacramento Public Library*.

became part of the War Manpower Commission) had trained 175 young men in aviation jobs from throughout the state at Grant Union High School. Alongside their studies, the men worked for pay at McClellan.[89] In addition, Grant Union High School started up its own Grant Technical Junior College in Del Paso Heights in 1942. The school offered technical courses that trained 1,703 workers for air depot assignments by March of that year.

When Sacramento's NYA program ended in 1942, a new training program for female machinists was established at Grant Union High School. The women were housed at the former NYA residence center on the high school campus and studied at the California State Fairgrounds. Training enabled them to receive job placement through the U.S. Employment Service. A *Sacramento Bee* article from July 1942 marveled at the spectacle of women performing work in the program: "Milady—with the soft hands and tinted nails—is experiencing such work day hazards as skinned knuckles, arc blindness and metal burns. The women are learning the machinist, sheet metal, welding and forge shop trades."[90]

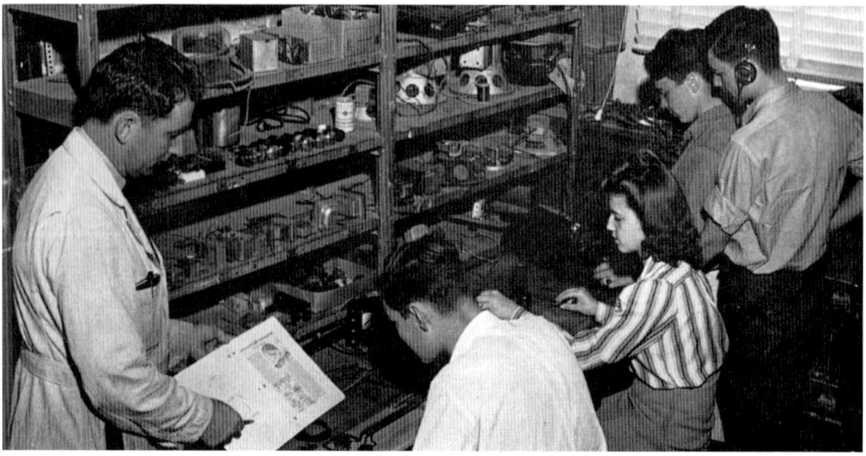

Sacramento City high schools offered pre-induction training and war production training courses. Pictured here is a radio shop class, circa 1942. *Sacramento Public Library*.

The sight of women working in jobs traditionally held by men, which was such a shock at the beginning of the war, became commonplace. Sacramento war workers were as varied as their work. Housewives joined the workforce in growing numbers. Government workers used their unique skill sets for the war effort. Incarcerated men at Folsom Prison were contracted out to harvest at local farms and create war art. Prisoners of war from Germany and Italy were put to work in building and agricultural projects. And conscientious objectors found indirect ways to support the war effort at farms and forestry camps. Because so many young men enlisted or were drafted into the military, Sacramento's defense workers would have to be made up mostly of women, youths and older workers—those physically or legally disqualified from military service. Women and minorities would need to be actively recruited for defense jobs to meet the growing need. George Bodie, of the U.S. Manpower Commission, addressed resistance to integrating workplaces that had been relatively homogenous before the war: "The prejudices of unions and employers must give way."[91]

At the outset of the war, married women's work was limited to the domestic sphere, and single and older women took jobs outside the home in fields like secretarial work, teaching or nursing. But that would very quickly expand to include war production jobs for both married and unmarried women. Sacramento policymakers first proposed the idea of incorporating women into traditional war work in early 1942. Roy C. Donnally, manager of the U.S. Employment Service in Sacramento, predicted that the extension of the draft age to forty-four would necessitate hiring female laborers at McClellan, a move that was successful elsewhere: "There is no reason why women cannot be fitted to jobs as riveters, aircraft inspectors, or radio repairmen. Southern aircraft factories use the feminine touch and find it highly efficient."[92] In January 1942, 11.4 percent of employees at McClellan were women; in November 1942, women comprised 40 percent of the workforce.[93]

By 1943, the federal government set a target to add three million to the United States workforce. Sacramento was asked to recruit three thousand housewives and unemployed young women as part of the national drive. The U.S. War Manpower Commission cited the use of women in Great Britain, where estimates showed that several years into the war, upward of 35 percent of all war workers were women—including 80 to 90 percent of workers in munitions plants. At the time, married women were a relatively untapped labor pool, as many resigned from work upon marrying, whether by choice or involuntary dismissal. Just a couple years earlier, attendees at the first annual convention of the California Federation of Business and Professional Women's Clubs in Sacramento voted for a resolution to ask both Republican and Democratic Parties to include planks in their national platforms guaranteeing women the right to work regardless of marital status.[94]

The recruitment efforts worked. At McClellan, women constituted 56 percent of the depot supply workforce, with 36 percent in maintenance and 49 percent at headquarters in 1943. Overall, they made up nearly half (46 percent) of civilians employed at the depot.[95] McClellan employed women in many pioneering areas, including as airplane mechanics and dispatchers. The depot held the distinction of producing the only plane on the West Coast overhauled, assembled and modernized by an entirely female crew.[96] Throughout industrial work in Sacramento, women expanded their roles. At the Southern Pacific Railyards, "railroadettes" were employed as war essential workers in both skilled jobs (riveters, machine tool operators) and support work (passing out tools, secretaries). By the end of 1942, Southern Pacific had employed more than three hundred women at the Sacramento and Roseville locations. Southern Pacific employed a peak of seven thousand at the shops near the Sacramento River during the war, nearly 40 percent of whom were women.

With so many women working long hours away from home, care was needed for children of defense workers. Nationally, nurseries were established with funding from the 1941 Defense Public Works law (popularly known as the Lanham Act). In addition, the California War Council submitted a bill

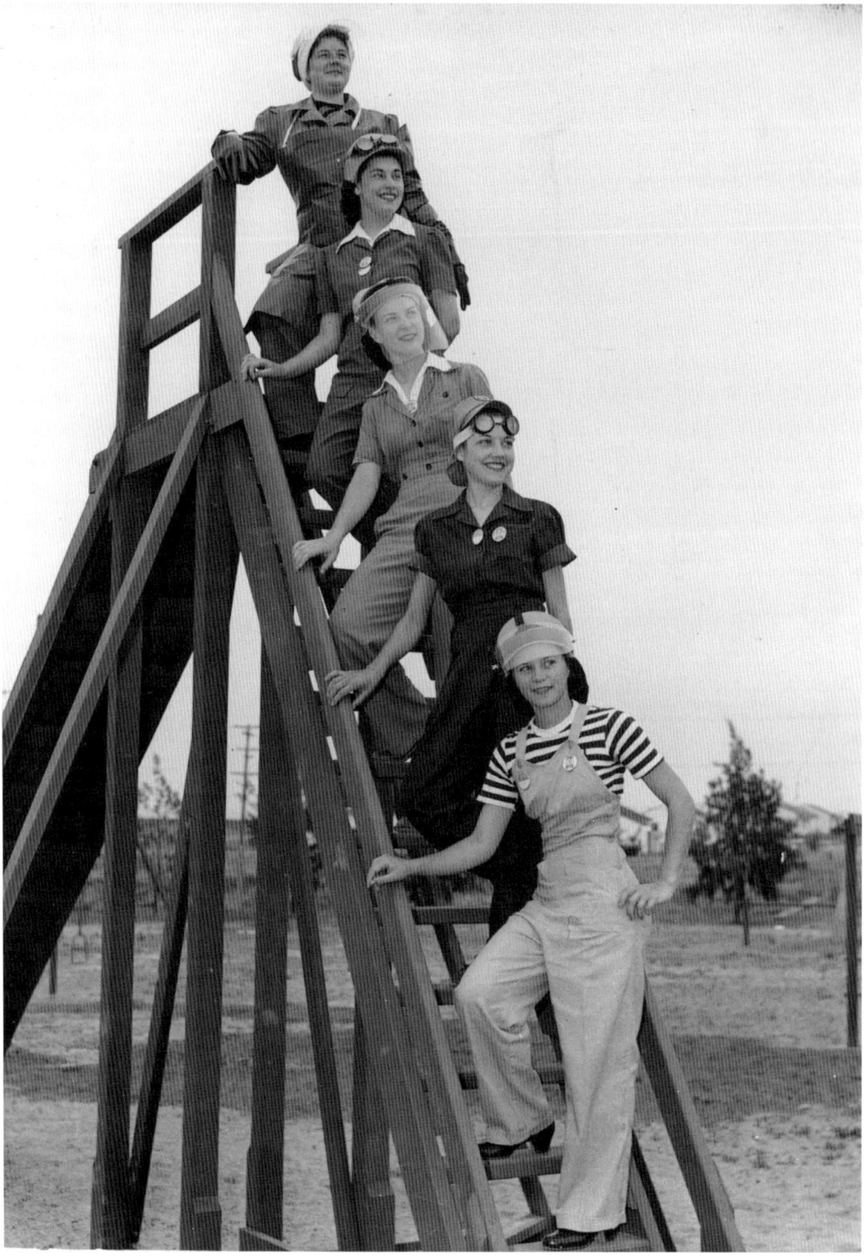

Defense workers pose on a stairway at McClellan Army Air Depot, where women made up nearly half of the civilian workforce during the war. *Sacramento Public Library*.

in 1943 to establish and maintain childcare centers for children between the ages of two and sixteen whose parents were employed in war industries. Several local elementary schools applied to open nurseries with money from the Lanham Act, and McClellan opened a twenty-four-hour center at Grant Union High School for the children of military and civilian workers who were engaged in work on three different shifts.[97]

The diversity of Sacramento's war workers extended beyond gender to include race and age. Older Sacramentans capable of working were encouraged to do their part to meet the need for manpower, and high school boys entered into apprenticeships in war manufacturing and mechanical trades while still in school. Although Sacramento had been an ethnically diverse city since the gold rush, workers of all backgrounds were challenged to work together for a common purpose during the war years.

The increasing ethnic diversity of Sacramento's military and civilian personnel was evident when the city opened the country's first interracial USO in the spring of 1942. The club was intended to serve black and Asian soldiers but was open to all and offered entertainment by all at 1024½ J Street. Ben Ellison, who had been youth activities director for the Los Angeles Coordinating Councils, moved to Sacramento to direct the USO, calling it "a fertile environment for the principles of the constitution of the United States and for the common rights of all Americans."[98] Entertainers and hostesses represented a variety of backgrounds. An International Show that fall included Chinese, Scottish, Italian, Spanish and "Anglo-Saxon" performers. When Lucille Hayward, wife of Camp Kohler's chaplain, took over from Ellison in 1943, she praised Sacramento as "a city which is noted throughout the United States for its fine understanding among the races" and declared it a time for racial unity: "Races should learn to appreciate one another. This is strictly war work, for this war is being fought so all races will have an equal standing under the sun."[99]

Conscientious objectors and prisoners of war found work not directly related to war industry, most of it agricultural. Ronald Chinn was a popular teacher of history and Americanization at Sacramento High School. He also was an active member of the local Sacramento Religious Society of Friends. When it came time to register for the draft, he asked for deferment from Draft Board No. 25 and declared himself a conscientious objector on religious grounds. Although Chinn was immediately suspended from teaching, his case came before the city board (and then the state board) to determine whether he should be permanently barred. His case gained prominence throughout the state. The board ruled that a person who was willing to perform noncombatant work did not violate the teacher oath. Along with other conscientious objectors, Chinn would be assigned to work at a camp through the duration of the war. He was granted extended leave by the district to work in the objector camp in San Dimas. Three years later, he returned to Sacramento and was rehired as an English teacher over protests from the local VFW.[100]

Thousands of German prisoners of war helped with projects throughout the region, most as agricultural laborers. Statewide, farmers enlisted some twenty thousand German prisoners to help with the 1945 harvest season. In the Sacramento Valley, prisoners performed a variety of work at sixteen prisoner-of-war camps in August 1945. German and Italian prisoners in Placer County installed fences and guard towers at Camp Flint, a relief camp for the unemployed opened in 1938 under the State Relief Agency (SRA) and WPA. Prisoners also helped maintain the grounds at DeWitt Army Hospital, located at Camp Flint. At Camp Kohler, about five hundred prisoners of war did laundry for Sacramento's military posts, eventually moving to a larger facility at McClellan.[101] Sacramentans were mostly in the dark about these local prisoner-of-war camps. When four German prisoners escaped their camp at the Signal Depot at Seventh and North B Streets in May 1945, the FBI, military police and local law enforcement revealed the presence of the camp only when asking local residents to be on the lookout for the fugitives.[102] More than three hundred German prisoners were encamped at the depot.

Prisoners from the Sacramento County Jail obtained special parole to work on local farms. Folsom Prison inmates likewise worked on harvest and forestry farms, and the state prison's large workforce volunteered for numerous other war projects. In October 1942, the machine and blacksmith shops at Folsom Prison were made subsidiaries of Mare Island Navy Yard, and the prison secured a contract to make nets, sheets and other linen goods for the navy.[103] At its peak production, hundreds of convicts were employed in the operation. More than one hundred inmates also received classroom instruction and practical training in firefighting and were on call by federal and state forestry officials for duty. In addition, inmates used their artistic sides to produce propaganda posters, which gained recognition. Lieutenant Colonel Hanover was impressed with the quality of work put out by the prisoners when he visited the prison in August 1942: "I've been all over the country and I've taken quite an interest in war posters. These posters I saw in Sacramento made by Folsom inmates, pack more punch than any others I've seen anywhere."[104] Among the artists was Ralph Pekor, who had been a successful artist prior to his imprisonment in the 1930s for manslaughter. Pekor painted patriotic posters and had many of his insignia designs accepted by McClellan air groups.

With confidence that America would be victorious, Sacramento began planning for a postwar economy in 1943. Officials did not anticipate a postwar economic boom, but rather a depression. Governor Warren addressed a conference of governors from western states in April 1943. While he touted that the war had brought about "the greatest economic transformation in the history of California," he also warned, "History records that following each great war we stumble and fall into the depth of a depression. This being the greatest war in history, it might be reasoned that we should prepare for the greatest plunge in history."[105] On the eve of the Japanese surrender in 1945, local and state officials met to develop a postwar plan. Since 1943, it was reported, the state had experienced a decrease in 250,000 defense jobs, and California prepared for many thousands more. Policymakers were also concerned with unemployment. E.P. Sherwin, Sacramento city manager, pledged 400 public works jobs at one dollar per hour pay for returning veterans, while the state anticipated a $250 million increase in unemployment insurance claims.[106]

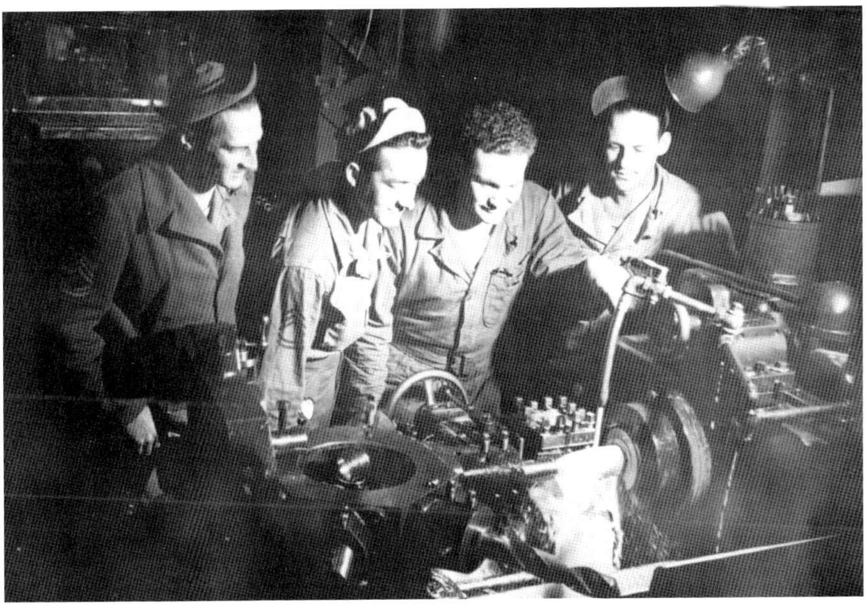

Sacramento soldiers celebrate producing one million airplane parts in a year. Angelo (Fred) Mallegni (*second from right*) went on to work at McClellan for thirty-seven years. *Linda Osuna.*

Despite preparing for an economic downtown, Sacramento translated its wartime economic successes into a postwar economic boom. California experienced the largest growth of any state between 1940 and 1944. While the nation as a whole broke even in workforce size, California's working population grew by more than 30 percent as hundreds of thousands migrated to the state.[107] The war in the Pacific opened new trade routes, where it was hoped that during the "reconstruction period," Sacramento would be called upon to serve more than 800 million consumers. Sacramento's unemployment rate dropped from 16.5 percent to 6.5 percent, and the labor force increased by nearly 50,000. Area military bases de-escalated postwar, but they continued to employ thousands more workers than they had before the war—workers like army veteran Angelo (Fred) Mallegni, who returned from combat to work for more than three decades as a civilian at McClellan Air Force Base, retiring as a toolmaker foreman in 1979. In addition to more temporary influxes of workers for war industry jobs, sectors already in place in the city that supported the war effort, like the railroads and canning, saw huge growth. Canning and preserving jobs grew to 20 percent of the city's payroll.[108] At the Southern Pacific Shops, the average number of employees peaked during the war years at 4,175 in 1943, making the operation the second largest of its kind in the nation. In the postwar era, Sacramento would be the center of expanding markets, raw materials and transportation alongside a growing defense industry and state government. The war years were instrumental in bringing the city into the modern era, and postwar Sacramento emerged as a city diversified, modernized and thriving, due in large part to its enthusiastic response to Uncle Sam's call for homefront help.

4

INNOVATIONS VERSUS SHORTAGES: SACRAMENTO AGRICULTURE IN WORLD WAR II

By Eric Webb

An axiom of war holds that shortages of metals, transportation and labor are inevitable. This certainly held true for Sacramento during World War II, and of the three, labor provided the most formidable challenge. Intensified by the Japanese incarceration, shortages of farm workers dogged the region throughout the conflict. Only with the toil of itinerant laborers, most notably the Mexican braceros, along with women and schoolchildren, did Sacramento stave off utter calamity.

Proximity to the state's leading school of agriculture provided Sacramento with unique advantages. The University of California–Davis School of Agriculture and its Extension, the backbone of regional farming since its founding in 1905, coordinated the labor effort and utilized local demonstration farms to test new field innovations. While other less-urbanized counties, particularly in the San Joaquin Valley, outpaced Sacramento in crop production, Sacramento County and its surrounding regions still managed to increase overall crop yield during the war.

Infrastructure

In retrospect, one cannot underestimate the providence of the New Deal infrastructure projects of the 1930s and 1940s. By 1940, Works Progress Administration laborers cleared 40,000 acres of Sacramento County wetlands in favor of crop acreage and urbanization. Some 322 miles of highways and streets were also graded and paved, including 183 miles of all-weather rural roads, allowing farmers to get their produce swiftly to market.[109]

The Public Works Administration funded, to the tune of $700,000, historic improvements in Sacramento's water infrastructure. The waterworks, featuring twin towers capable of holding three million gallons each, were celebrated at the time as the largest reinforced-concrete elevated water tanks ever constructed.[110] These edifices allowed sufficient water pressure to travel to residences and ranches through the flatlands of Sacramento. Five hundred emergency wells were drilled on farms throughout the county in addition to a large number of single-chamber septic tanks.[111]

The construction of Shasta Dam, which began in 1937, was an engineering rarity in that it was completed twenty-six months ahead of schedule in 1945. And it was additionally fortuitous that even before its completion it started to pay dividends, the most important of which was the generation of electricity for California factories during the war. The dam also provided a measure of stability for Delta farmers. They had long hoped for a reservoir that would release fresh water during dry months, thus preventing saltwater intrusion, and control floods during the winter months. The dam captured water for irrigation supply not only for farms in the Delta but also for the fields of the San Joaquin Valley through a system of canals.[112]

Climate and the Agricultural Regions

A successful war effort also requires simple good fortune. The recurrent droughts since the 1970s, most likely influenced by climate change, helped heighten public awareness of historical weather trends. Fortunately for Sacramento, the years from 1942 to 1945 ran a very normal course climatically. Precipitation was 91 percent of average during these years, and the median temperature held as expected. Rains did come early in 1943, which hampered the tomato harvest, but the losses were minor.[113]

According to the University of California, there were three distinct zones of agriculture in Sacramento County. First were the lowlands, consisting of the Delta districts of the Sacramento, American and Cosumnes Rivers where "the type of agriculture is so entirely different from that in the upland sections."[114] In the Delta, a vast array of vegetables, including a large

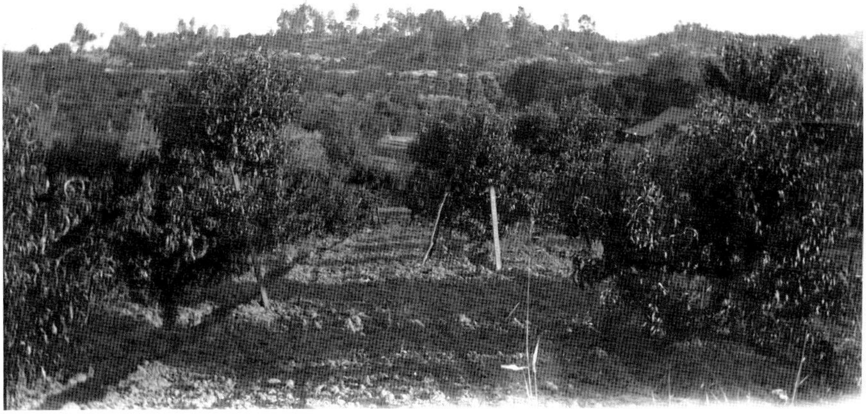

One of the many orchards in the hills of Loomis. *Center for Sacramento History.*

amount of asparagus and tomatoes, were grown in its fertile alluvial soil. The pear orchards surrounding Courtland served as a notable exception to the surrounding row crops.

A few miles to the east, where pockets of hardpan made the soil somewhat less favorable, vast swaths of deciduous fruit trees stood, from peaches and cherries to olives and apricots. Citrus trees, particularly mandarins, were grown in this area but much less so after the great freeze of 1932, which had effectively wiped out the county's citrus crop.[115] Cattle and sheep ranches dotted the foothill sections along the eastern borderlands adjacent to El Dorado and Amador Counties.

The final zone of Sacramento agriculture, according to university officials, consisted of the numerous home gardens and small part-time ranches found in the urban core. This urban cohort would swell in stature during the war because of the Food for Victory program. All told, one hundred different crops were grown in these subdivisions.[116]

Similarly, the university counted three types of Sacramento agronomists. Aside from the gardens and hobby farms of the urban areas, there were three thousand farms and ranches that were characterized as "professional." Their owners were typically active in farm organizations and had many years of experience. Most of these family farms had been passed down through several generations, and the families themselves led industry organizations, such as the Farm Bureau and 4-H clubs.

In contrast, there was an equally large group of about three thousand smaller farms. An agriculture commissioner observed, "[They are] not necessarily organization-minded and demand a great deal of service from the extension."[117] To a large degree, these parcels were operated by new farmers who had taken over the fields left vacant by the Japanese internment. In addition, the purchase of farms was brisk during the war on account of rising commodity prices. One report noted the rural appeal: "Some urbanites desire farm and ranch house life."[118]

Farming and the University

Since its inception, the University of California–Davis School of Agriculture viewed the Sacramento region as a playground for agricultural experimentation. With the onset of war, it now saw a region in need of crisis support. The Extension coordinated with both the state and county departments of agriculture to conduct thousands of meetings with local farmers during the conflict. In 1945 alone, there were 707 Farm Bureau meetings attended by 16,105 farm men, women, boys and girls.[119] University of California Agriculture Extension chief executive Elmer L. Stanley stated its goal: "Our program is designed to serve these agricultural conditions of various kinds to the best of our ability with limited personnel." He further defined the need: "After the Japanese were evacuated new growers taking over these plantings were very much interested in these meetings."[120]

These seminars addressed a wide array of topics and took place on the campus demonstration farm in Davis as well as on other demonstration farms throughout the county. Right from the start, the School of Agriculture took corrective action. After testing soil moisture in the Delta tomato fields during the late spring of 1942, they found that "new growers oftentimes added irrigation to already wet soil and were told to hold back."[121]

As one could imagine, irrigation was a hot topic. Water levels varied radically throughout the county from the shallows of the Delta to the hardpan soil and deep water tables on the eastern side of the county. Simple techniques such as furrowing with reversible chisel and mouldboard ploughs broke through this hardpan and enabled farms to irrigate their crops without the overuse of expensive fertilizer. The Andrew Brian farm in the Florin District featured a demonstration vineyard that illuminated these methods of irrigation application. Both the quality and tonnage of grapes

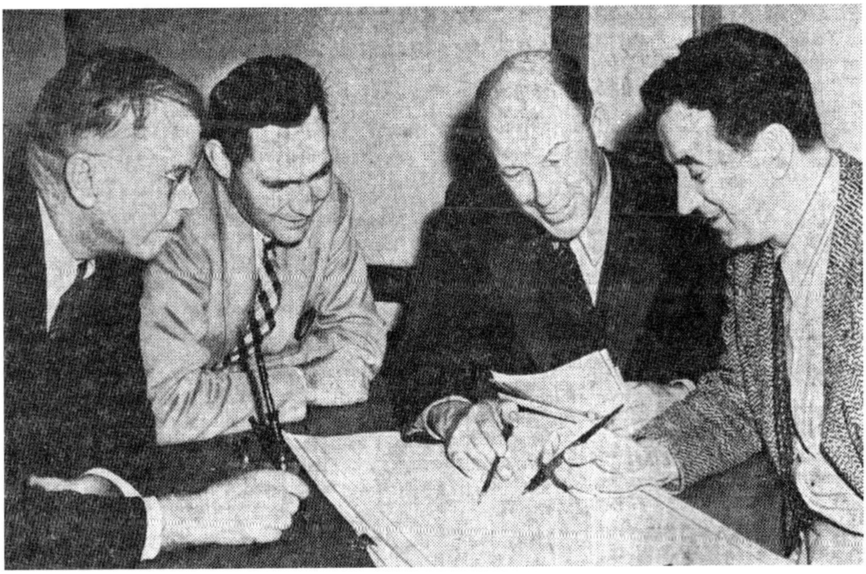

Elmer L. Stanley, head of the University of California–Davis Agricultural Extension, is on the far right. He led the extension from 1928 until his death in 1949. *Center for Sacramento History.*

immediately increased. A similar demonstration was also held on the L.A. Scott farm in Fair Oaks. Just as in Florin, soil posed difficulties in the rolling hills of Fair Oaks and Orangevale. These improved furrowing techniques also led to an increase in the production of the orange and olive orchards on the Scott farmland.

Conversely, drainage was the primary concern down in the Delta. A particularly dramatic intervention occurred at the Fay pear orchard just south of Walnut Grove. Constant flooding had the Fay family on the verge of abandoning their land. The university once again came to the rescue as noted in their annual report:

> *In cooperating with J.B. Brown, an Extension specialist, a drainage program was laid out and Mr. Fay agreed to keep the orchard another year to see whether or not he would get any results. This orchard has steadily improved and now it is one of the finest orchards on the Sacramento River. Every pear grower on the Sacramento levee has seen these results and has been influenced by these results. Most of them now have recognized that drainage is one of the most important factors having to do with the growing of pears.*[122]

INNOVATION

The effort to increase agricultural production continued with ideas big and small in rapid succession. In March 1942, local dairymen and the veterinary school at UC Davis formed a nonprofit cooperative that sought to create an artificial breeding program for cattle. The university also found that sheep had a particular fondness for sugar beet pulp, which was particularly beneficial, since crop production increased due to ongoing sugar shortages. These two improvements led to an increase in the number of "small unit" dairy farms and sheep ranches, particularly in the foothill sections of the eastern county.[123]

Methods characteristic of large-scale farming gained wider acceptance. For much of the preceding century, Sacramento County's legendary hop fields stretched along the Cosumnes and American Rivers from Sloughouse to the present-day grounds of Sacramento State University. By the mid-1890s, the county was the nation's top hop grower, churning out about one-third of U.S. production.

E. Clemens Horst, who oversaw the county's largest hop farm, invented a mechanical harvester in 1909. Although his harvest was fully mechanized the following year, his machine did not catch on with other growers, partly because of labor strife and also because the apparatus was not cost-effective for smaller farms.[124]

Prompted by the labor shortage, however, twenty-three of the thirty county hop growers installed harvesting mechanisms in the summer of 1942.[125] By 1945, the entire crop was mechanically picked.[126] Sacramento caught a break in comparison to other hop-growing counties, such as Mendocino and Sonoma. There, higher relative humidity levels at harvest time moistened the hop flowers, gumming up the machines. For these farms, manual labor was a necessity.[127]

But mechanization could only do so much. Joseph Green, head of the Sacramento County Land Use Committee, noted that sugar beets were being plowed under due to the labor shortage. Mechanical thinners offered little solace since they "result in a 20 to 30 percent loss when a 100-percent crop is vital to the nation." And he was not terribly impressed with the available labor either: "Many of those now listed on farm placement rolls are not physically able, or willing, to perform the work required."[128]

Undaunted, the university continued to innovate. Engineers improved seedbed drills to hasten the planting process on the tomato farms and improvements in insecticides and herbicides led to broader application by

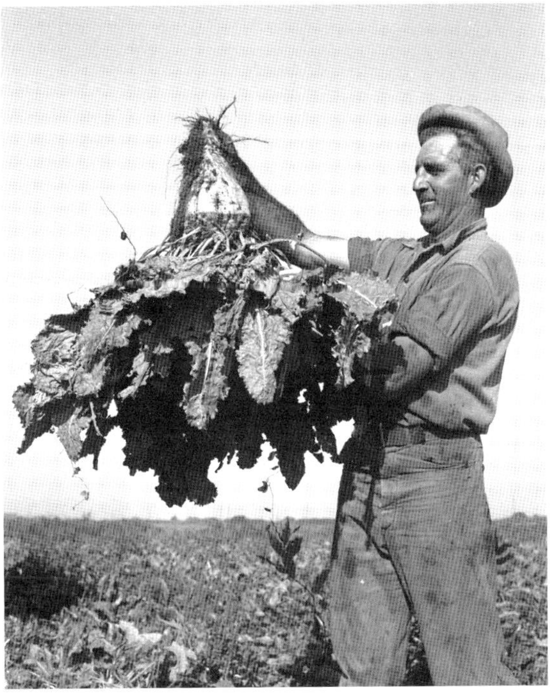

Right: Sugar beets were an essential crop due to sugar shortages. *Center for Sacramento History*.

Below: Farm workers picking hops in the 1920s. By the end of World War II, hops were harvested exclusively by machine in Sacramento County. *Center for Sacramento History*.

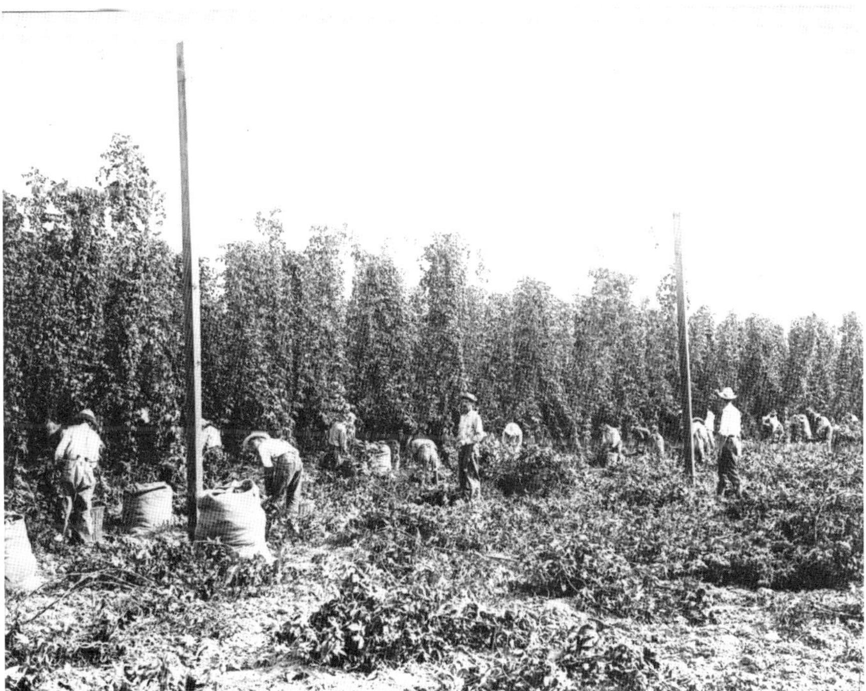

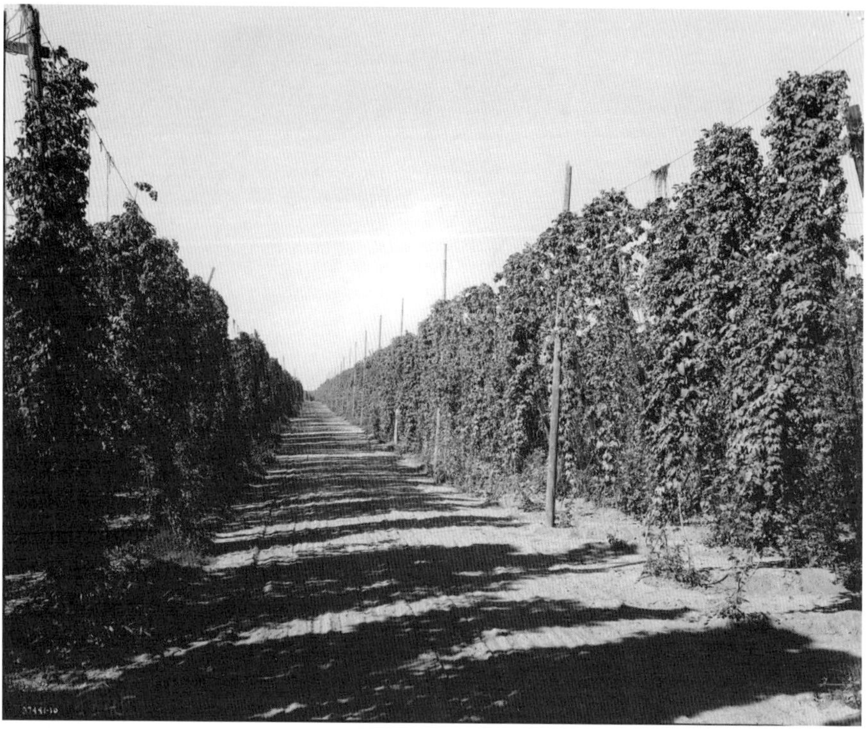

Hop vines at the E. Clemens Horst ranch in 1943. Horst invented a hop-harvesting machine in 1909, and his fields were fully mechanized by 1910. *California State Library.*

airplane crop dusters. The School of Agriculture also promoted increased refrigeration and storage capacity on the ranch. One critical advance came when the school invented a cooler that was able to store two thousand eggs at a time, which benefited the twenty-six poultry farms in the Rio Linda and Elverta region, which, at the time, was one of Northern California's largest egg-producing areas.[129]

Once in a while, ingenuity was reciprocated. Henry Sturmer, who owned the county's largest poultry ranch in Alta Mesa (Wilton), created a new highly efficient bulk feed storage system. Bins of various grains were fed into a grinder operated by a two-horsepower motor. The feed from the grinder then went into buckets, which in turn were dumped into a mixer where the various grains were combined according to a University of California recipe. This mixture was ultimately stored in two large metal tanks, and the entire operation was housed in a structure to protect it from the elements.

Sturmer, who had actually started this bulk storage system in 1940, found its benefits to be twofold: not only did he save thirty cents for every one hundred pounds of feed processed, but he also noticed that the new feed mixture improved the health of his chickens. Sturmer was happy to share his idea with fellow poultry farmers, and by 1942, most of the county had adopted some variation of this technique.[130]

Since metals were earmarked for military use, farm equipment was in short supply. Field machinery occupied three main categories. Category A consisted of power equipment, and Category B consisted of machinery attachments, both of which were tightly rationed. Category C included farm hand tools, which were not rationed—a nod to the essential role of the home gardener.[131]

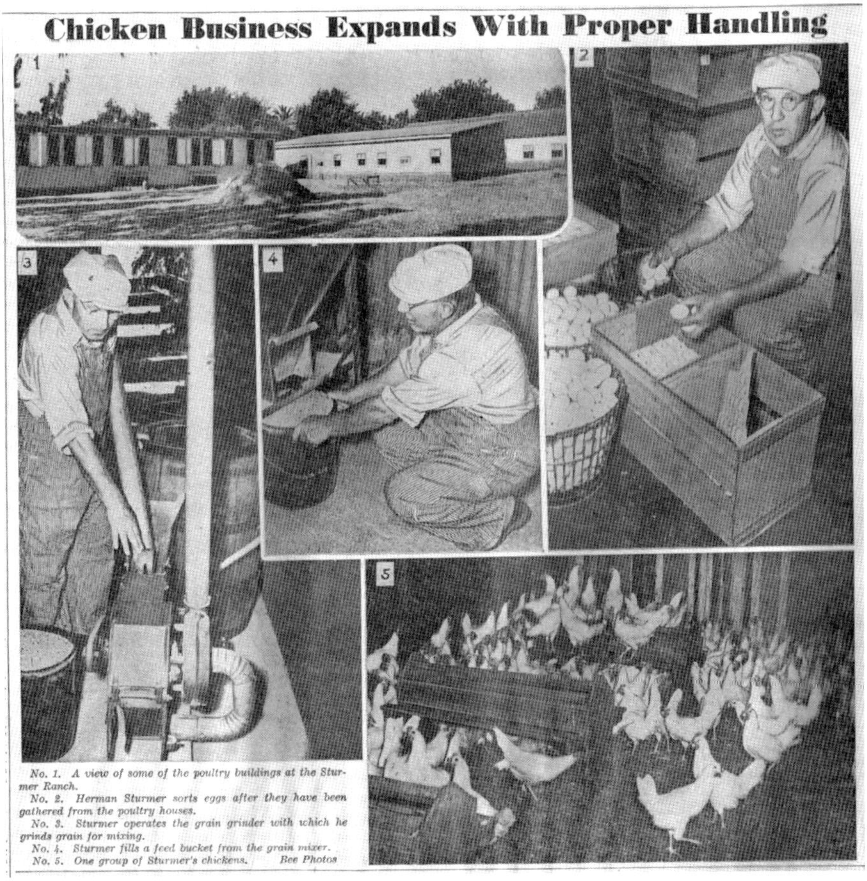

Henry Sturmer of Wilton. He developed a process of chicken feed production that was shared with other poultry farmers during the conflict. *Center for Sacramento History.*

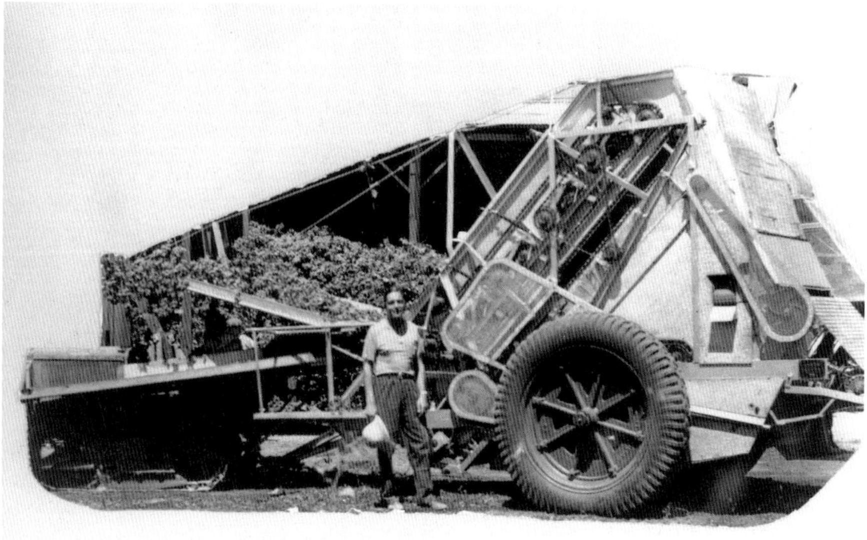

A 1942 photograph of a crop loader at the Bercut-Richards cannery. *Sacramento Public Library.*

This rationing placed the onus on maintaining heavy equipment. Right after the Pearl Harbor attack, UC Davis held its thirteenth annual farm machinery meeting on January 9 and 10, 1942.[132] This meeting, obviously fortuitous in its timing, not only provided a forum to discuss wartime farm production but also laid out a strategy for equipment repair.

Subsequently, the university held numerous classes on farm equipment upkeep both on campus and on demonstration farms throughout the region, with 120 sessions in the spring of 1942 alone.[133] A spirit of resourcefulness ensued, similar in spirit to the mechanics of present-day Cuba, who employ their wizardry in maintaining automobiles from the 1950s and 1960s.

Shortages and Transportation

On occasion, shortages provided a windfall for farmers. Fruit crops in general fetched high prices, but olives became particularly valuable. Wartime blockades made it impossible to ship olives from the Mediterranean basin, and California became the nation's sole domestic source.[134] A rush to expand olive acreage ensued. As demand for nursery stock skyrocketed, orchards in Fair Oaks, then the county's center of olive production, increased output,

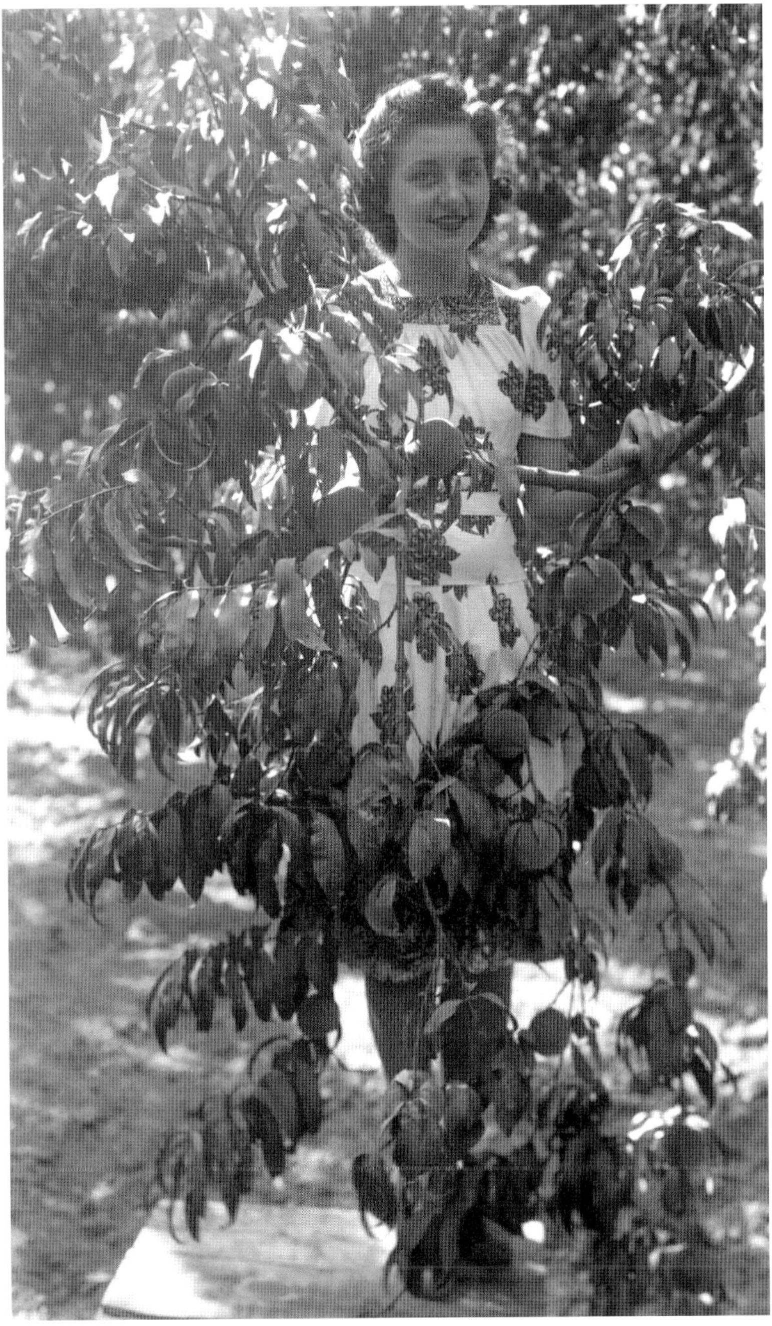

Betty Gropke demonstrates the proper technique for picking peaches in this 1942 image. The photograph was taken at the thirty-acre peach orchard adjacent to the Bercut-Richards cannery. *Sacramento Public Library.*

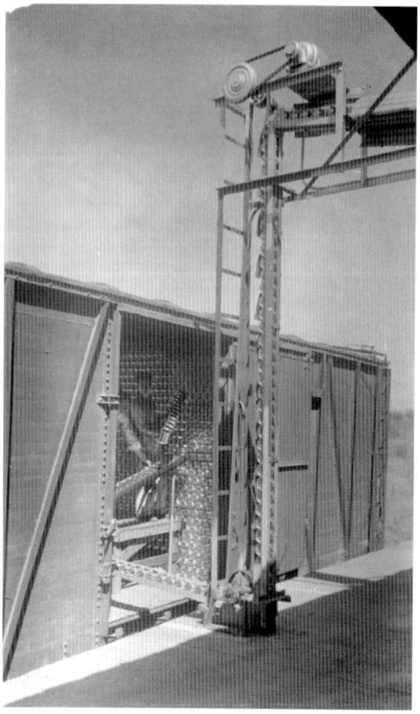

Empty cans are unloaded from a rail car in 1942 at the Bercut-Richards cannery. *Sacramento Public Library.*

and other groves sprang up throughout the region. Trees were meticulously harvested so as not to waste any fruit, and even then, supply could not meet national demand. Roseville-based Orsi Olive Oil Company and both the Fair Oaks Fruit Company and Phoenix Brothers, which packaged the olives for shipment, flourished in these economic conditions.[135]

Issues of transportation not only affected imports but local exports as well. In January 1942, UC Davis agriculture officials met with local pear growers at Courtland Grammar School to discuss improving the "transit quality" of Bartlett pears. These "improved" pears were then sent to the wholesale produce markets that had popped up throughout the region, such as the bustling Terminal market in downtown Sacramento at Sixteenth and B Streets, which served as an intermediary between farmer and transport. At these markets, fresh produce was packed for rail, truck and ship.[136]

Preserved fruits and vegetables, however, were Sacramento's strong suit. Along with the railroad, canneries had long dominated the Sacramento landscape. In the 1940s, the vast majority of fruits and vegetables were funneled through three major operations, all having easy access to at least one line of railroad, thus allowing for efficient transport from field to troops and allies. Bercut-Richards, the largest independent cannery in California, was the leading local processor of tomatoes and featured a thirty-acre peach orchard adjacent to its property.

The second of the "big three," the Libby-McNeil plant, was bounded by Thirty-First Street (now Alhambra Boulevard), R Street and Stockton Boulevard. The California Packing Company, based in San Francisco, featured the Del Monte brand and operated four plants in Sacramento. The biggest was located at Seventeenth and C Streets (now the Blue Diamond headquarters). By the 1920s, both the Libby-McNeil and Del Monte facilities were considered to be the largest canneries in the world.[137]

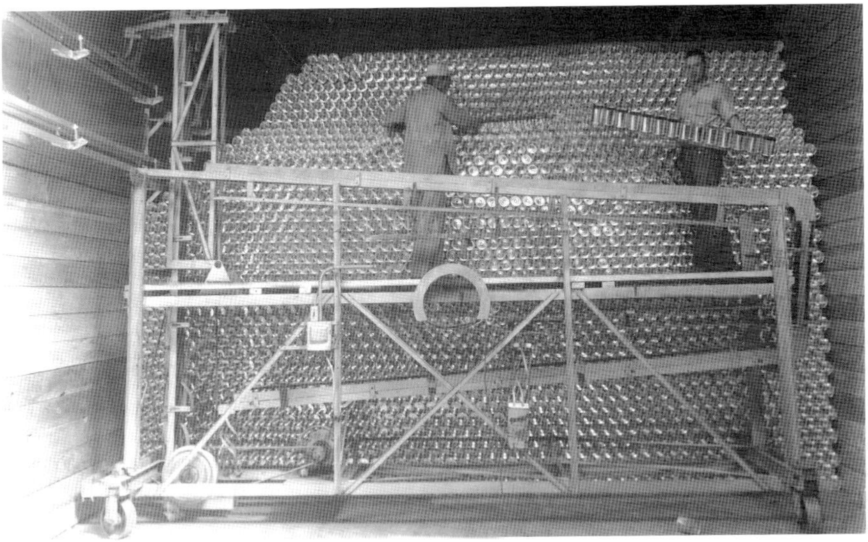

Stacks of cans and a loading belt at Bercut-Richards, August 1942. *Sacramento Public Library.*

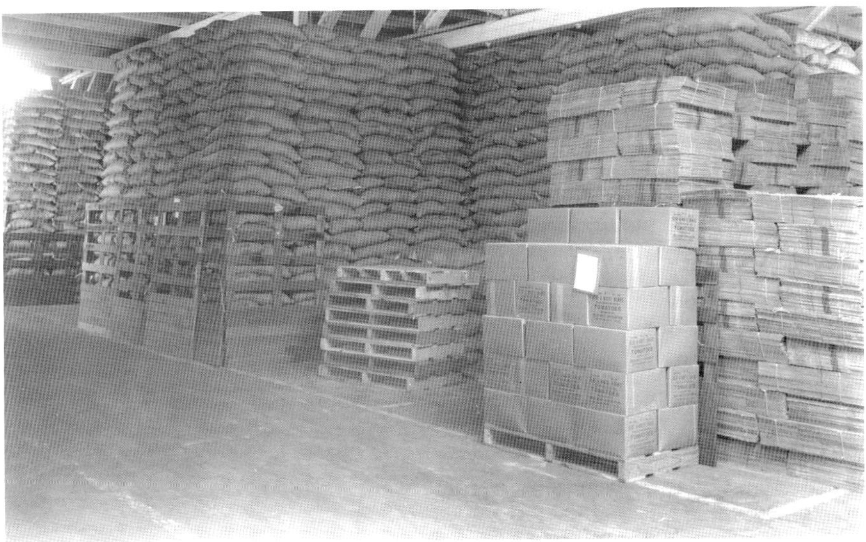

Sugar bags and fiberboard cases at the Bercut-Richards warehouse, August 1942. *Sacramento Public Library.*

Expanding the Labor Force

As men entered military service, the Libby-McNeil, Bercut-Richards and Del Monte–California Packing Company canneries increasingly depended on immigrant labor and women to work the lines. Aside from a few "Dust-Bowlers," about half of the cannery workforce was Mexican, with the remainder mostly consisting of women.[138]

Mexican neighborhoods popped up along the Franklin Boulevard corridor due to the work found at the nearby Libby-McNeil cannery. Alkali Flat, with its proximity to the Bercut-Richards plant on North Seventh Street and the massive CalPak–Del Monte operation, became the "Barrio Centro" by the early 1940s. This neighborhood featured a bustling commercial district along Twelfth Street, which "flourished with shops and various clubs like Los Reyes, La Mexicali, El San Diego, and El Xochimilco."[139] The neighborhood persevered well into the 1960s, producing such luminaries as poet José Montoya and his compatriots in the art collective "Royal Chicano Air Force."

Women literally "rode in to rescue" the canneries. Ads and newspaper columns beckoned them with appeals to patriotism and offers of flexible working conditions. One desperate plea in the *Sacramento Bee* begged, "Women needed in Del Monte canneries to work last half of night shift, 12

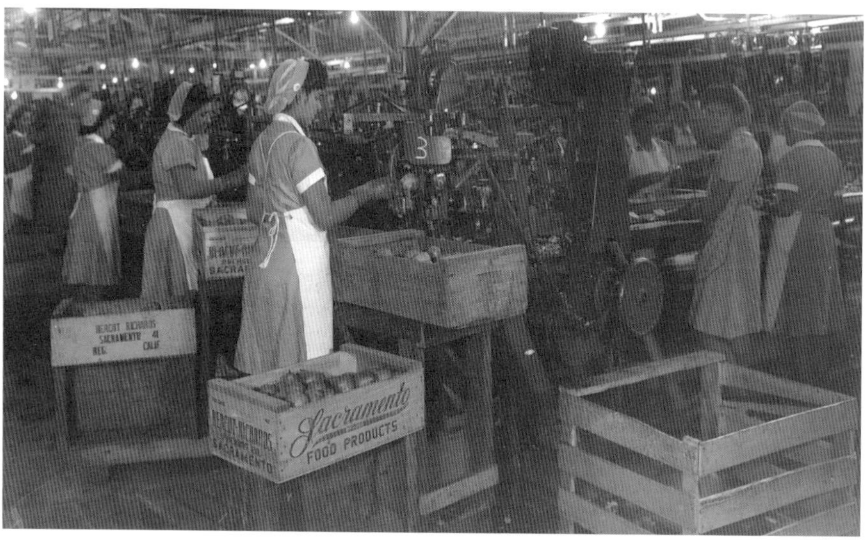

Packing crates at the Bercut-Richards cannery. Women were essential in keeping the canneries operational all day and night. *Sacramento Public Library*.

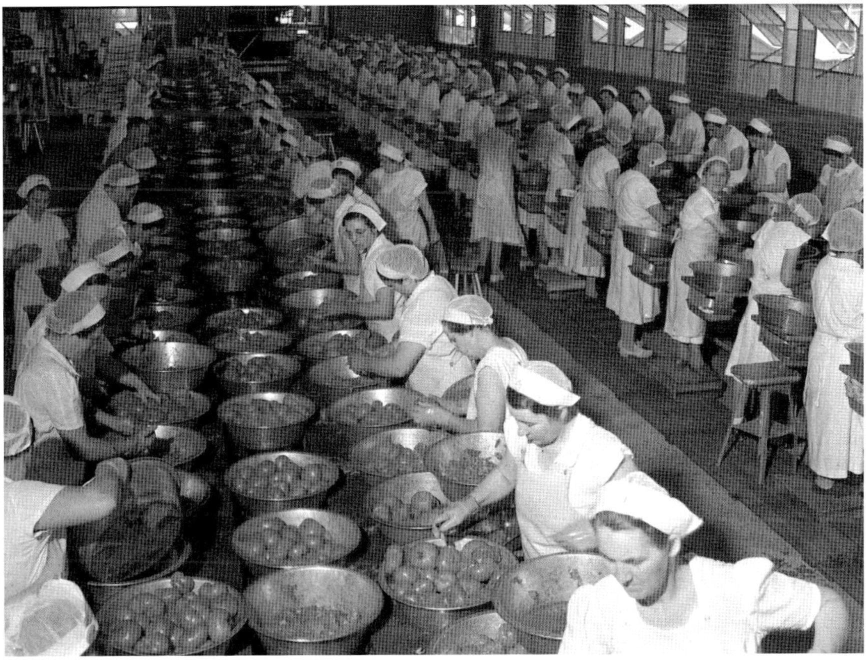

Women peeling tomatoes at Bercut-Richards. The cannery asked women to join the "WTP." *Center for Sacramento History*.

midnight to 6 a.m. help us finish this peach pack, which ends in about 10 days. Every worker counts. No experience necessary."[140]

A few months earlier, in October 1942, the Bercut-Richards cannery offered women a somewhat more elaborate and patronizing offer of work. Employing the New Deal–era love for acronyms, they called on them to join the "WTP, the army of Women Tomato Peelers":

> *Just put on a house dress, hop into your car with three or four other women, and drive out the Twelfth Street Road to the Bercut Richards Company's cannery, sign in at the timekeepers and then and there you are, a member of the new army.*

Further appealing to patriotic fervor, the company insisted that 100 percent of the tomatoes were destined for the "Army and Navy and other government agencies." Employees were paid by the unit, which incentivized production, as cannery officials explained: "If you fill a dozen cans, that is what you get paid for, and if you fill dozens of them the pay is multiplied accordingly." Additional reassurances came forth: "No uniform is required for the piece worker except a house dress and apron." A cap was required to cover hair, but only to meet "federal health regulations." And finally in a sort of prime directive, the cannery insisted, "When she gets tired there is a bench to sit and rest for her. When she wants to quit, well, that is her business and away she goes."[141] Whether because the offers were irresistible or, more likely, out of a simple sense of duty, women flocked to Sacramento's canneries at all hours of the day and night.

The Japanese Exclusion

As women filled vacancies in local canneries, an air of inevitability surrounded the Japanese internment. Anti-Japanese sentiment had been simmering for decades and was the latest incarnation of a longstanding anti-Asian bias in California. At first, Japanese immigrants were welcomed, as they filled the labor void left after the Chinese Exclusion Act of 1882. But as the Japanese population increased, so did the persecution. This was particularly intense in the agricultural community, where, in much the same fashion as the Chinese found work on the railroads, the Japanese increasingly had found a home in the fields.

In 1905, the Japanese and Korean Exclusion League was formed. By 1908, the organization had grown to 110,000 members on the West Coast and included a star cast of California's social and political elite. The nominal head of this organization was Valentine McClatchy, the publisher and editor of the McClatchy-owned *Bee* newspapers in Sacramento, Fresno and Modesto. Sacramento native Hiram Johnson, a San Francisco city attorney and future governor of California, joined the group along with his boss, Eugene Schmitz, the mayor of San Francisco. The league prompted the California legislature to consider a bill that precluded Japanese non-citizens from owning land, but President Taft, concerned about relations with Japan, interceded, and the bill was dropped.[142]

However, anti-immigrant advocates would have more success upon Johnson's return to Sacramento as governor. The Alien Land Act was passed by the legislature and signed by Johnson in 1913. This law disallowed Japanese, the law's primary target, as well as Chinese, Indian and Korean noncitizens from owning land or leasing land for any period longer than three years. The law was amended in 1920 and added further restrictions.

These changes forbade leasing of land altogether, precluded the right to purchase stock in any company that owned or leased agricultural land and "prohibited aliens from being appointed guardians of minor children whose estate consisted of real property."[143] In other words, the authorities wanted to prevent Japanese noncitizens from purchasing land in the name of their citizen children.

The Exclusion League teamed up with other anti-immigrant groups to form an umbrella organization called the California Joint Immigration Committee. This committee had an ambitious objective: "the total exclusion of all Japanese from the United States."[144] In an ominous foreshadowing, a young Earl Warren, who was at that time a deputy attorney for the city of Oakland, signed on to the organization. He was joined by a number of prominent civic entities, including the American Legion, the California State Federation of Labor and the California Federation of Women's Clubs.

Anti-immigrant forces struck a major achievement with the passage of the Federal Immigration Act of 1924. Embedded within this legislation was a measure specifically singling out the Japanese. Calvin Coolidge expressed ambivalence for the act because of this particular clause, stating, "If the exclusion provision stood alone, I would disapprove it without hesitation." The ambassador to Japan, C.E. Woods, had a more vociferous response. In his resignation letter, he exclaimed, "The Japanese government, I believe, would be willing to agree to almost any form of restrictive treaty, but the exclusion provision of the immigration bill has struck a blow to their national pride."[145] Indeed, the Immigration Act of 1924 ended any hope of a meaningful relationship between the United States and Japan. The die had been cast.

THE CONSEQUENCES OF EXCLUSION

Aside from moral considerations, the forced Japanese exile was a self-inflicted and nearly catastrophic blow to local agriculture. Sacramento County had the fourth-largest population of Japanese in the United States at the beginning of the war, so the internment not only left a void of immeasurable experience and talent but saddled the region with an intractable labor shortage as well.[146] Despite all the obstacles, a full 70 percent of Sacramento County produce was farmed by the Japanese at the onset of World War II.[147]

In a salient observation, especially in context of the 1913 Alien Land Act, and perhaps with a tinge of sympathy, the 1942 University of California–Davis Agriculture Extension report offered the unsolicited observation that more than two-thirds of the exiled Japanese were, in fact, American citizens.[148] Susumu Satow, whose family grew strawberries, grapes and raspberries on a twenty-two-acre farm in the Mayhew area of the county, offered a representative take on the forced relocation:

> *It was the middle of the harvest...and yet we had to abandon it and leave. You know this is just the beginning and they may very well send us back to Japan. In my heart I know my loyalty belongs to America. I went to school, pledged allegiance every morning in grammar school and so forth. To think I may be sent to Japan was...horrendous.*[149]

Indeed, much of the acreage in the county that was farmed by the Japanese was taken over by either landowners or new tenants through foreclosure. The crops that were already planted for the 1942 growing season were brought to harvest, "although some of the poor acreage was abandoned."[150] The Extension further commented in its 1942 annual report, "The farm labor problem was greatly increased with some crops by the evacuation of the Japanese farmers early in the year. The problem is still an extremely serious one."[151]

Important crops were significantly affected in 1942. "Throughout the tomato season there was an acute shortage of available labor to properly take care of the tomatoes in the field when it reached its peak at harvest time."[152] The Japanese accounted for almost all berry production, and the internment effectively suspended commercial strawberry output in the region. For a time, a Sacramentan was hard-pressed to find a strawberry at market; only a home or community garden would have produced this fruit.

A massive transition took place in 1942. UC Davis officials noted that "much of the acreage in the county was taken over by new people. Much individual service was given these people in the growing of these crops."[153]

In February 1942, within two months of the Pearl Harbor attack, the region's farmers met with University of California and Sacramento County agriculture officials in Woodland to discuss the labor shortage. Farmers requested draft deferments for farm laborers. This demand fell in line with calls throughout the agricultural community in California and the rest of the country. A bill to institute draft deferments was introduced in Congress during the 1943 session but was met with overwhelming resistance by the

War Department and died in committee.[154] Undeterred, farmers latched on to any hint of good news. One agrarian observed, hopefully, that "many dust bowlers are returning to California. These unskilled laborers cannot find jobs at defense plants so they are expected to take their place on the farm."[155]

In 1940, there were approximately 2,200 Mexicans in Sacramento County, accounting for about 1 percent of the population. Many were initially brought in to work the "Great Harvest" of 1920, but because of the restrictions imposed on southern and eastern Europeans by the Immigration Act of 1924, a majority of Mexicans found work away from the fields in favor of the higher pay at the Southern Pacific railyards and the local canneries. They lived in nearby communities such as Alkali Flat, Gardenland, across the Sacramento River in Broderick and Sacramento's "lower" or "west end."[156]

In an effort to quell the farm labor crisis, the Roosevelt administration instituted the Bracero Program in 1942, bringing Mexican workers to the United States. Although this guest worker program reached its zenith after the war in the mid-1950s, a dramatic surge of Mexicans immediately came to Sacramento. A few found work in the railyards and the canneries, but an additional 1,500 were tending the fields by 1944.[157] Agricultural workers mostly harvested asparagus and sugar beets and strung hop vines, which were subsequently harvested by machine.[158]

IMMIGRANT NEIGHBORHOODS

Today, tourists in Old Sacramento are surprised to discover that this historic district was once known as the "most infamous skid row west of the Mississippi." Ernesto Galarza, in his memoir *Barrio Boy*, remembers, "Among the salons, pool halls, lunch counters, pawnshops and poker parlors was skid row, where drunk men with black eyes and unshaven faces lay down in the alleys to sleep."[159] During the war, just as in the preceding decades, county officials attempted to "clean up the liquor situation in the lower end of the city."[160]

This description of Sacramento's "lower end," featured in a 1968 thirty-minute local public television documentary and a favorite trope of city tours and barroom discussions, paints a small part of the picture. The "lower end" or "west end," as it was often called, bounded by the American River to the north, the Sacramento River to the west and Fifth and Y Streets (now Broadway) to the east and south, respectively, was in fact a vibrant, if marginalized, community.

North of K Street, there was the Chinese neighborhood, with the Japanese living between L and N Streets. Filipinos made their homes "scattered about the barrio" to the south. Galarza finishes the illustration:

> *Hindus from the rice and fruit country to the north of the city stayed in the rooming houses when they were in town, keeping to themselves. The Portuguese and Italian families gathered in their own neighborhoods along Fourth and Fifth streets southward toward the Y Street levee. The Poles, Yugoslavs and Koreans, too few to take over any particular part of it, were scattered throughout the barrio. Black men drifted in and out of town, working the waterfront. It was a kaleidoscope of colors and languages and customs that surprised me and absorbed me at every turn.*[161]

Although Galarza's description preceded the war by several years, it was apt save for one spectacular exception—the disappearance of the Japanese.

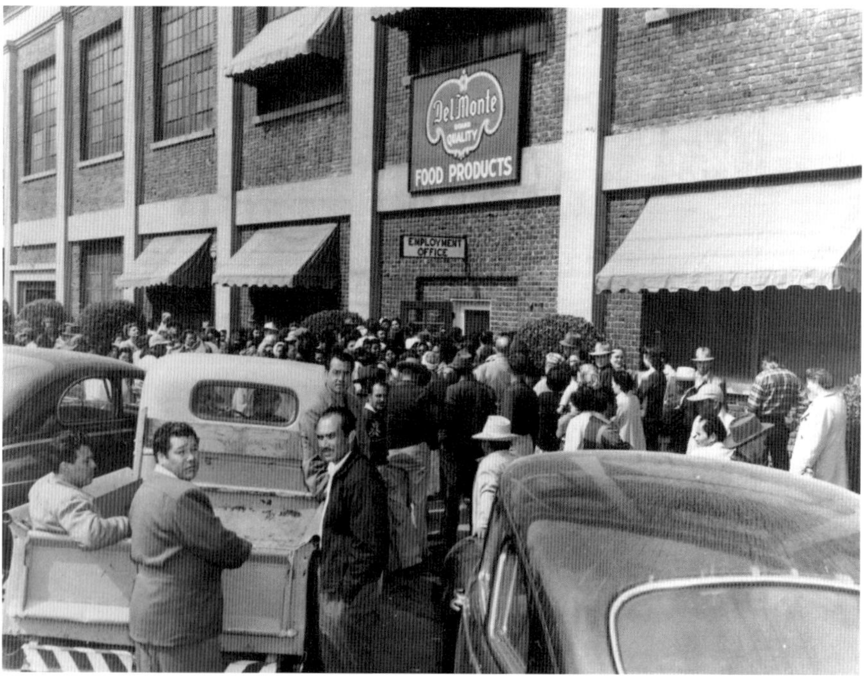

Laborers congregating at the Del Monte Cannery. *Center for Sacramento History.*

Against this backdrop, an epic congregation of laborers gathered daily at Second and K Streets between 1942 and 1945 to seek, as Galarza put it, their *trabajo*. The Agricultural Extension exclaimed, "On one day more than 2000 farm workers were placed from the farm labor office on Second Street and the season average will be more than 500 workers placed per day." Many were the Mexicans brought in by the Bracero Program, along with Filipinos, "dust bowlers" and a slew of others, including "a few Jamaicans."[162] These men were sent far and wide, from the orchards in the eastern part of the county to the farms in the Delta to the south.

Other itinerant workers were shipped out to neighboring counties, including the tomato fields in Yolo County to the west and the rice paddies in the Natomas Reclamation District of Sutter County to the north. By the end of the conflict, the University of California surmised that this labor office "had probably placed more farm workers than any single farm labor office in the United States."[163] Approximately 100,000 people found work at this intersection in 1944 and once again in 1945. All told, more than a half-million prospective workers passed through Second and K during the war. The county agriculture commissioner boasted, "It is doubtful if any county in the United States attained that high figure."[164]

Other Remedies to the Labor Shortage

The University of California–Davis Agricultural Extension employed other methods to meet the labor shortage. Soldiers on leave or stationed at nearby bases pitched in, but their restricted availability limited their efficacy: "Release of soldiers from the army and the release of war workers from many plants on the coast has so far not materially assisted in the seasonal and year round farm labor problems in the county." The Extension further noted the primacy of guest workers: "Imported farm workers are again going to be necessary if we continue to harvest our record production of crops without loss."[165]

Youth from the Sacramento region and beyond provided a somewhat more dependable source of labor. Examples abound of Bay Area children venturing to the Sacramento area to aid in farming. The Oakland YMCA sent boys to work the orchards of Loomis in the summer of 1942. Sleeping in tents, they enjoyed a local swimming hole while earning some extra pay.[166]

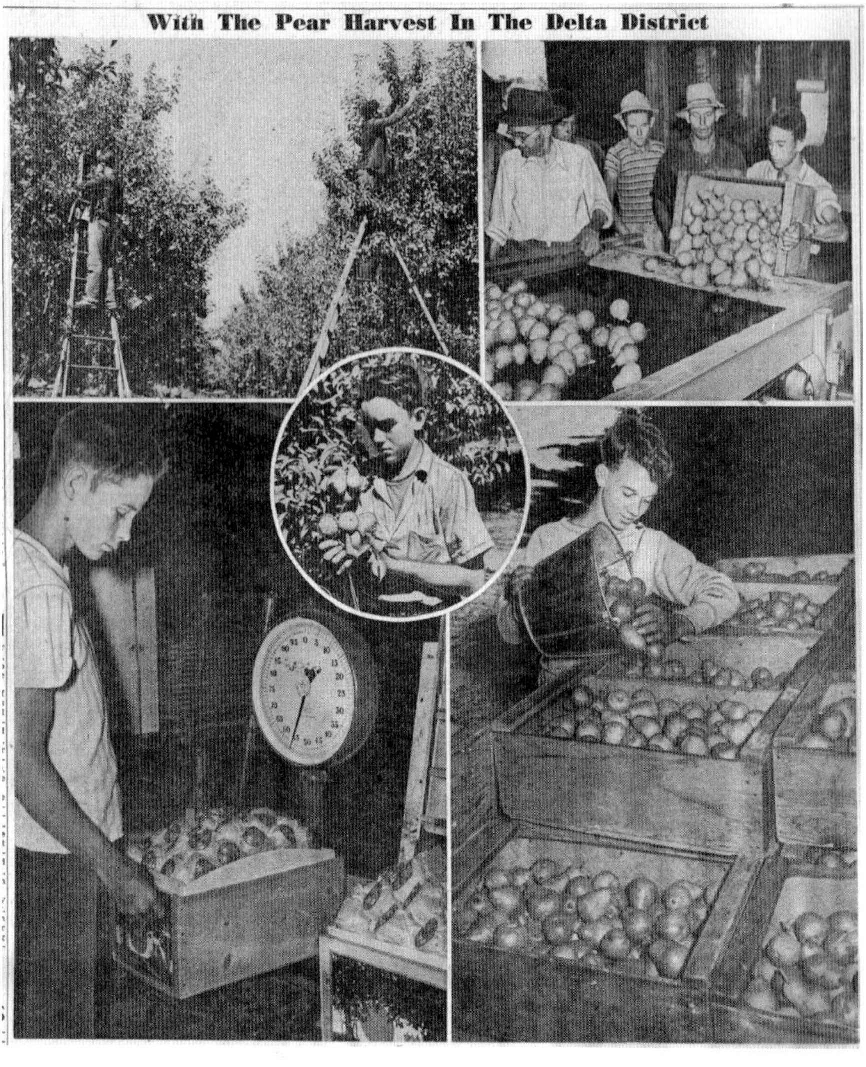

Scenes from the 1943 pear harvest in Courtland. Students played a large role at harvest time during the war. *Center for Sacramento History.*

Simultaneously, girls from Bay Area schools flocked to the Delta to assist with the tomato harvest. Closer to home, the 514 4-H organizations sent approximately 70 percent of their members to help in the fields. Also in the summer of 1944, the Sacramento YMCA set up camp for two hundred in Courtland to pick pears. Local schools, as well as UC Davis, adjusted their schedules during harvest time.[167] Phalanxes of school-age children were a common sight in the orchards and fields after school and on weekends.

CONCLUSION

All of these efforts paid off. The University of California–Davis Agricultural Extension, which took control of the county's labor program in July 1943, managed to stave off disaster:

> *Placements by the extension service has increased over one hundred percent over last year. There has been no loss of crops this year due to the farm labor shortage. Better cooperation was a factor and more thorough organization of the farm labor programs including volunteers, student camps, Mexican nationals and the utilization of transient labor made the difference.*[168]

In fact, the county farm output actually improved slightly during the war. Gross farm receipts escalated from more than $32 million in 1942 to more than $35 million in 1944 and $37 million in 1945. Acreage and tonnage also increased.[169] Of course, the unsung heroes were the workers themselves, the students who worked the fields outside of school, the women who kept the canneries running day and night and, perhaps most of all, the guest workers from Mexico who helped fill the void left by the exiled Japanese.

The legacy of this era of agriculture in Sacramento is complex, although some of the transitions are obvious. The dominance of farm labor shifted from the Japanese to Mexicans, Central Americans and Filipinos. European Americans consolidated control of the farms themselves. Of the 6,764 Japanese expelled from Sacramento County, only 4,000 returned. A few of them reconnected to farming, mostly in the Pocket and Elk Grove areas.[170] Traditional neighborhoods, however, most notably the "Japan Town" or "J-town" along L, M and N Streets in the west end and the Florin district, were decimated, if not wiped out entirely.

As the labor market normalized in the postwar era, an exploited underclass of mostly immigrant farm labor became entrenched. Although the Bracero Program was introduced in 1942 with promises against worker discrimination, the postwar backlash was fierce. Just as the program reached its zenith in the 1950s, the vindictive Eisenhower-era "Operation Wetback" was deployed to root out illegal immigrants. In hindsight, this operation was a human-rights disaster that, among other things, dropped suspected illegal immigrants into the Sonoran Desert without food or water, killing eighty-eight people in July 1955 alone. By the 1960s, the Bracero Program had little independent oversight and was rife with abuse.

The final blow came in 1963, when thirty-two braceros died in a bus crash in Salinas. U.S. Representative Adam Clayton Powell commissioned Ernesto Galarza, who was then a professor at Columbia University, to investigate and issue a report. The erstwhile Sacramentan, who had long disdained the guest worker program, unveiled a thorough and damning conclusion citing "extreme negligence" in the workers' deaths. The tragedy and Garza's contribution did much to pave the way for Cesar Chavez and the formation of the United Farm Workers.[171]

In some respects, Sacramento agriculture reverted to prewar conditions. After the conflict ended, California's olive crop, which had just exploded in production, retrenched as exports from the Mediterranean were reintroduced. Many of the olive companies disappeared, and others shrank. Acreage diminished in Sacramento County, save a few olive orchards and stray trees that can still be found in open space.[172]

But canned olives and other fruits and vegetables went on an entirely different trajectory. Emil Mrak, the UC Davis food scientist and future chancellor, "helped perfect army rations" during World War II. In fact, both world wars not only promoted improvements in canning techniques but popularized canned goods as well. The thinking was that what fueled the troops must be perfectly good for civilians. In 1910, canned goods accounted for 10 percent of household consumption, but by 1945, Americans were eating as much of it as fresh food.[173]

As a greater number of Americans entered the workforce, most notably women, household incomes increased, prompting a corresponding uptick in per-capita food consumption. Americans spent more on food, both in absolute terms and as a percentage of household income, than before the war.[174] The nation now had less time to prepare food, thus ushering in an era of frozen pizza, cake mixes and the iconic TV dinner. Away from home, restaurants inventoried more frozen and canned foodstuffs in an effort to speed up service.

The University of California–Davis, which already had a prominent role in Sacramento agriculture before the conflict, cemented its supremacy afterward. Mrak, due largely to the fame from his war innovation, was appointed chancellor in 1959, becoming the first food scientist in America to head a major university. With the local farming community as the university's virtual wartime laboratory, advances in irrigation, refrigeration and feed storage, among other things, were now shared by agricultural engineers and economists throughout the world.

Yet as they were making advances in canned food rations during the war, Mrak and his colleagues in the Food Science Department were experimenting

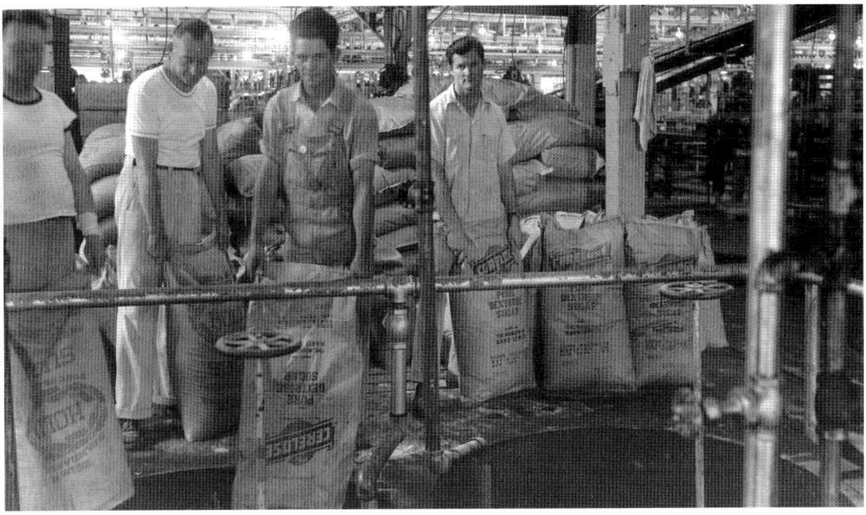

Men processing sugar syrup at Bercut-Richards, August 1942. They would pour one-hundred-pound bags into a vat for mixing. *Sacramento Public Library.*

with food chemistry. They deconstructed food with "advanced work on milk components, enzymes and flavors." This revolution gained traction with the 1946 Research and Marketing Act, and by 1960, over half the products on grocery shelves had not existed in 1945.[175] The logical conclusion came later in the 1960s, as "derived" foods appeared featuring components such as starches, proteins and sugars intertwined into palatable creations like potato crisps and instant soup.[176]

Meanwhile, the large canneries in Sacramento hummed along for a few decades after the war, but urbanization and a changing American palate exacted a steady toll. By the early 1980s, the "big three" canneries had disappeared. In similar fashion, the fields of the eastern county were torn asunder by development, the latest notable casualty being the Tomich Brothers orchard, which ended operations in August 2017 after 120 years of production.[177] Farms in the fertile sections of Natomas have also vanished, but a few notable exceptions still hang on. Delta farming remains strong for now but is under threat by rising tides, weakening levees and the impending "water wars" surrounding the proposed "Delta Tunnels" project.

Sacramento, under the tutelage of the University of California, which had done so much to help usher in the era of industrial agriculture, has now seen its farms largely disappear. Yet with an ideal growing climate, fertile soil and a nearby agricultural college, the war offered a stage perfectly set for an agricultural renaissance.

5

HOME TO FORK: VICTORY GARDENS IN THE VALLEY OF EDEN

By Eric Webb

Business and civic leaders in the late nineteenth and early twentieth centuries promoted a unified vision of the Sacramento region. Steeped in the prevailing Romantic-era ideal of "rural virtue," which lamented the effects of industrialization while simultaneously glorifying nature, these local boosters beckoned potential residents with elaborate portrayals of an agricultural and environmental paradise. Sacramento and its environs were a veritable Garden of Eden, they exclaimed, a place "where even Adam and Eve would feel at home."[178]

Future landowners would find themselves surrounded by vast wetlands and their unique flora among the oak woodlands and wild oats of the prairie. Stands of sycamores, willows, oak and ash formed riparian forests that stretched more than five miles beyond the banks of the Sacramento River, not to mention the myriad creeks and streams.[179] Such descriptions echoed an account from Spanish explorer Gabriel Moraga's 1808 expedition: "Canopies of oaks and cottonwoods, many festooned with grapevines, overhung the blue current. Birds chattered in the trees and big fish darted through the pellucid depths." The members of the expedition "drank in the beauty around them."[180]

One historian noted that an abundance of fauna prospered in these riparian habitats with numbers and diversity "unsurpassed in any region in North America."[181] William Davis, the captain of Johann Sutter's ship *Isabella*, observed upon their arrival in 1839 that "a large number of deer, elk and other animals of the plains were startled, running to and fro, while

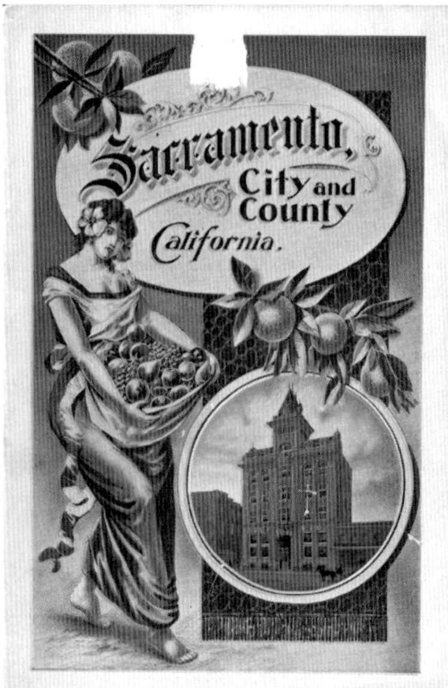

Center for Sacramento History.

from the interior of the adjacent woods the howls of wolves and coyotes filled the air, and immense flocks of waterfowl flew wildly about the camp."[182]

The "boosterism" reached an apex in 1888 with this grand declaration by the chamber of commerce: "The Valley of Sacramento is a garden and Sacramento is the *urbs in horto* [city in a garden] of it. It is our first glimpse of the celestial flowering kingdom of the Christian world."[183] Enthralled with this evangelism, migrants from the American Midwest and South, particularly after the Civil War, snapped up real estate and established ranches throughout the region.

The notion of the Sacramento region as an agrarian paradise, hyperbolic as it may seem, does have some basis in fact. One chamber of commerce publication noted the area's superior Mediterranean climate: Sacramento "had both sacred and beautiful soil and perfect climate, superior even to idyllic Italy's average temperature of sixty degrees and two hundred twenty clear days with its own average temperature of sixty-one degrees and two hundred thirty-eight clear days."[184]

Sacramento indeed lies in the center of the California Floristic Province, one of the planet's "hot zones" of plant biodiversity. Over five thousand species of flora live in this zone, which stretches from southern Oregon to northern Baja California. And over one-fourth of these species exist in a relatively small number of square miles that surround the foothill sections north of El Dorado Hills.[185] Perhaps unknowingly, these civic propagandists were on to something.

Even though Sacramento's business and civic leaders took great pains to paint an idyllic natural landscape for prospective landowners, there was another side of this coin. For them, the more relevant aspect of this "rural ideal" was nature's subservience to human will and domination. In contrast to the Native Americans, who had lived harmoniously with their natural surroundings for centuries, California's natural resources, in the settlers' view, demanded exploitation.

By the 1860s, the miners of the gold rush had already dredged and excavated much of the landscape. Now, the abundant soil begged to be tilled and planted and the water reclaimed. Over the ensuing decades, large swaths of intensive farming developed, from row crops in the Delta to the fruit orchards of the eastern valley. What remained of the valley's expansive riparian forests was soon lost to "the march of reclamation."[186]

A central tenet of the Romantic spirit was hero worship. Readers were always looking for a good story, and the exploits of early trailblazers such as Kit Carson and the tragedy of the Donner family captured the imagination of Americans and the outside world. James Beckwourth, who established the northern passage that traversed the Sierra from Nevada to Marysville, wrote an autobiography that became a bestseller in Europe.

An eager public gobbled up the latest exploits of other colorful California characters, from the outlandish stage performer Lola Montez to the miners and gamblers chronicled by Bret Harte. Now, with the late 1800s rolling along and the gold rush a memory, Sacramento's civic leaders saw a new era at hand. It was time for a new chapter to be written, one that has the "heroic farmer" taking his rightful place in the heart of this "vast agricultural empire."

Yet there was more to this story. At the turn of the twentieth century, the "agriopolis" of Sacramento and its agriculture-centric suburbs, or the so-called "agriburbs" of Orangevale, Fair Oaks and Citrus Heights, formed, in their view, a small but "bustling metropolis."[187] Civic leaders extolled Sacramento as a hub of transportation, with the transcontinental railroad, an inland port and a web of transnational and trans-valley roadways.

Throw in its status as the state capital, they maintained, and there was unlimited potential for commerce and, in turn, cultural life. Sacramento offered the urbanity of town with the bounty of country and, in this way, was superior to other California cities such as San Francisco and Los Angeles.

With this origin story in mind, Sacramentans were primed, and perhaps even felt some pressure, to take on the Roosevelt administration's Food for Victory program. The goal was simple: every home should maintain a vegetable garden, and every available open space should have a plot. Public schools and colleges, the press and business community and most notably, the University of California, all enthusiastically supported this endeavor, appealing to local patriotism and creating an atmosphere of community engagement.

By war's end, the victory garden program proved to be one of the city's most successful civic endeavors, with Sacramento standing out as a national

A WAR EMERGENCY PROCLAMATION

VICTORY HARVEST COMMITTEE
OF THE
SACRAMENTO CHAMBER OF COMMERCE

TO THE PEOPLE OF SACRAMENTO:

FOOD IS A WEAPON OF WAR!

The most important war job every one of us has to do this summer is to help harvest and can our crops.

Our soldiers, sailors and marines, and the 35 million families here at home are depending on us to do this job.

Give all the time you can during this emergency to the harvesting of fruits and vegetables or to work in the canneries—especially during the critical months of August and September. You are needed for:

1. A full shift, six days or nights a week, or
2. A half shift, six days or nights a week, or
3. A half shift, three days or nights a week, or
4. A full shift or half shift full time during your vacation.

You say you have never worked in a cannery, or picked peaches and tomatoes? You can learn very quickly. Remember, there's many a soldier from Sacramento who never shouldered a gun before this war began.

You are a housewife and have your hands full at home? A few hours each day during the peak emergency may save the life of some boy who is fighting for you and your loved ones, on a ship at sea or in the all-out battles on land and in the air thousands of miles away.

You are already working 8 hours a day at your regular job? Well, think what our fighting men are giving up for us. A few more hours on the evening shift surely aren't too much to give by comparison.

You need a vacation? Your compensation for helping harvest, or working in a cannery, will be more than money—it's the satisfaction you will always have of knowing your time went to help win this war, and win it sooner.

People of Sacramento, this is a real war emergency right here in our own community. The eyes of the world are watching to see how we accept the responsibility Uncle Sam has placed on our shoulders.

When you are asked to "sign up," do so, if you possibly can — and urge your friends and neighbors to do likewise.

Yours for Victory,
SACRAMENTO CHAMBER OF COMMERCE
VICTORY HARVEST COMMITTEE
ROSS E. PIERCE, Chairman

B. A. BARRY, HOMER BOUCHER, JOHN BURTON, J. J. CERRUTI, HAROLD DEXTER, WM. L. DORIAN, ROY HIBBITT, MERLE HUSSONG, T. A. KLABAU, MRS. FRED J. KLAUSS, T. J. LABHARD, E. C. LE COUNT, L. A. LEWIS, THOMAS McMAHON, A. E. MORRISON, W. O. ROSS, WADE SARGENT, FERD. H. SCHEID, E. L. STANLEY, DWIGHT STEPHENSON, THOMAS WARDLAW, GEO. B. WELCH, JAMES R. WILSON.

"FOOD IS NO LESS A WEAPON THAN TANKS, GUNS, AND PLANES."

FRANKLIN D. ROOSEVELT, President of the United States

This Sacramento Chamber of Commerce "War Emergency Proclamation" implored citizens to maintain victory gardens and work in the canneries. *Sacramento Public Library.*

leader. Even more significantly, the home gardening effort of the 1940s stood in juxtaposition to the increasing industrialization of the modern farm. It also offered a blueprint for today's burgeoning "farm to fork" and community gardening movement.

If Sacramento's powerful local agricultural ideology provided the aesthetic motivation, rationing offered the practical incentive. Food rationing during World War II largely followed the point-based paradigm used in the United Kingdom. War Ration Book One—also known as the "Sugar Book"—was issued in May 1942. Sugar, which was the first commodity subject to restriction, was apportioned to half a pound per person per week, roughly halving the average American's consumption. Special allowances were made for certain households that demonstrated a significant output of fruit and vegetable preserves. This proved particularly advantageous for Sacramentans, who had maintained a long tradition of producing these homemade products. Canneries, most notably Bercut-Richards, solicited residents to drop off their extras to assist in the war effort. Out in the fields, increased sugar beet acreage helped fill the deficiency.[188]

In January 1943, the point-based rationing system expanded to include stamps for processed vegetables and fruits as well as juice. Each product was assessed a point value based on type and quantity. Individuals were then given booklets that allotted forty-eight points per rationing period. A certain flexibility was allowed: stamps could be traded and products exchanged, households could combine individual booklets and stamps earmarked for a subsequent period could be used at the end of a previous one. Just as with postage, authorities encouraged citizens to use their larger denominations first so that smaller values could be used to gap purchase prices later.[189]

Rations also were imposed on meat. Children younger than six were allowed three-quarters of a pound per week; those nine to twelve one and a half pounds; and those older than twelve were granted two and a half pounds. Strategies such as having the occasional "meatless day" were suggested. Most typical, however, was the plethora of recipes that either offered a "meat alternative" or the less-appetizing "meat extender."

Some of the alternative—or better put, vegetarian—recipes ranged from "Tomato Rabbit," which actually did not contain any rabbit but was, in fact, creamed vegetables and eggs over toast, to a very simple soybean salad. The so-called meat extender recipes were, after an initial glance, quite decent, offering such staples as "Meat Pie with Catsup Biscuits" and the inevitable "Meat and Bean Loaf."

Organ meats also were encouraged and featured in such delectable entrées as "Stuffed Hearts" and "Liver Loaf." Finally, there were dishes only a zombie could love, such as "Breaded Brains," "Creamed Brains" and the requisite "Scrambled Eggs with Brains."[190]

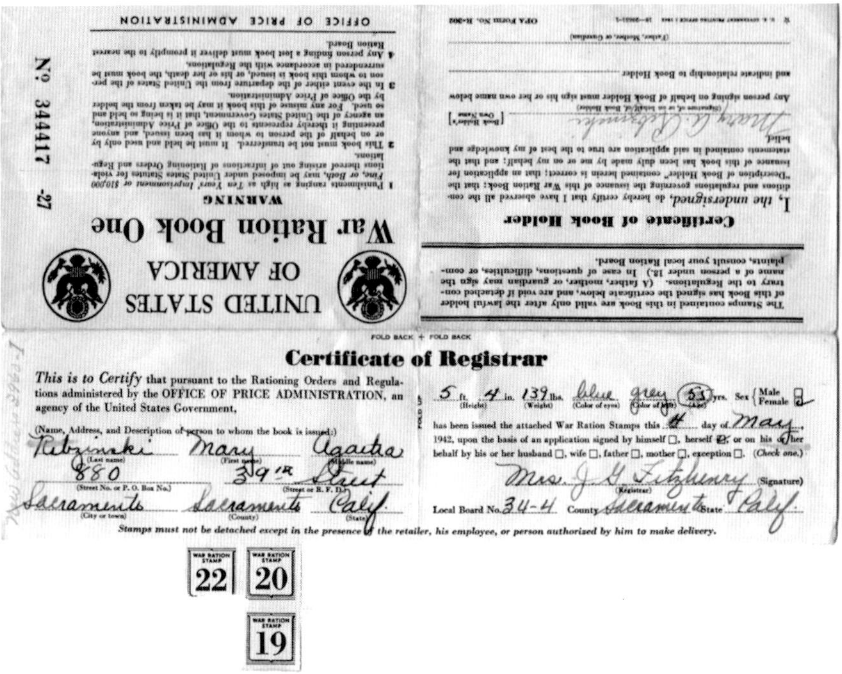
UNITED STATES OF AMERICA

War Ration Book One

Certificate of Registrar

This is to Certify that pursuant to the Rationing Orders and Regulations administered by the OFFICE OF PRICE ADMINISTRATION, an agency of the United States Government,

(Name, Address, and Description of person to whom the book is issued:)

Ribzinski Mary Agatha

880 39th Street

Sacramento Sacramento Calif.

5 ft. 4 in. 139 lbs. blue grey 53 yrs. Sex Female

has been issued the attached War Ration Stamps this 4 day of May, 1942, upon the basis of an application signed by himself ☐, herself ☒, or on his or her behalf by his or her husband ☐, wife ☐, father ☐, mother ☐, exception ☐. (Check one.)

Mrs. J. G. Fitzhenry (Signature) (Registrar)

Local Board No. 34-4 County Sacramento State Calif.

Stamps must not be detached except in the presence of the retailer, his employee, or person authorized by him to make delivery.

WAR RATION STAMP 22 | WAR RATION STAMP 20 | WAR RATION STAMP 19

Issued in 1942, War Ration Book One was also known as the "Sugar Book." *Sacramento Public Library*.

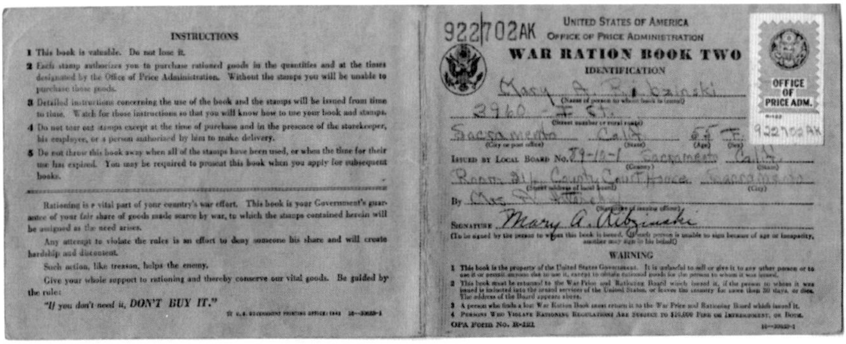
INSTRUCTIONS

1 This book is valuable. Do not lose it.

2 Each stamp authorizes you to purchase rationed goods in the quantities and at the times designated by the Office of Price Administration. Without the stamps you will be unable to purchase those goods.

3 Detailed instructions concerning the use of the book and the stamps will be issued from time to time. Watch for those instructions so that you will know how to use your book and stamps.

4 Do not tear out stamps except at the time of purchase and in the presence of the storekeeper, his employee, or a person authorized by him to make delivery.

5 Do not throw this book away when all of the stamps have been used, or when the time for their use has expired. You may be required to present this book when you apply for subsequent books.

Rationing is a vital part of your country's war effort. This book is your Government's guarantee of your fair share of goods made scarce by war, to which the stamps contained herein will be assigned as the need arises.

Any attempt to violate the rules is an effort to deny someone his share and will create hardship and discontent.

Such action, like treason, helps the enemy.

Give your whole support to rationing and thereby conserve our vital goods. Be guided by the rule:

"If you don't need it, DON'T BUY IT."

922702AK

UNITED STATES OF AMERICA
OFFICE OF PRICE ADMINISTRATION

WAR RATION BOOK TWO

IDENTIFICATION

Mary A. Ribzinski

3960 - F St.

Sacramento Calif. 55 F

Issued by Local Board No. 34-4-1 Sacramento Calif.

By Mrs. J. G. Fitzhenry

Signature Mary A. Ribzinski

OFFICE OF PRICE ADM.

WARNING

OPA Form No. R-121

War Ration Book Two, which was released in 1943, restricted canned fruits, vegetables and juice. *Sacramento Public Library*.

While farm tools and power equipment were rationed due to metal shortages, the Roosevelt administration had the foresight to leave basic gardening tools unrestricted. Since large-scale agricultural production was set aside for troops and allies, Sacramentans, armed with their instruments, started digging up their front and backyards. Civic leaders consistently reminded citizens that fresh produce from the home was not only good for the country; it was good for them, too. "Grow vitamins at your kitchen door" was a common refrain.[191]

The University of California–Davis School of Agriculture, with the assistance of the local press, embarked on a comprehensive public education campaign right after the Pearl Harbor attack in December 1941. Elmer Stanley, the county agent for the University of California, and Ferd Scheid, the Sacramento County Home Food Production manager, led the effort and were ubiquitous figures throughout the war.

Stanley immediately hosted a weekly victory garden broadcast on radio station KFBK that lasted throughout the conflict, and both he and Scheid conducted and oversaw hundreds of meetings in Sacramento. By March 1942, the UC Davis Agricultural Extension had ramped up its printing press, producing thousands of brochures promoting the Food for Victory program.[192]

Virtually every civic organization could be counted on for an informational session. UC Davis representatives held classes for civic stalwarts such as the Elks Club, the chamber of commerce, Boy Scouts and Girl Scouts and 4-H clubs. The Sacramento Garden Club, as well as the Sacramento Fuchsia Club, saw fit to join the act, and the Sacramento High School Faculty Wives Club entertained seminars. Even an occasional informal neighborhood meeting was held in a private residence.[193]

For older Sacramento residents, many of whom had come from the Dust Bowl and the South, tending a home vegetable plot was second nature, reminiscent of the Edwardian farms of yesteryear. Nonetheless, as most adults were called to perform war work, it fell upon the public schools to reacquaint their children with basic gardening practices.

If not called up for military duty, many adults filled positions in civil defense. Women, in particular, could be found signing on for work at the bustling canneries such as Libby-McNeil, Del Monte and Bercut-Richards. As a result, the youth of Sacramento enjoyed a featured role in the victory garden program.

The greatest impact of the informational campaign was found in the alliance between the UC Davis Agricultural Extension and the region's

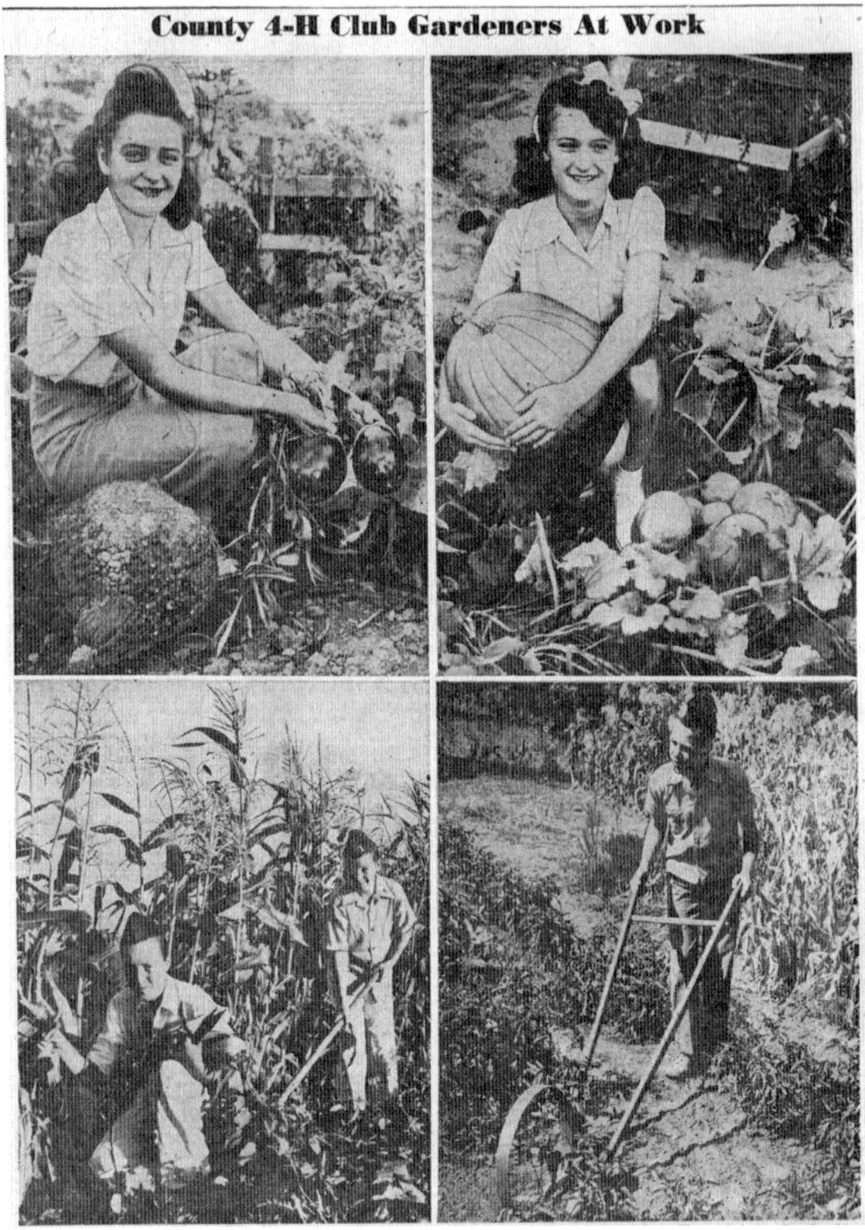

In November 1942, the Munz sisters tend the Fruitridge 4-H garden, and the Mohr brothers of Elk Grove work on the Franklin 4-H farm while James Broadley plows the land in Fair Oaks. All of these farms provided food for neighborhood families. *Center for Sacramento History.*

educational institutions. The university implemented curricula in every public school and initiated course offerings at Sacramento Junior College.

Schools also served as settings for seminars intended for the general public. One representative course was held in January 1943 on the campus of Sacramento Junior College. Sponsored by the state Department of Agriculture and the University of California, this six-week class covered the basics of home gardening and was attended by 150 adults.[194] Dozens of similar gardening courses were tendered during the wartime era.

The Sacramento Public Library also got into the act. It offered "up to the minute" instructions on victory gardening. A wide array of books and pamphlets were provided, leading one patron to exclaim, "We're glad to know that you don't have to be a green thumb to be a good gardener."[195]

Efforts to reclaim land for vegetable and fruit gardening got off the ground in early 1942. Sacramento mayor Tom Monk declared a citywide "Clean Up and Plant" week that started on April 13. Residents began plowing and planting in earnest. Plots sprung up at residences, and a vegetable garden was immediately sown at C.K. McClatchy High School. Sacramento High School quickly followed and ultimately had two hundred individual student sections.

With seed brought in from area farms, every public school in the city, and most in the county, had some type of vegetable garden by the end of the year.[196] In that same month of April, 80 percent of the county's ranches also maintained a victory garden as a sign of solidarity.[197]

In November 1942, the City Parks Department opted to include victory gardens in every city park. Mentored by the Elks Club, hordes of students immediately descended upon McClatchy, Land and Southside Parks. East Portal and McKinley soon followed, with the smaller parks close behind. The plant science departments of the junior college and high schools, under the tutelage of the UC Davis School of Agriculture, oversaw garden maintenance in the parks throughout the city and county.[198]

Federal, state and county officials sought to squeeze every square inch of available land for vegetable gardens. The downtown post office maintained a plot and donated its produce to needy Sacramentans. Radishes, turnips, carrots and other staples found a home at Capitol Park, and similar crops were also grown at Sutter's Fort.[199] In August 1942, the New Helvetia subdivision off Broadway included a vegetable garden behind its 310-unit apartment complex.[200]

In an effort to establish community gardens, Sacramento County executive Charles Deterding took an inventory of available open space. He partnered with Carl Klein, president of the Sacramento Realtors Board,

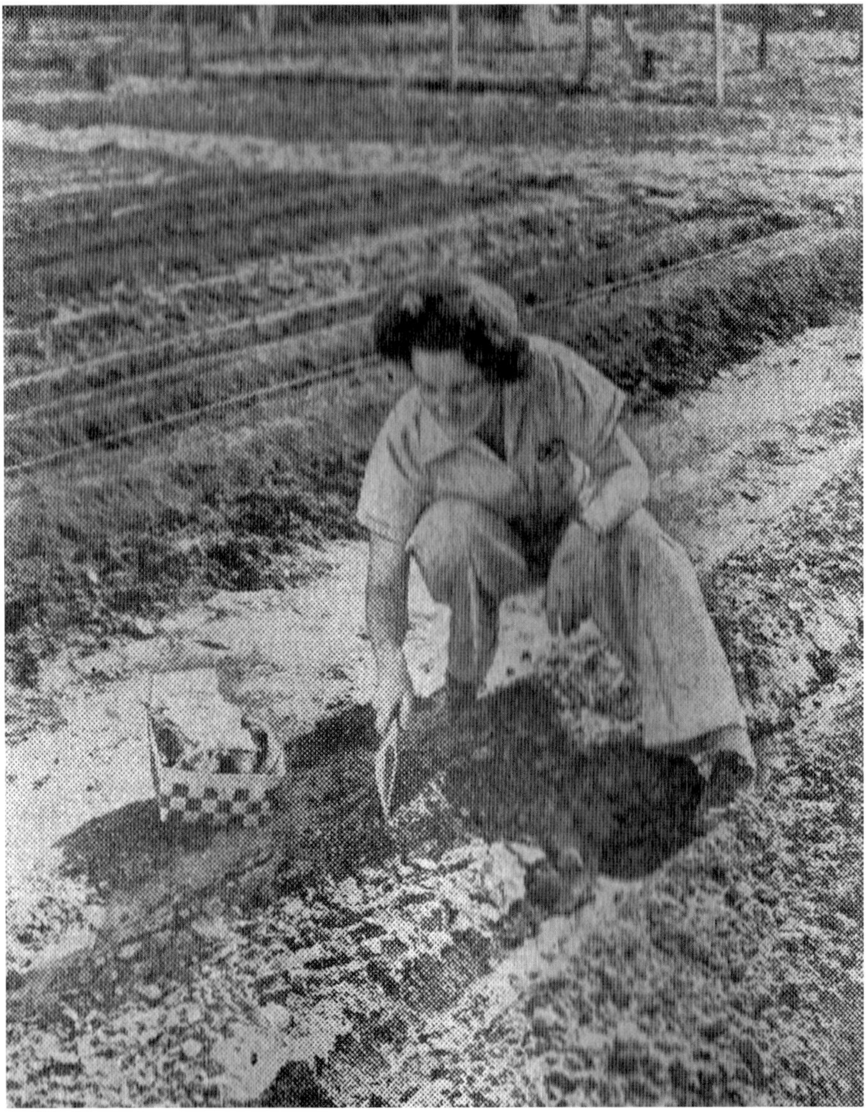

In March 1943, Mrs. A.A. Whitaker cultivates her victory garden at 1375 Forty-Fourth Street in East Sacramento. *Center for Sacramento History*.

who chipped in and announced, "Sacramento realtors are making Victory Gardens part of their war activity and are seeking to plant vegetables on all vacant lots in the city."[201]

Private landowners quickly heeded the call and donated parcels to the cause. Acres of vegetables popped up at Land Park addresses such as

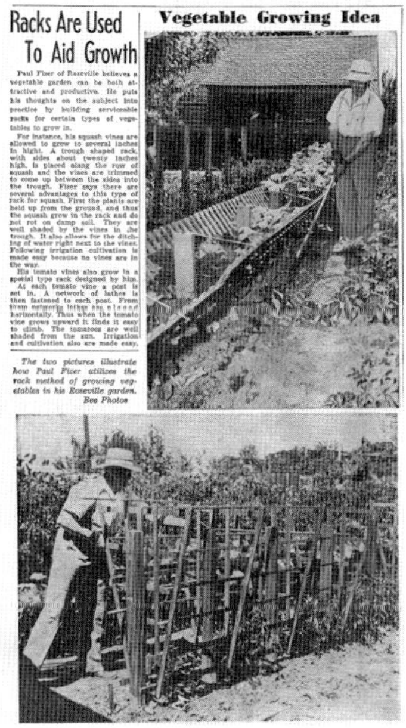

Racks Are Used To Aid Growth

Paul Fizer of Roseville believes a vegetable garden can be both attractive and productive. He puts his thoughts on the subject into practice by building serviceable racks for certain types of vegetables to grow in.

For instance, his squash vines are allowed to grow to several inches in hight. A trough shaped rack, with sides about twenty inches high, is placed along the row of squash and the vines are trimmed to come up between the sides into the trough. Fizer says there are several advantages to this type of rack for squash. First the plants are held up from the ground, and thus the squash grow in the rack and do not rot on damp soil. They are well shaded by the vines in the trough. It also allows for the ditching of water right next to the vines. Following irrigation cultivation is made easy because no vines are in the way.

His tomato vines also grow in a special type rack designed by him. At each tomato vine a post is set in. A network of lathes is then fastened to each post. From [illegible] lathes are placed horizontally. Thus when the tomato vine grows upward it finds it easy to climb. The tomatoes are well shaded from the sun. Irrigation and cultivation also are made easy.

The two pictures illustrate how Paul Fizer utilizes the rack method of growing vegetables in his Roseville garden.
Bee Photos

Vegetable Growing Idea

Paul Fizer of Roseville installs racks to grow tomatoes in July 1942. *Center for Sacramento History.*

3216 Fourth Avenue, 1037 Ninth Avenue and the major intersection of Land Park Drive and Vallejo Way, adjacent to what is now California Middle School.[202] The intersection of Eleventh and V Streets also featured a community garden. In the early spring of 1943, Ferd Scheid estimated that 50 percent of the population of Sacramento planted gardens. Within six months, participation increased to 75 percent.[203]

The University of California–Davis Agricultural Extension offered state-of-the-art advice not only for the agricultural community but also for the amateur gardener. Stanley consistently reminded residents that a successful garden did not require a large section of land. An area measuring twenty feet by twenty feet against a back fence would do.

Yellow tomatoes, for example, could be grown on one side, lima beans on the other, interspersed with a wide range of other vegetables, such as spinach and broccoli. In a wink to the organic gardener, flowers such as marigolds were recommended to stand sentry adjacent to the plot. Such borders attract beneficial insects and reduce the need for insecticides.

Occasionally, amateur gardeners did not measure up to this sage advice. One reader of Stanley's weekly *Sacramento Bee* column wondered why his watermelon crop was unsuccessful. Other readers could envision Stanley biting his lower lip as he politely indicated that watermelons were probably not best suited for a narrow strip of soil next to a driveway. After lauding the reader for attempting to cultivate such a small parcel, he went on to suggest that radishes or onions would probably be a better bet.[204]

Victory gardens spilled into other areas of popular culture. A long-running and popular *Sacramento Bee* column, authored by the pseudonymous Katherine Kitchen, offered seasonally appropriate recipes that featured common produce from home gardens. So, in spring, one might come across recipes for the simple "Stuffed Eggplant." In summer, "Vegetable Fritters" were on the menu, as well as the inviting "Beer Casserole."[205] During fall, recipes for "Nut Bread" and "Pecan and Rice Loaf" were on the docket.[206]

The Katherine Kitchen column also delivered advice on canning vegetables and preserving fruit, including a free brochure for those who sent in a stamped envelope or attended one of the informational sessions throughout the area.

It comes as no surprise that gardening establishments, such as Lagomarsino's Seed Store and the East Lawn and Capital Nurseries, benefited mightily from the Food for Victory program. Other retailers also sought to cash in. The venerable department store Weinstock-Lubin merchandised what could be called "Victory Garden kitsch." Displays of fashionable garden tools and paraphernalia adorned the downtown establishment.

The department store also introduced a smart, fashion-forward denim onesie geared toward young ladies aged seven to fourteen. Suitable for work in the garden, this particular garment highlighted the importance of young women in this civic movement.[207]

A good community program requires healthy competition. Foreshadowing larger events to come, a number of victory garden contests sprang up in 1942 and 1943. The Tuesday Club of Sacramento held an annual "miniature" victory garden contest that featured prizes and a lecture by Elmer Stanley. California state employees also held an annual garden competition.

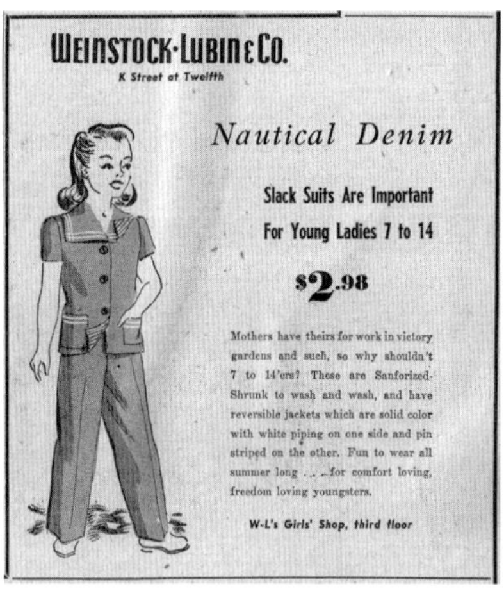

Young women figured prominently in the victory garden movement. *Center for Sacramento History.*

Most prominent, though, was the chamber of commerce garden contest. Residents competed based on size of plot, ranging from small parcels of less than one thousand square feet to larger gardens of more than two thousand square feet. The June 1942 contest had winners such as W.E. Perry of 4464 H Street in East Sacramento and W.W. Workman of 1851 Seventh Avenue in Land Park. The contest also included a school division, with Tahoe and El Dorado Elementary Schools coming out on top.[208]

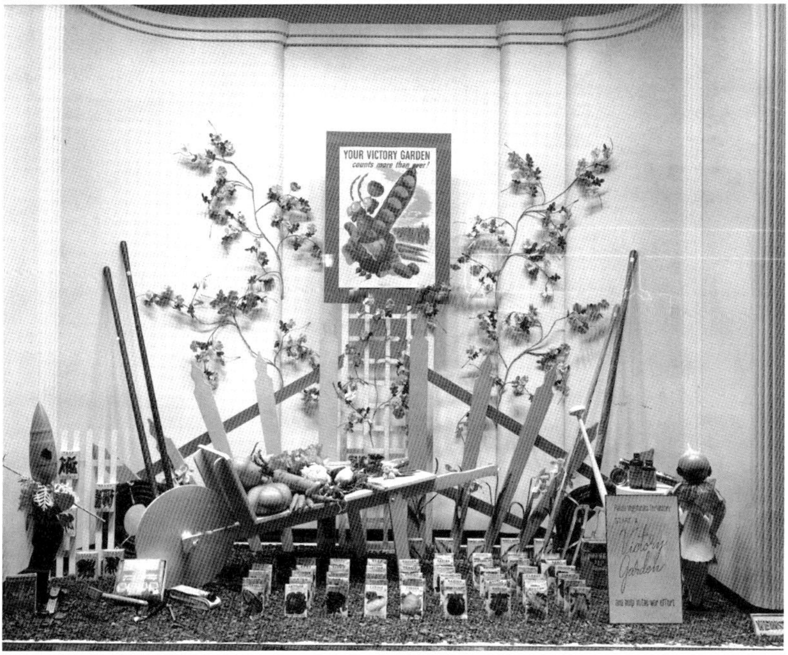

This page: Victory garden displays were a common sight at the Weinstock-Lubin department store. *Center for Sacramento History*.

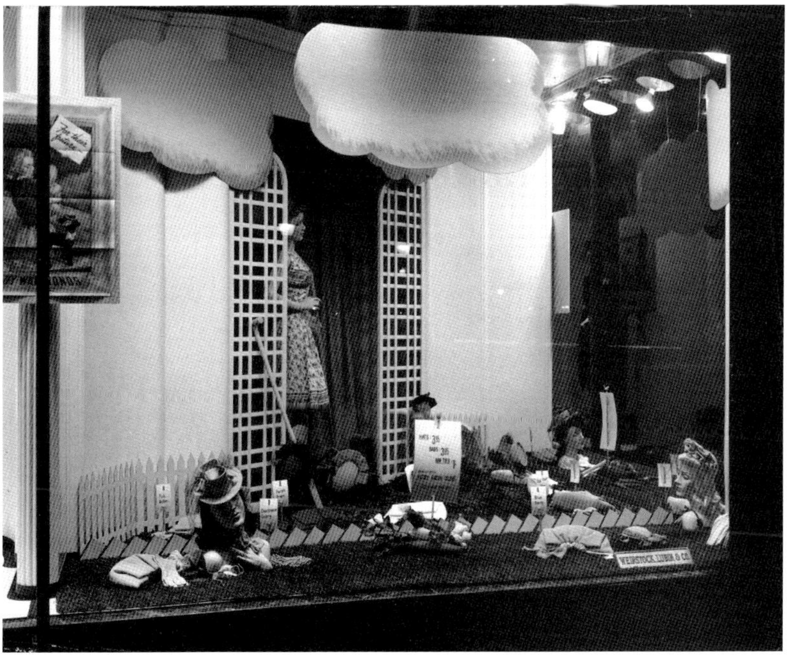

With all systems humming, one peculiar headwind arose. Along the Del Paso corridor in North Sacramento, as well as a couple of neighborhoods in the southern area of the city, packs of stray dogs harassed residents. Complicating matters was their fondness for digging. Sacramento city manager Elton Sherwin noted, "City officials have received a large number of complaints from Sacramentans who are cultivating Victory Gardens that dogs are destroying their crops." Frustrated residents "indicated that if the annoyance continues they will kill the offending animals."[209]

County executive Charles Deterding jumped on the case and found that Fairfield had a similar problem and had implemented a series of traps to capture the fugitive canines. Corresponding measures were enforced in Sacramento, with apprehended dogs sent to the pound. Fortunately, the majority of them were reunited with their owners, since the dogs were licensed. Sherwin wagged his finger at residents, complaining that "even though a $1 permit has been obtained for a dog does not mean the animal can run loose."[210]

The stray canine issue ultimately proved to be a minor annoyance, and these initial efforts began to pay off. According to the annual UC Davis county agriculture report for 1942, twenty-five thousand home gardens were established. In addition, there were four thousand home poultry flocks, four hundred rabbit hutches and two hundred additional herds of cattle in Sacramento County.[211]

With momentum on its side, Sacramento brought out the heavy hitters to promote the Food for Victory program. McClatchy empire stalwarts KFBK radio and the *Sacramento Bee*, as well as the county Department of Agriculture and the University of California, sponsored an annual harvest festival. Held at the Memorial Auditorium, it occurred on the first weekend of August from 1943 to 1945.

With the state fair on hiatus during the war, the three festivals met pent-up demand and averaged an overflow crowd of fourteen thousand. Enticed with music, contests, prizes and patriotic appeals, Sacramentans flocked to the Memorial, creating one of the best attended series of non-sporting events in city history.

In July 1943, the County Board of Supervisors signed on to support the festival. Days later, Governor Earl Warren, who had started his own garden at the governor's mansion, unleashed a gleeful challenge to the county's victory gardeners, which by now numbered thirty thousand: "You can count on a display of vegetables from the Warren Victory Garden and

I'll say right now that if any of the products of Sacramento gardens can taste any better than those we are now harvesting from our garden, they are entitled to a prize."

On a more serious note, Governor Warren went on:

> *It is my hope that the Sacramento Victory Garden festival will provide inspiration and knowledge causing thousands more home owners in the area to plan fall and winter gardens. During the year one-fourth of our total food products will be required by our armed forces and our allies. This demand plus the labor problems which have arisen in many farming areas makes Victory Gardening both a patriotic duty and an economic necessity. Certainly it is a prudent precaution for every family with space available for ordinary vegetables and greens. You can count on me to lend encouragement to any program which will give emphasis in the desirability of Victory Gardening.*[212]

The head of the California Department of Agriculture, Merle Hussong, added a stark humanitarian plea in his support for the festival: "We must produce food for the 500,000,000 starving victims of Axis aggression who must be fed both now and after the Allies have achieved victory."[213]

With the governor's marching orders in hand, volunteers opened the doors for the inaugural Victory Garden Harvest Festival at 1:00 p.m. on August 5, 1943. The Emil Martin orchestra greeted the crowd and played big-band hits throughout the two-day affair, with a collection of "prominent" military performers rotating through the sets.

While the band performed on the main stage, about one hundred Girl Scouts escorted onlookers as they surveyed the various entries scattered on tables throughout the main auditorium floor. The hours of 2:30–5:00 p.m. and 5:30–7:00 p.m. were set aside for informational lectures and short films in the adjacent Little Theater.

Underlining the ultimate goal of the event, however, were one hundred representatives from local garden clubs and the University of California–Davis School of Agriculture who gave out advice throughout the festival. The formal starting ceremonies were held shortly after 7:00 p.m. with county Food for Victory coordinator Ferd Scheid as the master of ceremonies and Mayor Tom Monk as the keynote speaker. The festivities wrapped up each day at 10:00 p.m.[214]

The harvest festival contest itself had a very similar format to the chamber of commerce competition. In the days prior to the event, judges fanned out

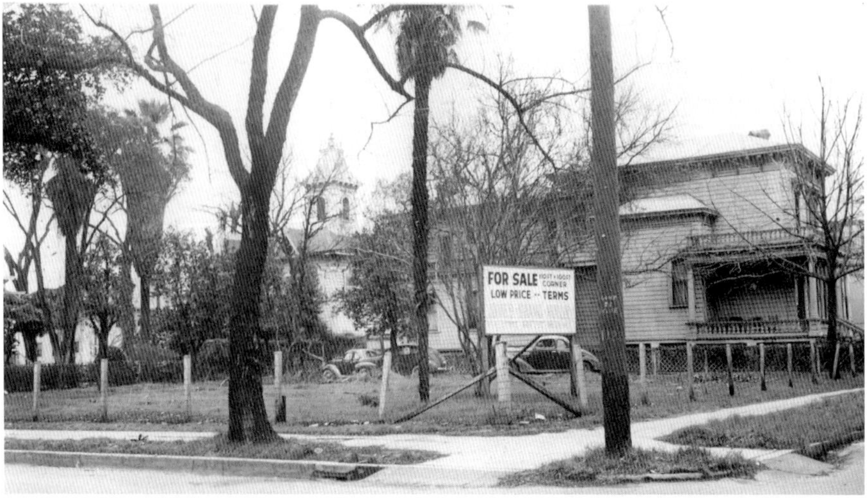

This is a 1941 photograph of the parcel where Governor Earl Warren and family planted their victory garden. The Governor's Mansion is in the background to the left. *Center for Sacramento History*.

to local victory garden participants in the area. With coveted war bonds and war stamps as the incentive, entrants were rated based on presentation, crop yield and ingenuity of garden technique.

Just as with the chamber competition, categories were based on lot size: small (less than 500 square feet), medium (less than 1,500 square feet) and large, with some of the biggest residential lots exceeding 5,000 square feet. The community garden category had no limit on square footage.

Meanwhile, inside the auditorium, judging took place in the individual vegetable, fruit and display categories. Attendees ogled the various entries as they navigated their way through the building. There was, of course, the mandatory "largest watermelon" category, but every fruit and vegetable was judged not only on size but also on the more important qualities of taste and appearance, with the more exotic entries having the best chance at winning a prize.

Displays of every incarnation, from vegetable bouquets to fruit poster boards, came from all corners of the region. Along with residential participants, Sutter's Fort and Capitol Park as well as the city schools and parks entered the fray. Preserved fruits and vegetables were the largest category of the competition. Ultimately, all of the submitted jars and cans were given to the Bercut-Richards cannery and were distributed with the signature "V" label.[215]

At the 1944 festival, one winning entrant tested the bounds of imagination. In an homage to the dreaded and ubiquitous garden pest, a competitor constructed a large, menacing insect out of fruit and vegetables. The thorax consisted of a zucchini, the legs rhubarb. The creature possessed eyes made of red berries, a green berry mane and ears of succulent leaves. A nifty white bow tie topped off the costume. By all accounts, this dapper monstrosity was the star of the pageant.[216]

After the initial 1943 harvest festival, KFBK and the *Sacramento Bee* decided to take their marketing efforts a step further by producing a film that both promoted the next year's edition as well as victory gardening in general. This thirty-eight-minute silent film, which used intertitles to convey scene changes and information, was shot and directed by *Sacramento Bee* photographer Harry Handsaker.

The movie became a local classic in spite of the fact that it was Handsaker's first attempt at filmmaking. Handsaker recorded the documentary in color on 16mm film, and since he did not have post-production editing facilities, he edited it on his camera.[217] The movie consisted of two parts, the latter featuring scenes of the 1943 festival.

The first part of the film is particularly noteworthy in that it features a local telephone linesman, Prentiss Ferguson, and his wife, daughter and son at their residence across from Land Park. Mr. and Mrs. Victory Gardeners, as they were called, were shown planting, irrigating and otherwise tending their home garden on Seventh Avenue.[218]

This section of the movie also featured the gardening efforts of Ferguson's neighbors both at home and in the community.[219] The film debuted at the KFBK studios and then made the rounds throughout 1944 and 1945, showing at community centers and movie theaters, including the Alhambra and the Little Theater at the Memorial, and at every conceivable meeting hall.[220]

Anticipation and uncertainty filled the air as the last harvest festival opened its doors once again at 1:00 p.m. on Saturday, August 4, 1945. Along with the rest of the United States and its allies, Sacramento had celebrated the surrender of Nazi Germany on May 8. The slog continued in the Pacific, however, but significant gains had been made: the fall of Iwo Jima in March, the British conquest of Burma in early May and the American takeover of Okinawa in June. The demise of Imperial Japan seemed imminent, so much so that the Allies demanded unconditional surrender at the Potsdam conference on July 27. But Tokyo refused, and the fighting continued.[221]

The festival had a similar format as in years past but this time carried a "country fair" theme. F.M. Sandusky, the newly appointed head of the California State Fair, presided over the festivities, which included more than one thousand exhibits "ranging from cucumber and tomatoes to canned string beans and currant jelly."[222]

Katherine Kitchen, the *Bee*'s resident home economist, set up shop on the west side of the auditorium foyer just as she had done in years past. At her desk, Kitchen distributed literature and "consulted on nutrition problems," and on the floor of the auditorium, she offered wisdom in "the home preservation section." In another corner of the auditorium, the university extension displayed the latest in home refrigeration.[223]

On the second day of the festival, at 4:00 p.m. on Sunday, August 5, about three thousand festival-goers were enjoying the last hours of the event. As usual, the strains of Emil Martin's big band filled the hall as attendees milled about the exhibits. Others crammed the adjacent Little Theater, watching one of the many instructional films on home gardening. As people were taking notes and perusing the displays of rhubarb, broccoli and asparagus, the "Enola Gay" dropped the atomic bomb. Hiroshima lay in ruins.

The next twenty-four hours produced a news cycle that local editors would never forget. Not only did news of Hiroshima break that evening on the radio and the next day in the *Sacramento Union* and *Bee*, yet another story, one of particular significance for Sacramentans, broke as well. At 6:45 a.m. on Monday, August 6, Hiram Johnson, native son, former California governor and current U.S. senator, died of a stroke at Bethesda Naval Hospital.[224]

Johnson's death, which was not entirely unexpected since he had been in a coma for a couple of weeks, had a ring of irony. On one hand, he had expanded certain rights and battled corruption as a Progressive Era champion. As governor, he helped bring the franchise to women; established the initiative, referendum and recall process; regulated public utilities and the railroad and instituted labor reforms. But he also possessed an antipathy for East Asians, most notably the Chinese and Japanese, and will be remembered for his relentless quest to restrict their immigration and property rights.

After Japan signed the treaty of surrender on September 2, 1945, and the celebrations died down, locals took stock of the community's performance in the Food for Victory program. Starting in 1943 and throughout the remainder of the war, the county had held steady with thirty thousand victory gardens. In the United States, approximately 80 percent of residences maintained a plot, and about 40 percent of produce consumed came from a home or community garden. Sacramento County exceeded these averages with upwards of 90 percent of residences participating and more than half the produce grown at home or in the neighborhood. According to the state Department of Agriculture, Sacramento had one of nation's best programs and was "the per capita leader of the west coast."[225]

The harvest festivals were a sensation and reported forty-two thousand in attendance over the three years. Later in 1945, Eleanor McClatchy, the matriarch of the family media empire, received a personal letter from Eleanor Roosevelt commending her for the harvest festivals and promoting victory gardening in general.[226] Sacramento had indeed lived up to its lofty agrarian heritage.

The later years of Prentiss Ferguson, the "Mr. Victory Gardener" of the Robert Handsaker film, were fittingly emblematic of postwar America. Ferguson clearly had an interest in gardening and the environment, as records indicate his membership in the local chapter (Sacramento Valley) of the California Native Plant Society (CNPS).

Although documents prior to 1968 have been lost, it is most likely that he was one of the twenty founding members of the society at its inception in 1965. He was a thoroughly active member of CNPS, becoming its vice president in 1969 and its president in 1970.

In those and subsequent years, Ferguson led a multitude of field trips, including botanical walks, throughout the capital region.[227] Sacramento's most prominent home gardener had evolved into a familiar figure in post-1960s America—citizen scientist and environmental activist.

The current home gardening movement, including Sacramento's claim as America's "farm to fork" capital, has now come full circle. Just as they did in the 1940s, city and county residents can once again maintain gardens in their front and side yards and sell produce without a permit. Lists of seasonal varieties, the use of sentinel plants and other gardening advice found in the thousands of victory garden pamphlets are now codified in the University of California Master Gardener's Manual. Photos and biographies of local organic farmers adorn produce sections in local markets just as restaurateurs who utilize this produce are featured in local and national publications. The harvest festivals at the Memorial Auditorium have morphed into the "farm to fork" festivals of today.

Indeed, the "heroic" farmers of yesteryear have not disappeared—they have merely come home. The victory gardeners ran interference for an industrial agricultural machine that fed troops and allies and, in later years, sustained an increasingly hungry nation.

But their civic duty also offered an alternative. Ferguson and his disciples have sought to rectify some of the environmental damage done by intensive farming to perhaps restore, in some small measure, the other half of the "rural ideal" trumpeted by Sacramento's forefathers. They had taken to heart Rachel Carson's admonition: "'The control of nature' is a phrase conceived in arrogance, born of the Neanderthal age of biology and philosophy, when it was supposed that nature exists for the convenience of man."[228]

But now, the stakes are even higher. The home gardeners of today and those of World War II share one last and most important trait: an enemy. For the victory gardeners of the 1940s, it was the Axis powers; for today's home gardener there is a no less immediate and formidable foe—climate change.

6

THE TWO DRAGONS: THE SACRAMENTO SOLDIER EXPERIENCE

By James C. Scott

Hey Jack, Lucky won't jump!" were the very last words that Lieutenant Jack Voss needed to hear as his near-engineless B-24 Liberator, the "Ceaseless Cindy," spiraled downward into the emerald green of China's Canton Province. "Well, kick his ass out!" was the best he could manage just seconds before he, himself, had to jump. As Voss floated earthward, none of it seemed real—the ability or even the need to make the quick, life-or-death decisions that most twenty-three-year-olds shouldn't have to make. And, yet, this was war, and he was a million miles away from being the kid who, just three and a half years earlier, had been picking oranges for ten cents a lug on a certain Sunday in December 1941 in Fair Oaks, a town located thirteen miles northeast of Sacramento proper. It was after breaking for a few moments that the orchard's owner, a Mr. Harper, told Voss, "Well, it looks like you are going to be in the service"—essentially the old man's way of telling Voss that Pearl Harbor had been attacked and that his life was going to change very quickly.

I was fortunate enough to sit down with Voss in June 2003 and talk to him about his World War II experience. As we chatted in the comfort of his Rosemont home, his affability and boyish excitement guided our conversation with a seamless ease. Looking back, I don't think I asked him even one of a bundle of precoordinated questions that I had so nervously clung to with previous subjects. A year earlier, another local World War II veteran, Joe Wayne Fong, welcomed me to his home in Sacramento's

Land Park neighborhood for a talk as well. Like Voss, Fong was a lifelong Sacramentan and could also tell a terrific story.

This chapter is a narrative of those two interviews. The intent is to feature the somewhat separate, but easily relatable, lives of two Sacramento boys who became two Sacramento soldiers and, ultimately, two men worthy of being called the "Two Dragons," the fearsome mascot of their shared and beloved alma mater, Sacramento High School, which graduated Voss in 1940 and Fong in 1944.

****

WITH THE STING OF Pearl Harbor still fresh, Voss kept a determined cadence, continuing school at Sacramento Junior College, playing baseball, bowling, golfing and finding work where he could, including a stint at the downtown YMCA at Fifth and J Streets where the lifeguard-certified Eagle Scout taught students, mostly children, how to swim for thirty-five cents an hour. His most awkward, if not serendipitous, pupil came in the form of an adult, whom Voss described as a "big, robust" army officer. That very officer came to see something special in the young lifeguard, which prompted him to ask if flying was something that had ever interested Voss, who happily replied, "Yes, Major, ever since I saw John Wayne in the *Flying Tigers*."[229] With that, Voss's course was set. After a series of intake tests and a short stint at the University of Tennessee–Knoxville, he was on this way to pre-flight training with the U.S. Army Air Force, first at Maxwell Field in Montgomery, Alabama, and then Cochran Field in Macon, Georgia.

It was at Cochran that Voss, having already soloed back in Knoxville, claimed, in his words, the "most outstanding accomplishment" of his time as a cadet. Every trainee had to face the daunting task of taking off and landing during the darkness of night, doing so with a common trainer of the time, the BT-13 Valiant. One evening, Voss and three other classmates were maneuvering at an altitude of roughly four thousand feet for their very first night landing when his engine suddenly stalled. After calling "mayday," he was ordered to go through a checklist of fixes. With none working and his altitude dropping to a perilous three thousand feet, Voss was ordered to bail out of the plane by his superior, a Captain Benson. Voss would have none of it. With a mortal fear of both snakes and alligators and situated so close to Georgia's swampy Piedmont Region, Voss refused: "Sir, I'm not going to bail out of this thing....I'm

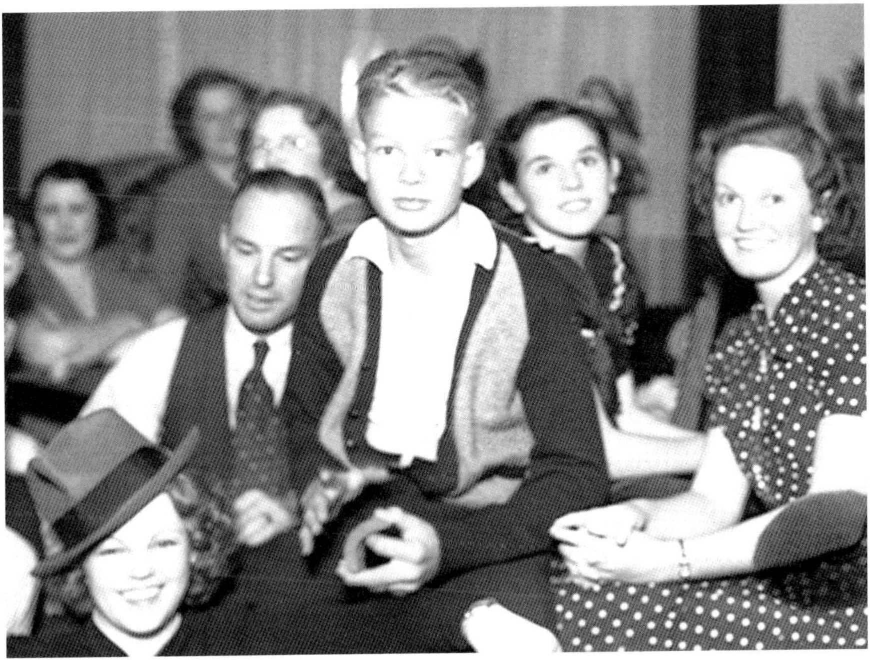

Surrounded by family in 1932 is ten-year-old Jack Voss. His mother, Edythe, is wearing a fedora. *Mick and JR Voss.*

going to bring it in." Voss recalled that, after saying so, it "got real quiet on the other side."[230] Losing both altitude and air speed at a rapid pace and after what must have seemed an eternity, he finally heard Benson say, "Well, don't talk anymore—I'll talk to you." After having put the Valiant into a slow, gliding circle, Voss was repeatedly told by Benson to control his airspeed and be mindful of braking too much when making contact with the soft field. He did both to perfection, landing the plane to the relief of all, mostly himself.

Voss may have been alive, but he had also disobeyed a direct order. Without any contact with Benson for an agonizing three days, the two finally met. With few words spoken, Voss was formally disciplined by way of an official statement that was placed into his personnel file, but he was also able to keep his cadet status. In the time he had left, Voss made the most of it. Not long after graduation, he made the long walk to Benson's office, intent on thanking the captain for both his leniency and a transfer to advanced pilot training with two of his closest friends. At the end of a very cordial meeting, Benson looked at Voss and said, "I want to tell you something. You

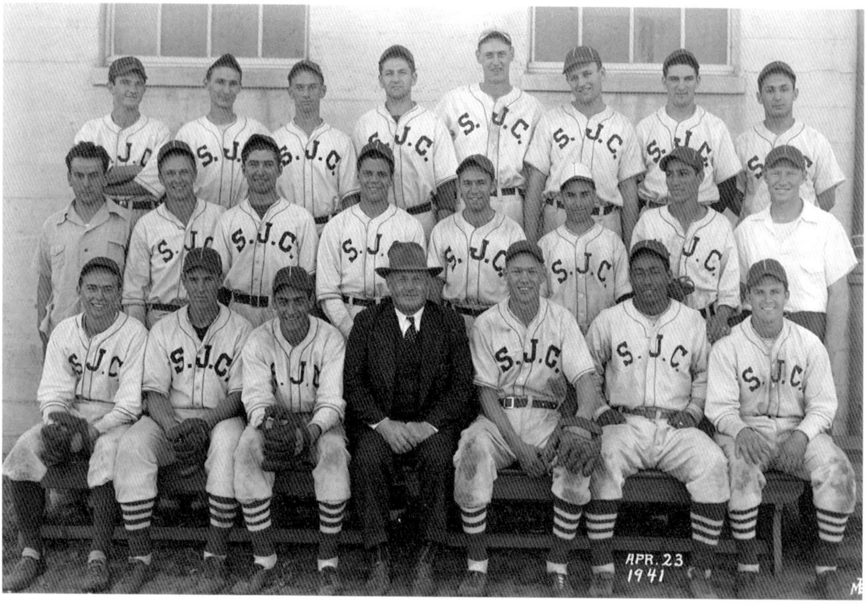

Above: In spring 1942, Jack Voss (*seated fifth from the left*) poses with the Sacramento Junior College baseball team. *Mick and JR Voss.*

Right: This 1945 image captures Jack Voss, clad in dress uniform and somewhere in the Philippines. *Mick and JR Voss.*

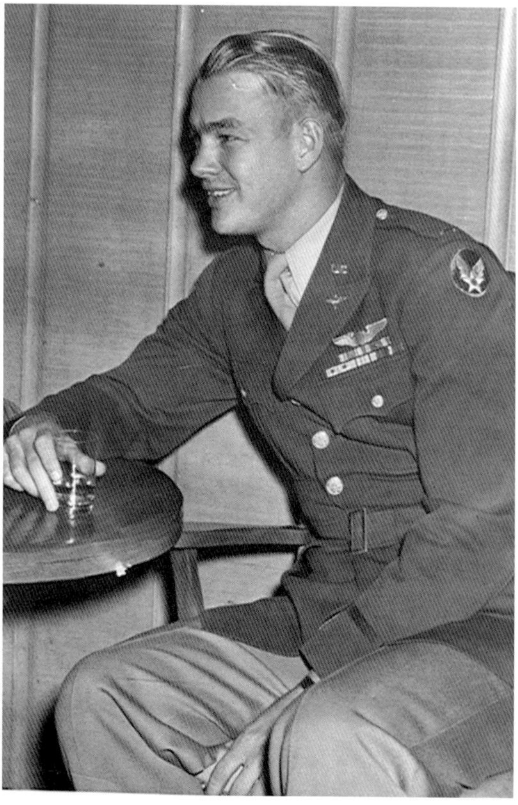

did something that's unheard of. For a cadet to land at night, dead stick, no power, is impossible."[231]

In receiving his coveted second lieutenant's commission, Voss assumed that he was off to single-engine fighter training. Instead, either because his height of six feet, three inches made him too large for fighters, or perhaps even dancing with the wrong girl at the wrong time, he was tapped to fly one of the more effective, albeit unattractive, long-range strategic bombers of World War II, the Consolidated B-24 Liberator. It could fly higher and longer and carry more ordnance than the more durable, if not glamorous, B-17. But its appearance was summed up in this common quip by American aviators of the time: "The B-24 is so ugly that it looks like the packing box that the B-17 came in." Nonetheless, in a matter of weeks, Voss went from doing acrobatics with his T-6 to what he saw as the equivalent of "driving a truck."[232] After Liberator instruction at Panama City, Florida, he was finally going to war as a copilot with the Fifth Air Force and member of the storied Ninetieth Bombardment Group, informally known as the "Jolly Rogers." Operating out of Mindoro, an island on the eastern side of the Filipino archipelago, Voss flew eighteen

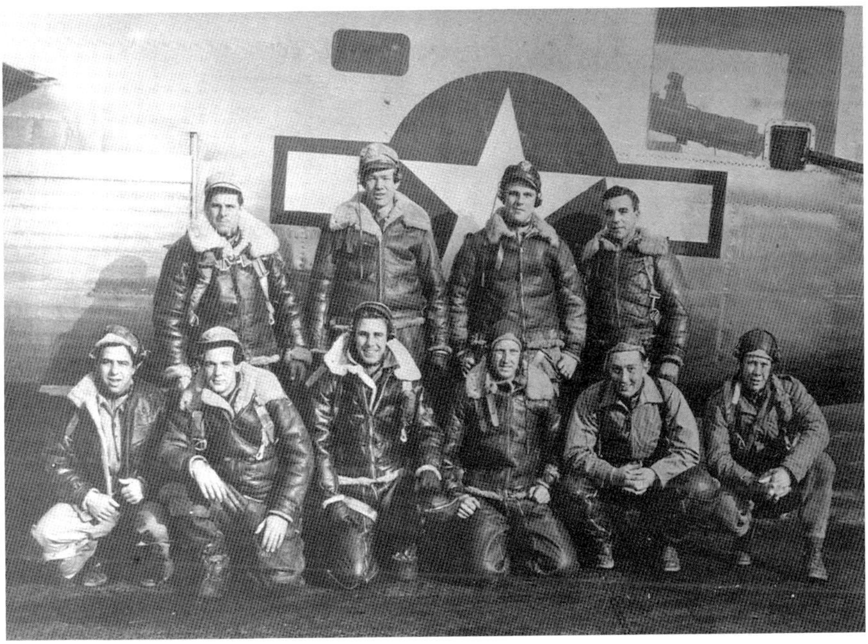

Jack Voss (*standing second from left*) posing with the crew of the "Ceaseless Cindy." *Mick and JR Voss.*

missions, most of them with the "Ceaseless Cindy." As the reader will see, and for a number of reasons, trip number eighteen—taking place on July 12, 1945—would stand as the most remarkable.

The mission's objective was a simple one. Fly 750 miles and drop two two-thousand-pound bombs on the supply warehouses of a beleaguered and retreating Japanese Imperial Army in Canton Province, China. The long trip, one that took the crew over hundreds of miles of open ocean, was uneventful. However, as Voss and pilot Harvey Del Fatti approached the Chinese coastline, en route to linking up with the rest of their formation north of Hong Kong, they noticed a sharp drop in the oil pressure in one of their supercharged Pratt and Whitney engines. Seconds later, a fusillade of antiaircraft fire hit the B-24, knocking out the malfunctioning engine and taking out another. The plane, however, Detroit-built and state-of-the-art, could still fly on two engines. With the "Ceaseless Cindy" committed to reaching its objective, bombardier Edward Novak took control of the B-24 by way of his Norden bombsight, gently guiding it to a direct hit with each of the massive bombs.

However, with a return to Mindoro out of the question, the crew had to then pivot to the prospect of bailing out either over the South China

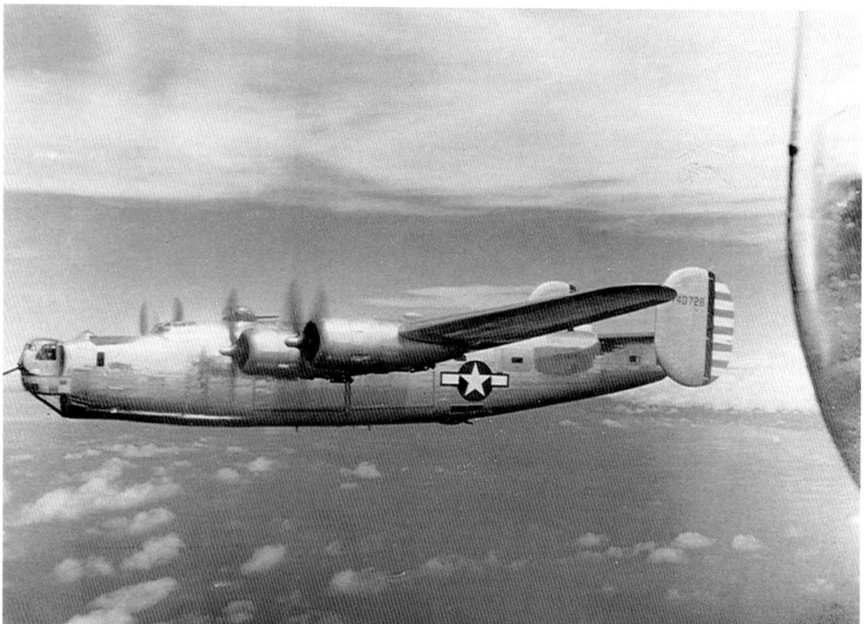

Jack Voss shoots a picture of a formation mate from the cockpit of the "Ceaseless Cindy" in 1945. *Mick and JR Voss.*

Sea (as prescribed by Air-Sea Rescue) or by taking their chances behind enemy lines. Voss, perhaps drawing on his years of swim instruction, knew exactly what to do and immediately made it clear to Del Fatti that only a few members of the ten-man crew could actually swim:

> *"Hey Harv, Jesus we can't have these boys..." Boys I call them, I was twenty-three years old, and Harvey was the same age, I said, "We can't have these guys bail out over the water, they don't even know what the ocean is. They all were from back east, eighteen, nineteen years old, the gunners, we can't have them bail out over the water, we'd lose somebody."*

Del Fatti, a native of Wisconsin, agreed. After getting inland, the two set the autopilot and put the Liberator into a slow circle, with the intention of having the entire crew land in roughly the same area. Years later, Voss recounted that every movement, every decision seemed to come second nature: "You don't even think about it, you're so well trained. You don't think about your own life. I never thought about me...[and] everybody got out of the aircraft," including a previously jittery, but quickly relieved, waste gunner that went by the nickname of "Lucky."[233]

All ten crewmen floated into a placid, green valley full of rice paddies and bounded by hills that reminded Voss of the Placerville area. After hitting the ground, Voss, who always carried a small one-pound Brownie camera, asked Novak to take a picture of him and the plane's radioman Sam Sparks, each draped in their parachutes and grinning ear-to-ear. Just minutes later, the group was surrounded—not by the Japanese, but by a unit of friendly Communist soldiers led by the affable General Tsoi King-kai. The fellow whom the aviators would come to simply call "General Tom" was determined to get the Americans to safety and, according to Voss, accepted the challenge as an honor and point of great pride.

Upon approaching the village that served as the unit's de facto headquarters, Voss recalled the near-hallucinogenic sight of a Caucasian man wearing a long beard, long hair and white robe and followed by "75 to 100 little boys." The stranger walked up to Voss and said, "Lieutenant, I'm Father Cellini." The stunned aviator replied, "Father Cellini, I thought you were Jesus Christ himself." Cellini, the soft-spoken leader of the village's Christian mission, then said, "I'm working on it, but I'm not there yet."[234] It was at that point, according to Voss, that he "got religious."[235]

So began the crew's thirty-day odyssey of escape. With a lofty bounty now placed on their heads by nearby Japanese units—said to be just two days

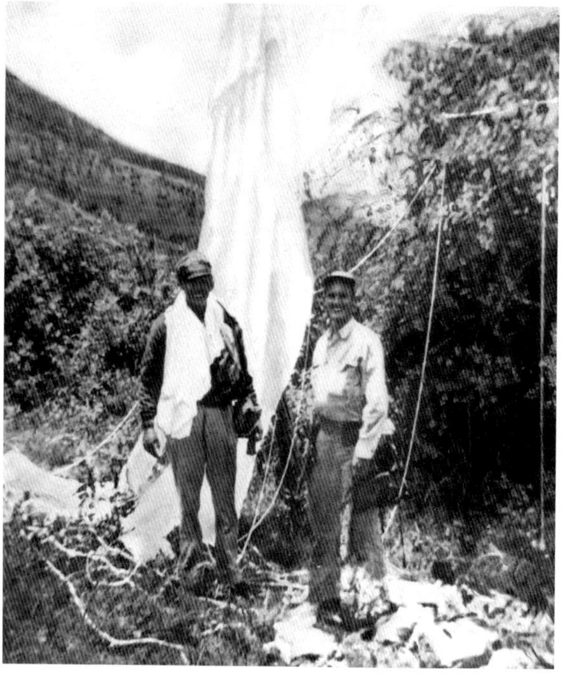

Jack Voss *(left)* and Sam Sparks enjoy a light moment after parachuting behind enemy lines in July 1945. *Mick and JR Voss.*

behind—the escape saw the airmen moved from spot to spot by foot, sampan (a flat-bottomed boat) and oxcart. Yet in the chaos that accompanied the extraction, Voss lost his cherished Brownie and, with it, the spontaneously magical "bailout image." While the drive to survive dwarfed the Brownie's importance, it didn't stop Voss from asking General Tom to keep an eye out for the camera.

Along the way, in the village of Lo Ting, the crew came across another priest, a Father Keneally, who, because of his size—six feet, six inches—was known to his Cantonese parishioners as "the Ox." Keneally's primary task was to minister the Gospel, but he spent most of his time operating an orphanage that was made up of neglected infants, mostly females, from the surrounding area. The priest asked Voss and his comrades more than once to help in collecting the multitude of little ones who littered the area's byways and village lanes, an experience that Voss recalled years later with great melancholy. They eventually moved on from the spot, but prior to leaving, and in a remarkable case of happenstance, the priest asked Voss to look up his aunt, who happened to be a nun in Sacramento.

At the end of nearly thirty days of travel, Voss and his crew finally reached the safety of Chinese Nationalist lines in Kunming. And amazingly enough, Voss's camera reappeared. Because the camera had ostensibly been stolen near the beginning of their journey, the general, fearing a loss of face, threatened to burn down the entire village if it wasn't returned to the Americans. The film was processed in Kunming but, in another curious twist, ended up in the possession of Novak, who, some thirty-two years later, would return the "bailout image" to Voss in what would become a reunion for the ages.

The crew of the "Ceaseless Cindy" had escaped through a combination of luck, leadership, guile and toughness. Years later, Voss would come to attribute the Boy Scout experiences of this youth, and the resourcefulness and confidence incubated therein, as playing no small part in seeing the escape through. One of the more character-revealing images of Voss comes from a digitized roll of film that is housed in the Special Collections of the Sacramento Public Library and the Boy Scouts of America Troop One Collection. It's there, in 1937, that one sees an already confident fifteen-year-old, clad in Scout garrison cap, powering his way up a trail into Camp Cody, Troop One's longtime backwoods sanctuary in the Sierra Nevada Mountains. Scouting was then, and for years to come, the locus of Voss's worldview and sense of family and community. What's also notable about the image was that it was captured while he and eight other Scouts (just one man short of a Liberator crew) were fulfilling the task of establishing Troop One's newly acquired Camp Cody. This was an experience that, albeit a bit out of scale, provided an interesting proving ground for future adventures, if not an opportunity to cultivate and understand the value of teamwork. The nine's toughness and pioneering spirit became legendary in Troop One circles, earning them the title of the "Big Brawny Bruisers." Ultimately, if either through the maintenance of dry socks to avoid foot rot or smiting the often verboten practice of an officer drinking alcohol (substitute in hot chocolate for the Scouting years) with his enlisted men as a way to nurture trust and unit cohesion, Voss could look at his journey through Scouting as a rich source of inspiration.

Voss came back to Sacramento by way of Mather Field's earlier-discussed "Sunset Project." Not long after touching down in his silvery new B-24, he called his father, Ray, and mother, Edythe, to come pick him up. The two, thinking that Voss was still in the Philippines, jumped into their car and raced out to Mather for what had to have been a joyous reunion. Voss stayed in the service for months to come, practicing bombing runs over several of the San Francisco Bay's bridges and serving out the balance of his commission. On one trip back to Mather from the Bay Area, Voss couldn't resist performing a low-altitude buzz of Land Park and his parents' house at 2809 Land Park

Drive, with navigator Novak using the Tower Theater at Sixteenth and Broadway as a pylon. In the words of Voss,

> *I put that ol' 24 right down on the deck…and I was just above the trees and the telephone poles and I'm going right toward the house and the kitchen window…and all that my dad could see was four engines coming right at the kitchen window. It was a Sunday morning, and he just happened to be at the kitchen window and he thought, "Holy Cow, here comes Jack!" I was a crazy pilot, but I am here to talk about it.*[236]

Voss also had a promise to keep. He made his way to the St. Joseph's convent and school at Ninth and G Streets in the hopes of finding anyone who could let Father Keneally's aunt know that he was safe and sound in China. Voss knocked on the door, and a nun answered. In a moment of nervous awkwardness, the best that the aviator could come up with was "I've just come back from China, and I've seen the 'Ox.'"[237] The nun nearly fainted, and it's not clear if Keneally's ninety-year-old aunt ever received word of her nephew's well-being prior to passing away, but Voss had certainly done his bit for his friend back in China.

Voss's World War II odyssey, one that would earn him the Chiang Kai-shek Medal of Valor, was done, yet he was also returning to a city full of nearly thirteen thousand veterans, most natives of the Sacramento area but nearly a fourth from other parts of the country who had no intention of leaving. That didn't include the thousands of civilian war-industry workers who would also choose to stay. He needed a plan. Following in a long family line of meat-cutters, he opted to become a business owner and butcher at Voss and Son's Meats, first at the City Market at Thirteenth and J Streets and then at 2717 Riverside Boulevard, attached to Hildreth's Grocery. He did so in concert with his father, Ray Sr., and brother Ray Jr., a navy veteran of World War II who went by the nickname "Moose" because of his large stature. The brothers would go on to provide meat for Governors Edmund "Pat" Brown and Ronald Reagan and be known to many longtime Sacramentans as the tallest, if not friendliest butchers in the Capital City.

Voss was also intent on building a family. In 1948, he married Ann Dell, a southern belle from Dothan, Alabama, who had been a civilian worker at Mather. They exchanged vows beneath the Byzantine-style dome at the Westminster Presbyterian Church at Thirteenth and N Streets before heading off for a Catalina Island honeymoon. They returned to Sacramento to raise three sons, Bill, J.R. and Mick, all of whom went on to become Eagle Scouts and successful Sacramento-area residents.

The butcher shop flourished for decades until it was felled by fire in 1971. But like he had so many times before, Voss landed on his feet, first as a meat-cutter and then as a customer service representative for Tony's Fine Foods of West Sacramento. He called it quits in 1989.

Voss's commitment to his beloved Troop One stayed true for the rest of his life, an experience made all the more meaningful with the presence of first his sons and then his grandsons. As a Sacramento food industry insider, he kept his eyes open for his Cody Scouts on the best deals for meats, produce and soups (particularly via the Campbell's Soup Factory on Franklin Boulevard) and made deliveries with his signature yellow-tone International Scout Jeep. It would become appropriate, then, that Voss, not long after passing away in 2004, would be immortalized through having the entryway into Cody—the same one used seventy years earlier by the "Big Brawny Bruisers"—renamed the Jack Voss Trail.

****

MORE THAN ONCE, JOE Wayne Fong described his childhood self to the author as a "brat," often falling into trouble at Folsom's Granite Grammar School by throwing modeling clay against doors and walls and then disavowing any knowledge of it. Over time, however, he transformed from wily troublemaker to a soul who loved playing baseball, basketball (C League city champs for Sacramento High School in 1942), working on cars and supporting his family by working at their laundry business at 315 J Street. As Fong told historian Philip Choy in 2008, "I used to iron shirts, 12 an hour! Not with an electric iron, with an iron heated over the stove! You have to know the heat. I never burned a shirt!"[238] Prior to moving to Sacramento, the Fongs lived in Folsom. It's there that Joe recalled how he and his brothers pulled a cart up and down the hilly avenues of Folsom—Wool Street, Riley Street, Figueroa Street—delivering clean laundry and picking up dirty linens. Perhaps Fong's greatest boyhood satisfaction came with his purchase of a Model A Ford, which he proceeded to chop the top from and paint in blue and white trim. Simply put, he was a "doer" who operated best when the task before him required a combination of imagination and skillful hands. Years later, he would claim that the ideal training ground for both came with an after-school job at the Union Garage located at Twelfth and I Streets.

Fong remembered little of the day Pearl Harbor was attacked. He was near Lincoln School, located at Third and Q Streets, when the news came down. The thought that swayed him the most related to the multitude of Japanese Americans whom he considered friends and how the attack would impact their lives. At the same time, he knew that his participation in the war was imminent. So, while Voss was flying in Asia, Fong was doing his bit in the European theater as a machine gunner in the 773rd Tank Destroyer Battalion Reconnaissance Company, an odd spot to end up for someone who wanted nothing more than to be wearing the whites of a sailor in the U.S. Navy. Yet with the increasing demands for infantrymen, Fong opted for the army and a trip to Fort Knox, Kentucky, where he was trained in the use of all things armor. After eight weeks there and a brief stay at Camp Shanks, New York, Fong was outrunning U-boats all the way to Europe on the RMS *Mauretania*.

After landing at La Havre, France, and participating in mop-up operations at the Battle of the Bulge in February 1945, his unit was moved into a blocking position along the Rhine River. His task was to man a .50-caliber machine gun on the back of an M-3 half-track, an armored personnel carrier that was moved by both wheels and treads. Fong recounted the frequent and juicy allure of firing at German BF-109 fighter planes, missing and, in the process, giving away his unit's position, almost always resulting in a stern shelling from the enemy. On one day, however, a German plane came whizzing by, one that, years later, Fong recalled to be a "funny-looking thing."[239] Again, he couldn't resist. He fired several rounds at the mysterious aircraft, and like so many times prior, the shelling of German .88s started. The unit was forced to move, but what differed this time was that Fong finally bagged his quarry. He had shot down one of Nazi Germany's prime wonder weapons, a Messerschmitt ME-262 jetfighter: a remarkably rare accomplishment, especially against a plane that had wrought so much damage—242 Allied planes shot down—in such a short period of time.

Fong's liberation experience continued with operations through the razed German towns of Oppenheim, Darmstadt and Nuremburg, in addition to sections of western Czechoslovakia. He and his "buddies" tiptoed through minefields; stalked enemy units; befriended wary French, Czech and German villagers; and eventually enjoyed a spell of rest and recuperation in Biarritz, France, where he "traded cigarettes for Cognac with a Frenchman named Bernard and a French girl named Josette." By the time he returned to Sacramento in 1946, he had been awarded the Croix de Guerre for his military service to France.

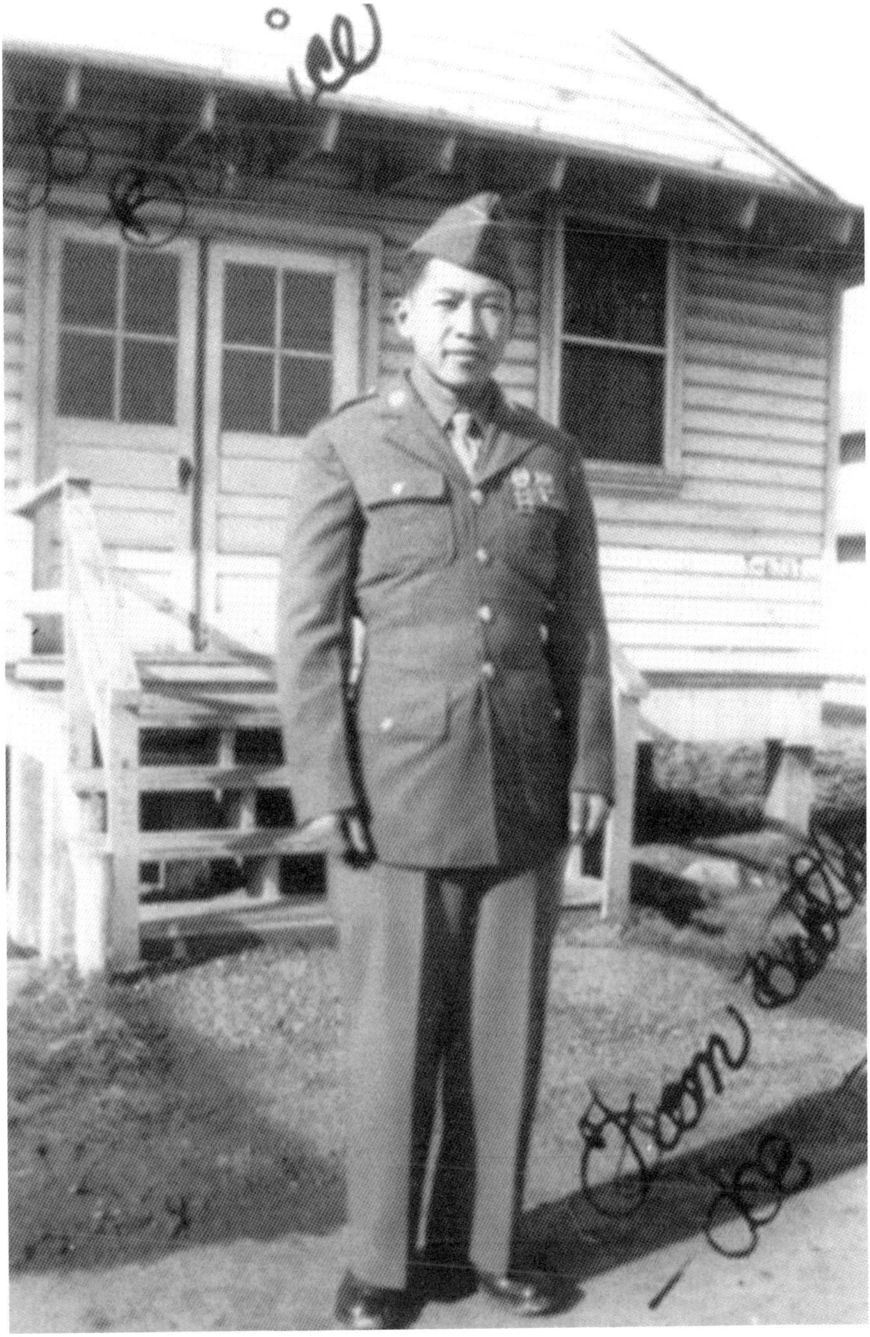

Joe Wayne Fong poses for a portrait just before his discharge from the service in 1946. *Patricia Woo.*

Like Voss, Fong came back to a city filled with veterans, yet that same burgeoning population would need services. Knowing as much, he started classes at North Sacramento's new Grant Technical College with an eye on refrigerator repair. Never one for school, however, Fong fell back on his first love—cars. By the end of the 1940s, he was operating a service station—Wayne's Auto Service—at Eleventh and S Streets with his brothers Bob and Jack. It was all part of what Fong called the "quest for my American dream." Seeing that dream through would be a combination of hard work and a series of cagey real estate deals during the city's redevelopment push of the 1960s and '70s. He was able to purchase and convert the old Goodwill Industries building at 707 Q Street, enabling him to park and service the cars of nearby state workers, primarily those at buildings 8 and 9. Fong quickly became a beloved fixture among civil servants. His kindness also made news in May 1972, when he randomly gifted some twenty home appliances to garage customers at a champagne party that he and his then wife, Dollie, threw as an expression of thanks.[240]

As time marched on, Fong's marriage ended, but he endured by holding tight to family, growing a large circle of friends and finding time for cats, pug dogs and, of course, cars. On occasion, he enjoyed a chat with friends over coffee at the Starbucks at Sixteenth and Broadway, and it was common to see Fong move about the city, mostly via bus and his own two feet, oftentimes with a visit to the public library in mind. He also never missed a Veterans' Day parade, clad in his cherished Eisenhower-style jacket and garrison cap.

Like so many who have experienced war, Fong went on to both savor and safeguard the world's many fragilities. Before visiting him one time in 2009, he made it clear during a phone conversation that I should never come to his front door for entry. Rather, because he was trying to protect a hummingbird nest that had grown out of an empty light fixture outside his large gray Land Park Drive home, I should always try to come around the driveway side. That's what I did. He waited for me at a side gate, where he carefully whispered a greeting. It was also near the last years of his life that Fong adopted a stray cat and fed it Chinese roast pork (also known as *char siu*) on a daily basis. He came to rely on the cat to wake him with a lick to the cheek during his many backyard naps.

The former Veterans of Foreign Wars commander (Chung Mei Post) died in October 2012 and is interred at the Sacramento Valley National Cemetery in Dixon, his ashes in a ceramic cookie jar in the shape of a cat.

****

There's no doubt that Voss and Fong experienced World War II like few others. Daring escapes and the downing of veritable spaceships were certainly out of the norm for your average aviator or GI. Their common experience of war makes for an exclusive club.

There's an additional connection between the two that is quintessentially Sacramento. It was Voss, a man of Norwegian American heritage, who fought to liberate the citizens of Canton Province, the genesis of so many Chinese American families—including Fong's—who immigrated to Sacramento in the nineteenth and twentieth centuries. In fact, years later, Voss recalled an exchange with one Chinese American colleague named Arnie Gee. After learning that Voss had flown missions over Canton, Gee quipped, "You tried to kill me!"[241] In fact, Gee, who Voss fondly remembered as "a great guy," had been living in Canton during the time that Voss was flying missions into southeast China. Gee, who eventually immigrated to join a strong family presence in Sacramento, long insisted that he would take Voss back to Canton for a less stressful experience, but the trip never happened. That Fong, on the other hand, was doing his bit to free those whose biological connection to Sacramento's European Americans—who ran West to "See the Elephant" of the California Gold Rush or escaped the fallout of Europe's Revolutions of 1848—was undeniable and clearly tantamount to the efforts of Voss. It should also be said that both knew what it was like to liberate Americans from the bonds of captivity—Voss by telling disbelieving prisoners of war that they were finally "going home" prior to ferrying them back to the United States and Fong by kicking down the doors of Wehrmacht-operated hospitals to the joy of Allied troops inside.

Each man also grew up in the Sacramento area, Voss in the splendor of the tree-lined avenues of East Sacramento and Land Park neighborhoods and Fong along the banks of the American River near Folsom and then Sacramento's Chinatown district. Despite differences in class, race and geography, their combined childhoods are what many Americans would fairly view as "storybook"—a time when children could leave the house after breakfast and then proceed to play, fail, learn and succeed, all before returning for dinner. What's more, as members of the "Greatest Generation," one must wonder if their growth and development during the Great Depression made for the best of all incubators for these little boys who would someday have to become men—saviors of the free world.

Although their entire lives would be spent walking the same streets and shopping the same markets, it will never be known if Voss and Fong knew one another. What is certain is that they set years of their youth aside to meet a calling for mother and country that neither had asked for but undertook as a matter of course. They did their bit, returned home to help transform and serve the city they loved and led lives of fullness, kindness and meaning. By "making it" and living the lives they did, there may have been no better way for either to honor the nearly five hundred Sacramento County men who gave their lives during World War II.

CONCLUSION

By Amanda G. DeWilde

Sacramento celebrated victory over Japan like most American cities, by descending on the city center by foot and car to take part in unrestrained revelry. After Japan's unconditional surrender was made public on August 14, 1945, thousands of people walked down K and J Streets, embracing and imbibing as they were showered with scraps from telephone directories and note paper. All taverns, businesses, banks and government offices were shuttered for the day. Only churches remained open, and they invited people to give thanks and reflect at special services. In Sacramento's Chinatown, residents lit illegal fireworks, covering the streets with firecracker paper.

For Sacramento, the end of the war didn't just mean the end of combat. It also meant no more gas rationing, no more food points and no more blackouts; it meant being able to buy nylons and leather shoes and drive over thirty-five miles per hour. Jubilation on August 14 gave way to solemn reflection in the following days as people looked forward to the return of their loved ones. Although victory over both Japan and Germany had been declared in 1945, it would take until the end of 1946 for Truman's official proclamation of the cessation of hostilities and five more years until a peace treaty was negotiated with Germany. In the year following the end of hostilities, many returned to Sacramento, while others departed. Those who returned would find work, build homes, start families and transform Sacramento into a modern postwar city.

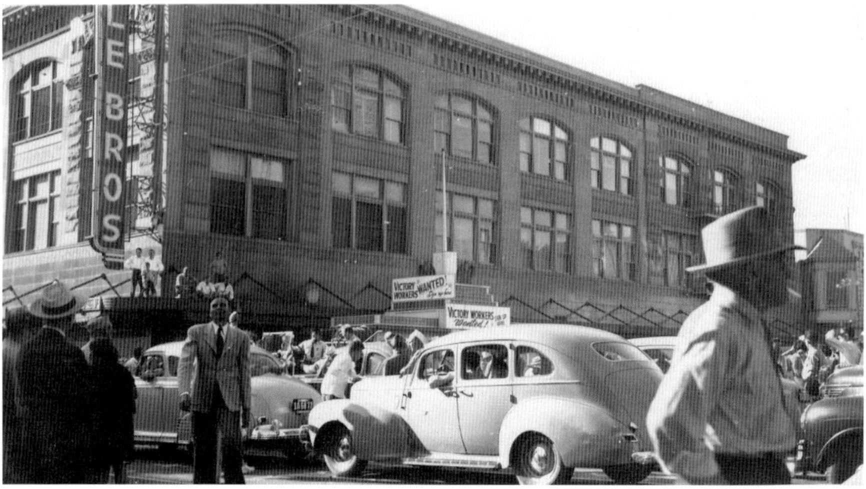

Sacramentans gather at the intersection of Ninth and K Streets in celebration of victory over Japan in August 1945. *Center for Sacramento History.*

Throughout 1945 and 1946, disparate groups returned to Sacramento. In small numbers, civilians imprisoned abroad at concentration camps like Santo Tomas in the Philippines or at work in California forestry camps as conscientious objectors filtered back into the area in 1945. Japanese American internees and war veterans comprised the biggest numbers, with tens of thousands making their way back. Confident of American victories in Europe and Japan, the United States began making plans to release interned Japanese Americans in late 1944, with release dates set throughout 1945. Many Californians who had been supportive of internment were wary of internees returning. Some groups even called for their deportation and permanent ban. This sentiment was expressed most in California's rural counties and to a lesser extent in the Sacramento area. The Native Sons of the Golden West, Sacramento Parlor No. 3, approved a resolution in April 1945 protesting "the influx of Japanese into California as a threat to our state and nation."[242] And Sacramento's American Legion Post 61 drew the criticism of War Relocation Authority area supervisor Charles F. Miller, who accused them of making "intolerant, inflammatory and un-American statements" with regard to using Camp Kohler to temporarily house and process returning Japanese.[243]

One shining light amidst the darkness of the Japanese tragedy can be found in the story of Bob Fletcher. A 1933 graduate of UC Davis, Fletcher quit his job as an agriculture inspector and stepped in to preserve the ranches of the Nitta, Okamoto and Tsukamoto families. Fletcher saw the forced exile of his Florin-area neighbors as a point of basic morality: "I did know a few of them pretty well and never agreed with the evacuation. They were the same as everybody else. It was obvious they had nothing to do with Pearl Harbor."[244]

On the eve of the internment, Al Tsukamoto proposed that Fletcher work the combined ninety acres of Tokay grapes and pay the mortgages and taxes in exchange for half of the profits. Over the next three years, he did just that, typically working eighteen-hour days. After three years of exile, the families returned in 1945 to their farms, which had been preserved just as they were when they left. The mortgages were paid off, and the balance of profits was returned to the families. For his service, Fletcher endured epithets and narrowly escaped a bullet fired into the Tsukamotos' barn.

Only in recent decades did Fletcher get recognition for his efforts. Including these three families, only one-fifth of the two thousand internees came back to Florin, with the rest scattering to destinations throughout the United States.[245] Fletcher's erstwhile colleagues at the University of California–Davis Agriculture Extension seemed to show a glimmer or two of sympathy for the Japanese in their annual Sacramento County reports. At the very least, these reports acknowledged the immense loss of their talent and experience. Perhaps Bob Fletcher was more influential than he realized.

Among those leaving Sacramento after the cessation of hostilities were German prisoners of war and many soldiers and civilians who had moved to the area for defense jobs. Local military installations began winding down their war mobilization beginning in 1943. From McClellan, Mather Field, the Sacramento Signal Depot and other locations, thousands returned home or were reassigned. Because peace negotiations took over a year and covered the return of prisoners of war, German prisoners remained in the area until well into 1946, long enough to raise concerns that they were lingering in jobs that should have gone to returning veterans.

Returning veterans from World War II fueled an expansion that tripled the prewar population in Sacramento County by 1960. After the region's brief flirtation with demilitarization, the Cold War kept many veterans on active duty at the local military installations. While a few even saw combat in Korea, even more left the service to find civilian work at the Army Depot, Mather and, most especially, McClellan. Some veterans joined the ranks of the newly formed Aerojet General Corporation in 1951. Aerojet, which supplied rocketry for the missile defense system and NASA, is still in business today.

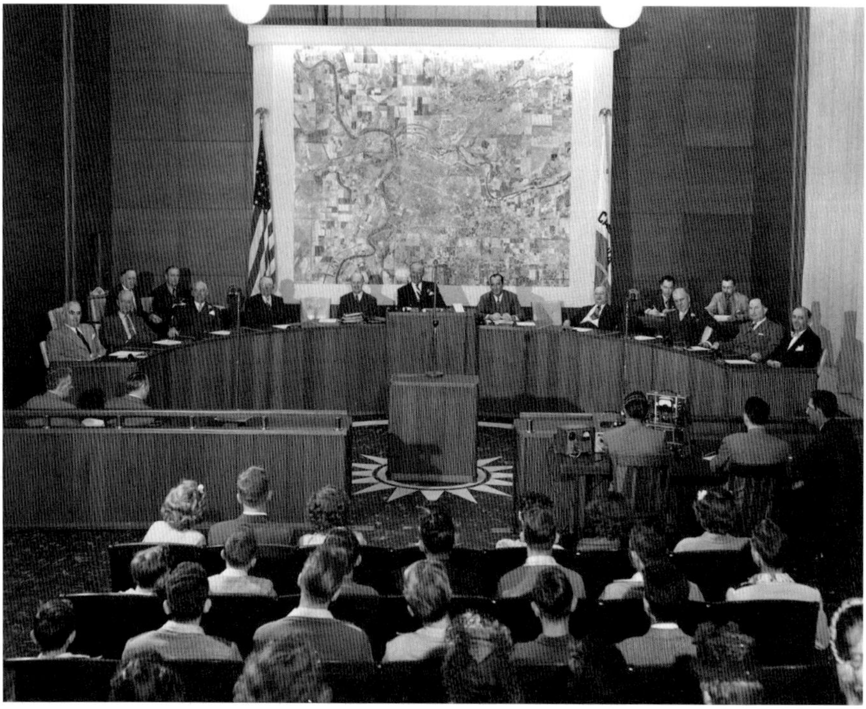

In 1946, the Sacramento City Council tackled postwar concerns like jobs for returning veterans, infrastructure and housing for a growing population. *Sacramento Public Library.*

Their greatest impact, however, was felt in local education. The Servicemen's Readjustment Act of 1944, commonly known as the GI Bill, is widely hailed as one of the most successful and revolutionary articles of legislation in American history. Those looking to take advantage of the GI Bill drove up the demand for institutions of higher learning. Sacramento Junior College exploded in size as American River College, which opened in 1955, was built on the grounds of the wartime Grant Technical College. Perhaps its most profound effect on Sacramento was the formation of Sacramento State University in 1947. Guy West, the dean of Upper Division at Chico State College and the future president of Sacramento State University, drafted a report for the legislature in 1945 that indicated a pressing need for a university in the capital city. The campus, which was originally housed on the grounds of Sacramento City College, welcomed a rapidly expanding roster of erstwhile servicemen.[246] John J. Collins, a veteran of the Pacific theater and Bronze Star recipient, was the lone member of the school's first graduating class in the spring of 1948.

In January 1948, George Strayer, a retired educator from Columbia University, assisted by the future dean of Sacramento State, Aubrey Douglass, coauthored a report that foreshadowed the master plan of California higher education adopted by the Brown administration in the 1950s. In the "Strayer Report," the mission of Sacramento State was established: it offered a liberal arts curriculum with an emphasis on teacher training.[247] Over the ensuing decades, the university's graduates shaped all facets of Sacramento life, with a multitude of veterans and their descendants finding a calling as educators in the region's burgeoning school districts.

For all who settled in Sacramento, the postwar era promised a hopeful, if uncertain, prosperity. The *Catholic Herald* observed, "Vaguely it had something to do with a future which included packaged homes, helicopters and wondrous gadgets."[248] World War II brought Sacramento into the modern age, with enduring changes in a number of areas.

First, the war provided an unexpected boost to the local economy. According to a 1946 report from the State Reconstruction and Reemployment Commission, during the war, Sacramento County was "lifted to a higher economic plane." Income shot up from $124 million in 1939 to $264 million in 1944, and per capita income rose from $738 to $1,354. Despite the fact that wartime incomes were buttressed by enormous payrolls of military installations, salaries continued to rise after the war. The county's per capita income remained at a wartime level into 1946 due to the persistence of military installations, population growth that spurred economic growth by creating larger markets for goods and services and accumulated credit in the form of war bonds and bank deposits.[249]

Second, postwar Sacramento became a defense city. During the war, the city's major military installations brought many jobs to the area at McClellan and Mather Air Force Bases, along with the Sacramento Signal Depot and Camp Kohler. Elsewhere in the state, peacetime jobs made up for losses in the defense industry. Although defense employment peaked during the war, Sacramento kept its bases and continued to employ thousands in defense jobs after the war ended. Some installations, like the Sacramento Signal Depot, expanded in the immediate postwar period. In 1945, the depot was moved from a few buildings at the Bercut-Richards packing plant to a 485-acre site off of Fruitridge Road. Defense work further expanded after the Korean War, while railroads and agriculture declined in importance. The bases were later joined by Aerojet General Corporation, which began building missile propulsion systems in the Rancho Cordova area in the 1950s, and Douglas Aircraft Company, which established a missile-testing facility in Sacramento

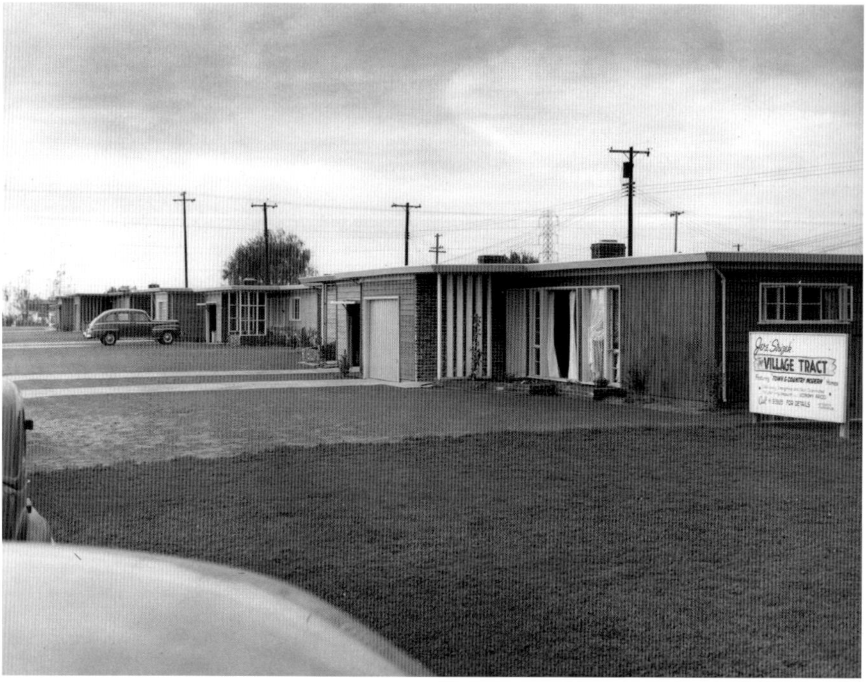

Veterans were given preference in purchasing tract homes in Jere Strizek's Town and Country Village. *Sacramento Public Library*.

during the same decade. By 1959, nearly 40 percent of basic employment in Sacramento was devoted to defense.[250]

Third, Sacramento moved to the suburbs. While suburbanization was a postwar theme in most American cities postwar, Sacramento's residents were especially quick to move outside the city. According to a Department of Commerce housing study from 1946, nearly a third of the estimated 13,000 World War II veterans living in the area desired to build or buy a home in the Sacramento area. With limits on construction and an increasing population, only 0.9 percent of the city's habitable homes were unoccupied, resulting in rapid new construction outside the city limits. Sacramento grew in size, both by population and land area, in the late 1940s. After the war, the population boomed to 137,572 residents in 1950 and 191,667 in 1960. Countywide, numerous cities formed and incorporated. Rancho Cordova formed from a nucleus of homes at the intersection of Zinfandel Drive and Folsom Boulevard, while both Folsom and Galt incorporated in 1946. The 1950 census marked the first time that the city claimed fewer residents than the rest of the county. Returning veterans and residents drawn by wartime

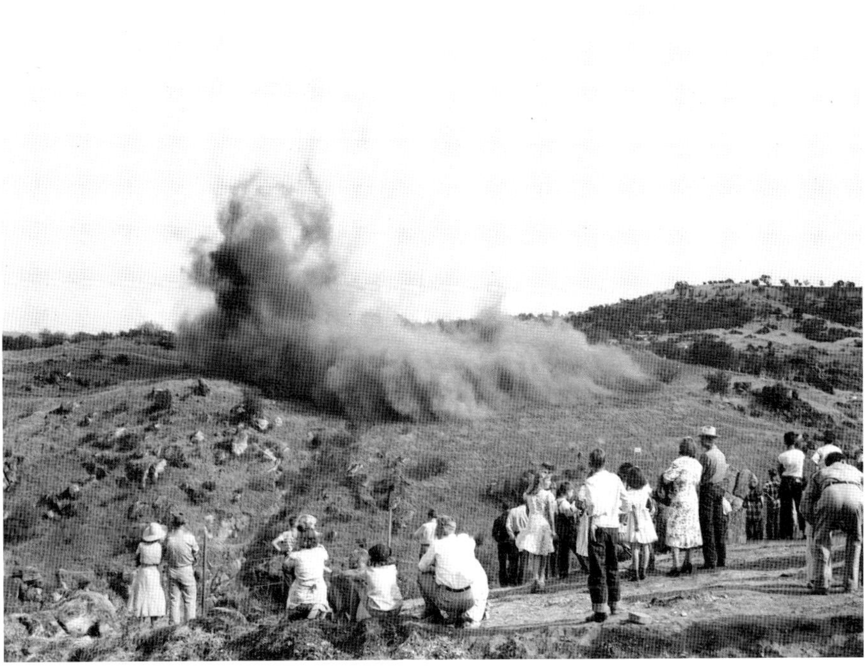

Residents gather to view demolition at the new Folsom Dam site, circa 1948. *California State Library.*

jobs needed housing, and new construction could begin on projects like Town and Country Village Shopping Center, built in 1946 by local developer Jere Strizek. Located in Arden Park, the center was one of the first of its kind in the world—a suburban outdoor mall surrounded by a neighborhood of tract homes. The development became a blueprint for suburban development throughout the country.

Just as the war drove life on the homefront during World War II, veterans and their growing families determined the trajectory of the city after the war. Sacramento made great battlefield and homefront sacrifices during the war years and met the challenges of scarcity and war production demands with dedication, ingenuity and unity. But while Sacramento took pride in supplying so much for the war effort, Japanese internment would leave a lasting stain on the legacy of the war for many residents of the county. World War II tested Sacramento in numerous ways, and the war years proved to be a formative period that continues to define the region today.

NOTES

Prologue

1. Florence Kawagoye and Bill Mahan, "Growing Up in Florin," *Golden Notes* (Winter 1994): 8.

Introduction

2. Steven Avella, *Sacramento: Indomitable City* (Charleston, SC: Arcadia Publishing, 2003), 102–3.
3. Joseph A. McGowan, *History of the Sacramento Valley* (New York: Lewis Historical Publishing, 1961), 287.
4. Marcos Breton and Steve Wiegand, "World at War 1940–1949—More than Any Other Period, the Years Surround World War II Changed Sacramento, Planting the Seeds of Growth that Would Spread from the Heart of the City," *Sacramento Bee*, December 31, 1999, OC21.
5. "Rites Are Held for Japanese Suicide," *Sacramento Bee*, December 15, 1941, 8.
6. "Japanese Girl Leads in Singing of U.S. Anthem," *Sacramento Bee*, December 8, 1941, 15.
7. Ada Weeks, "Life Goes On," *Sacramento Union*, December 13, 1941, 5.

Chapter 1

8. "Raid Brings First Taste of Trouble," *Sacramento Union*, December 9, 1941, 1; "Area Has First Blackout; Will Improve Setup," *Sacramento Bee*, December 9, 1941, 1.
9. "Capital Is 'Attacked' From Air; High Army Leaders Escape 'Raid'," *Sacramento Bee*, January 18, 1940, 1.
10. "Realistic Air Raid Will Lure Thousands to Stadium," *Sacramento Bee*, August 11, 1941, L6.
11. Franklin D. Roosevelt, "Proclamation 2352—Proclaiming a National Emergency in Connection with the Observance, Safeguarding, and Enforcement of Neutrality and Strengthening of the National Defense Within the Limits of Peace-Time Authorizations," September 8, 1939, accessed August 1, 2017, http://www.presidency.ucsb.edu/ws/?pid=15806.
12. California Department of Education, "Report of First Statewide Conference of Law Enforcement Officers to Discuss Specific Problems of Civilian Defense," Sacramento, California, Department of Education, 1941.
13. "General Warns of Sabotage Attempt by Axis in U.S.," *Sacramento Bee*, November 12, 1941, 6.
14. "Sacramento Japanese Section Placed Under Patrol of Police," *Sacramento Union*, December 8, 1941, 1; "State Defense Council Will Meet in L.A.," *Sacramento Bee*, December 8, 1941, 22.
15. "Any Apathy on Home Front Is Termed Form of Sabotage," *Sacramento Bee*, February 17, 1943, H12.
16. City of Sacramento, Ordinance 938, Fourth Series.
17. "New Official Blackout and Air Raid Rules Are Announced by Local Safety Council," *Sacramento Bee*, December 24, 1941, 10.
18. "Folsom Council of Civic Defense Issues Statement," *Folsom Telegraph*, December 26, 1941, 1.
19. City of Sacramento, Ordinance 942.
20. "Air Raid Drills," *Sacramento Bee*, December 11, 1941.
21. "City Distributes Sand for Use in Fighting Bombs," *Sacramento Bee*, December 16, 1941, 3.
22. "A Citizens' Army, Ready for Action," *Sacramento Bee*, December 26, 1942, M3.
23. "California's Quota—30,000," *Express*, March 13, 1942, 4.
24. "An Army of Sentinels Keeps Faithful Vigil," *Sacramento Bee*, June 25, 1942.

25. "Civilians in War: Home Nursing Classes Provide Many with a Chance for Special Aid," *Sacramento Union*, April 20, 1943; "Auxiliary Police Get Firearm Instruction," *Volunteer*, August 26, 1942, 1; "Capital to Sign Messengers for Defense," *Sacramento Union*, April 11, 1943, 2.
26. "The Rolling Pin Brigade in Action," *Sacramento Bee*, March 7, 1942, M5.
27. "Civilian Defense Official Warns of Complacency," *Sacramento Bee*, January 27, 1943, 9.
28. "Mock Bombs Bring Havoc Over City," *Sacramento Union*, April 20, 1943, 1; "Practice Raid Is Successful," *Sacramento Bee*, April 20, 1943, 12.
29. "Sacramento Civilian Defense Council, Citizens Service Bulletin, Block Plan Service, No. 3, Dec. 22, 1942," Sally Zentner Family Papers, MC 49, Sacramento Room, Sacramento Public Library.
30. "Behind the Lines Conservos Will Be Organized," *Sacramento Bee*, September 23, 1942, 4.
31. "PTA Makes Future Plans," *Californian*, June 11, 1942, 4; "You and the War," Sally Zentner Family Papers, MC 49, Sacramento Room, Sacramento Public Library.
32. "Display in Gallery to Launch Drive for Volunteers," *Volunteer*, February 6, 1943, 1; "All Groups to Get Actual Practice in New Program," August 26, 1942, 1.
33. "Japanese Balloons Landed in State but Caused Little Alarm," *Sacramento Bee*, August 17, 1945, 1.

Chapter 2

34. "Mather Field Is Inspected as Defense Project Site," *Sacramento Bee*, September 20, 1940, 13.
35. The installation was named after Major Hezekiah McClellan who died when the P-30 he was flight-testing crashed near Centerville, Ohio.
36. Representative Frank Buck, speaking on "Sacramento's Army Air Development," 74th Cong., 2nd sess., *Congressional Record* (Friday, May 8, 1936): 1.
37. "U.S. Discloses Air Power at Dedication," *Sacramento Union*, April 30, 1939, 4.
38. *Sacramento Air Service Command, McClellan Field–Sacramento: Chronological History* (Sacramento, CA: Sacramento Chamber of Commerce, 1943), 4.
39. *McClellan Remembered, 1938–1998: 60th Anniversary Commemorative Album* (Sacramento, CA: McClellan Commemorative Association, 1998), 113.

40. "Horses Once Roamed Air Base," *Sacramento Bee*, March 8, 1964, C3.
41. Maurice Miller, et. al, *McClellan Air Force Base, 1936–1982: A Pictorial History* (Sacramento, CA: Office of History, Sacramento Air Logistics Center, 1982), 54.
42. "Huge Engineering Shops at Depot Cover 13 Acres," *Sacramento Bee*, April 29, 1939, A4.
43. Brigadier General Christian F. Dreyer, USAF (Ret.), interview by Raymond Oliver, Office of History, Sacramento Air Logistics Center, McClellan AFB, California, June 1981.
44. "All-Out War on Japs Asked for Execution of Tokyo Raiders," *Sacramento Air Depot News*, April 23, 1943, 1.
45. "Skipper of 'Suzy-Q' Thanks McClellan Personnel for Welcome," *Sacramento Air Depot News*, April 30, 1943, 1.
46. *Sacramento Air Depot News*, April 10, 1942, 4.
47. Ibid., April 3, 1942, 7.
48. "U.S. Worker Transportation Crisis Is Seen," *Sacramento Bee*, June 26, 1942, 7.
49. Mila Landis, "At Your Service Captures First Night Audience," *Sacramento Bee*, October 16, 1943, 7.
50. Miller et al, *McClellan Air Force Base*, 57.
51. Ibid., 58.
52. McGowan, *History*, 318; Paul Rhode, "California in the Second World War: An Analysis of Defense Spending" in *The Way We Really Were: The Golden State in the Second Great War*, edited by Roger W. Lotchin (Chicago: University of Illinois Press, 2000), 97.
53. Tinker was a soldier's soldier, known for his affability, fairness and for flying his own fighter plane called "Bird-O-Prey." The first Native American to vault to the rank of major general, Tinker died in January 1942 while leading a raid on the Japanese-occupied Wake Island.
54. "Bombers Will be Trained at Mather Field," *Sacramento Bee*, October 30, 1940, 1.
55. Special Collections of the Sacramento Public Library, *Mather Field* (Charleston, SC: Arcadia Publishing, 2011), 75.
56. Ibid., 77.
57. "The West Point of the Air," *Popular Mechanics* 54, no. 1 (July 1930): 49.
58. "Queen," *Sacramento Bee*, April 25, 1942, 4.
59. Martin Kuz, "Wayne Thiebaud: The First 90 Years," *Sactown Magazine* (October–November 2010): 77.

60. Ibid.
61. Michael Amrine, *The Great Decision of the Atomic Bomb* (New York: G.P. Putnam's Sons, 1959), 195–96.
62. Richard Rodda, "Atomic Bombers, Here, Differ on Weapon's Future," *Sacramento Bee*, November 8, 1945, 1.
63. First Lieutenant Frederick L. Kohler was an Oakland-born Signal Corps officer. He died on March 12, 1942, when the overloaded cargo plane that he was a passenger on crashed into a Chinese hillside.
64. Danny M. Johnson, "Camp Kohler, California," *On Point* (Winter 2017): 46.
65. "Life Goes On as Usual in Relocation Camp," *Sacramento Bee*, July 18, 1942, 17.
66. McGowan, *History*, 310.
67. Steve Magagnini, "Detention Center Plaque Rededicated," *Sacramento Bee*, August 26, 2015, A3.
68. John Leggett, *A Daring Young Man: A Biography of William Saroyan* (New York: Alfred A. Knopf, 2002), 128.
69. Ibid., 129.
70. "Kohler Builds Village for Combat Training," *Sacramento Bee*, September 24, 1943, 23.
71. "Telephone Setup Is Installed for Forest Service," *Sacramento Bee*, June 24, 1944, 15.
72. "Relocation Head Rap's Chamber's Plea for Kohler," *Sacramento Bee*, November 7, 1945, 4.

Chapter 3

73. "McClellan Base Occupies Site of Historic Rancho," *Sacramento Bee*, March 1, 1961, M2.
74. *McClellan Air Force Base: 1936–1982, A Pictorial History* (Sacramento, CA: McClellan Air Force Base, 1982), 43.
75. *A Camera Trip through McClellan Field, California: A Picture Book of the Field and Its Activities* (Brooklyn, NY: Ullman Company, 1944), 2.
76. "Air Depot Shops Sign Up Women," *Sacramento Bee*, February 11, 1942, 14; Air Depot Announces Another Series of Aircraft Courses," *Sacramento Bee*, July 24, 1942, 3.
77. *Sacramento Air Depot: What New Workers Need to Know About S.A.D.* (Sacramento, CA: Sacramento Air Depot, 1942), 6.

78. Bonnie A. Olson, *Silver Anniversary History: Chronology, Sacramento Air Material Area, McClellan Air Force Base, California* (Sacramento, CA: McClellan Air Force Base, 1964).
79. "McClellan's Soldiers of Production Honored By Army, Governor Earl Warren at Huge Ceremony," *Command Post*, December 10, 1943, 1; "Big Military Rite at Air Depot Will Fete War Workers," *Sacramento Bee*, December 4, 1943, 1.
80. "Great Signal Corps Depot Operates Near Sacramento," *Sacramento Bee*, October 13, 1944, 1.
81. Myrtle Shaw Lord, *A Sacramento Saga: Fifty Years of Achievement* (Sacramento, CA: Sacramento Chamber of Commerce, 1946), 322.
82. "Concerns Work Round the Clock on War Contracts," *Sacramento Bee*, March 27, 1943, A7.
83. "Sacramento War Industries, Inc., Receives E Award for Efficient Production," *Sacramento Bee*, October 6, 1942, 6.
84. Long to Edward O. Strong, October 27, 1944, Edward O. Strong Collection, California State Library.
85. "War Work Will Continue to Present Many Problems to Public Works Department During the Year 1945," *California Highways and Public Works* 23, no. 1–2: 1945, 1.
86. Letter from donor Robert Rhodes to Sacramento Public Library, Margaret (Wilson) Rhodes photographs, PH 2017-30, Sacramento Room, Sacramento Public Library.
87. "Air Depot Will Bring Increase in Population," *Sacramento Bee*, June 16, 1941.
88. "Rules Adopted for Renting Homes in Housing Project," *Tribune-Progress*, March 5, 1942, 4.
89. "NYA Doing Vital Defense Job at the Sacramento Army Air Depot," *Desert Sun*, May 2, 1941, 4.
90. "School for Girl Machinists," *Sacramento Bee*, July 25, 1942, M5.
91. "Industries Must Call on Minorities," *Sacramento Bee*, October 17, 1942, 17.
92. "May Employ Women Laborers at Air Field," *Folsom Telegraph*, February 6, 1942.
93. Olson, *Silver Anniversary History*.
94. "National Leader Defends Right of Women to Work," *Sacramento Bee*, May 24, 1940, 14.
95. "It's A Women's War! Feminine Workers Are On Increase," *Command Post*, July 30, 1943, 1.

96. "Women Overhaul, Modernize Airplane by Themselves," *Sacramento Bee*, March 2, 1943, 23.
97. "Local Schools Ask for Nursery Assistance," *Sacramento Union*, April 10, 1943.
98. "In Charge of a War Melting Pot," *Sacramento Bee*, July 25, 1942, M5.
99. "Interracial USO Director Assumes Sacramento Post," *Sacramento Bee*, August 14, 1943, 2.
100. "VFW Post Protests Hiring of Objector," *Sacramento Bee*, February 15, 1946, 16.
101. "More Germans Will Be At McClellan," *Sacramento Bee*, March 23, 1946, 28.
102. "Escaped Germans Still Are Eluding Search Parties," *Sacramento Bee*, May 2, 1945, 2.
103. "War Work Contracts Are Awarded to Folsom Prison," *Folsom Telegraph*, December 4, 1942.
104. "Folsom Prison Artist Designs Shop Insignia," *Folsom Telegraph*, August 7, 1942, 2.
105. "West Must Plan to Own Postwar, Warren Tells Government Group," *Sacramento Union*, April 10, 1943.
106. "Local, State Officials Develop Postwar Plan," *Sacramento Union*, August 14, 1945.
107. Davis McEntire, *The Labor Force in California: A Study of Characteristics and Trends in Labor Force, Employment and Occupations in California, 1900–1950* (Berkeley: University of California Press, 1952), 10.
108. *Hub of Western Energy: Sacramento, California* (Sacramento, CA: Sacramento Chamber of Commerce, 1944), 25.

Chapter 4

109. Paul J.P. Sandul, "Both Country Town and Bustling Metropolis," in *River City and Valley Life*, edited by Christopher J. Castaneda and Lee M.A. Simpson (Pittsburgh: University of Pittsburgh Press, 2013), 189.
110. Ibid., 191.
111. "Co-operative Extension Work in Agriculture and Home Economics State of California, Sacramento County Annual Narrative Report, 1942," Sacramento County Cooperative Agricultural Extension Records 1979/041, Center for Sacramento History, 6 (hereafter "Co-operative Extension Work, *Year*").

112. Todd Holmes, "Rivers of Gold, Valley of Conquest," in *River City and Valley Life*, edited by Christopher J. Castaneda and Lee M.A. Simpson (Pittsburgh: University of Pittsburgh Press, 2013), 131.
113. "Precipitation for California-Sacramento County 1941–1945," Climate, Ecosystem and Fire Applications of the Desert Research Institute, accessed August 1, 2017, https://cefa.dri.edu/Westmap.
114. "Co-operative Extension Work, 1942," 6.
115. Carlos Alcala, *Sacramento Street Whys* (Sacramento, CA: Big Tomato Press, 2007), 138.
116. "Co-operative Extension Work, 1942," 21.
117. Ibid.
118. *Sacramento Bee*, "Sale of Farm Lands is Brisk," July 11, 1942, 16.
119. "Co-operative Extension Work, 1945," 16.
120. "Co-operative Extension Work, 1942," 21.
121. Ibid., 8.
122. "Co-operative Extension Work, 1944," 8.
123. "Co-operative Extension Work, 1942," 14.
124. Cheryl Anne Stapp, *Sacramento Chronicles: A Golden Past* (Charleston, SC: The History Press, 2013), 80–81.
125. "Many Sacramento Valley Hop Men Install Machines," *Sacramento Bee*, August 29, 1942, 14.
126. "Co-operative Extension Work, 1945," 7.
127. "Many Sacramento Valley Hop Men Install Machines," *Sacramento Bee*, August 29, 1942, 14.
128. "Leader Stresses Labor Shortage," *Sacramento Bee*, May 23, 1942, 16.
129. "Co-operative Extension Work, 1945," 2.
130. "Chicken Business Expands with Proper Handling," *Sacramento Bee*, August 15, 1942, 14.
131. "Sacramento Farm News: Rationing of Farm Machinery," *Sacramento Bee*, October 3, 1942, 18.
132. "Sacramento Farm News: Farm Machinery," *Sacramento Bee*, January 10, 1942, 16.
133. Ibid.
134. Judith M. Taylor, *The Olive in California* (Berkeley, CA: Ten Speed Press, 1999), 190.
135. "Harvest of Oil Olives Is in Full Swing in Valley," *Sacramento Bee*, January 10, 1942, 16.
136. "Pear Shipping Problems Will Be Given Study," *Sacramento Bee*, January 10, 1942, 16.

137. Cheryl Anne Stapp, *Sacramento Chronicles: A Golden Past* (Charleston: History Press, 2013), 82.
138. Avella, *Sacramento*, 108.
139. Ibid., 109.
140. "Canneries Need 90 Women This Evening," *Sacramento Bee*, August 21, 1943, 18.
141. "Here Is Your Chance to Help Women; Join the WTP," *Sacramento Bee*, October 1, 1942, 4.
142. Christopher T. Hiroto, "The Evacuation and Relocation of the West Coast Japanese During World War II—How It Happened" (special project, United States Army War College, Carlisle Barracks, Pennsylvania, 1991), 4.
143. Ibid., 5.
144. Ibid.
145. Bill Hosokawa, *Nisei: The Quiet Americans* (Boulder: University Press of Colorado, 2002), 112.
146. Benjamin J. Patterson, *Ethnic Groups USA* (Bloomington, IN: Xlibris Corporation, 2008), 167.
147. Co-operative Extension Work, 1942," 2.
148. Ibid.
149. Maggie Riechers, "War Stories: The American People in World War II," *Humanities* 28, no. 4 (2007): 4.
150. "Co-operative Extension Work, 1942," 10.
151. Ibid., 21.
152. Ibid., 10.
153. Ibid.
154. Congressional Record, *Furlough to Servicemen to Aid Agriculture* (Washington D.C.: United States 78th Congress, First Session, 1943), 1–18.
155. "Ranchers Urge Draft Deferments for Farm Labor," *Sacramento Bee*, February 18, 1942, 16.
156. Avella, *Sacramento*, 108.
157. "Co-operative Extension Work, 1944," 5.
158. Avella, *Sacramento*, 108.
159. Ernesto Galarza, *Barrio Boy* (South Bend, IN: University of Notre Dame Press, 1991), 172.
160. "Co-operative Extension Work, 1942" 6.
161. Galarza, *Barrio Boy*, 172.
162. "Co-operative Extension Work, 1945," 5.
163. Ibid.

164. "Co-operative Extension Work, 1946," 1.
165. "Co-operative Extension Work, 1945," 6–7.
166. *Sacramento Bee*, "Fruit Men Like Boy Volunteers," June 20, 1942, 16.
167. "Co-operative Extension Work, 1944," 20.
168. "Co-operative Extension Work, 1943," 6.
169. "Co-operative Extension Work, 1946," 20.
170. Avella, *Sacramento*, 108.
171. Lori A. Flores, "A Town Full of Dead Mexicans: The Salinas Valley Bracero Tragedy of 1963, the End of the Bracero Program, and the Evolution of California's Chicano Movement," *Western Historical Quarterly* 44, no. 2 (2013): 124–43.
172. Judith M. Taylor, *The Olive in California* (Berkeley, CA: Ten Speed Press, 1999), 190.
173. Richard A. Walker, *The Conquest of Bread: 150 Years of Agribusiness in California* (New York: New Press, 2004), 246.
174. Ibid., 247.
175. Ibid.
176. Ibid., 246.
177. "After 120 Years Orangevale's Last Commercial Orchards to Close," *Sacramento Bee*, August 16, 2017, B1.

Chapter 5

178. Paul J.P. Sandul, "Both Country Town and Bustling Metropolis," in *River City and Valley Life*, edited by Christopher J. Castaneda and Lee M.A. Simpson (Pittsburgh: University of Pittsburgh Press, 2013), 164.
179. Todd Holmes, "Rivers of Gold, Valley of Conquest," in Castaneda and Simpson, *River City and Valley Life*, 128.
180. Sandul, "Both Country Town," 158.
181. Titus Fay Cronise, *The Natural Wealth of California* (San Francisco: H.H. Bancroft and Company, 1868), 309.
182. Joseph A. McGowan and Terry R. Willis, *Sacramento: Heart of the Golden State* (Woodland Hills: Windsor Publications, 1983), 10.
183. Sandul, "Both Country Town," 163.
184. Ibid., 164.
185. Dylan O. Burge, "Botanical Diversity of the California Floristic Province," *Manzanita* 21, no. 1 (2017): 1, 12–13.
186. Holmes, "Rivers of Gold," 128.

187. Sandul, "Both Country Town," 165.
188. "Co-operative Extension Work, 1942," 10.
189. "Points Rationing of Processed Fruits and Vegetables," Sally Zentner Family Papers, MC 49, Sacramento Room, Sacramento Public Library.
190. "99 Ways to Share the Meat," Sally Zentner Family Papers, MC 49, Sacramento Room, Sacramento Public Library.
191. Michelle Obama, *American Grown* (New York: Crown Publishing, 2012), 29.
192. "Victory Gardens," *Sacramento Bee*, March 5, 1942, 8.
193. "Gardens for Victory Will Be Club Topic," *Sacramento Bee*, March 21, 1942, 9.
194. "Victory Garden Class will be Conducted Here," *Sacramento Bee*, December 22, 1942, 16.
195. "Library Has Books on All Phases of the War Situation," *Sacramento Bee*, March 21, 1942, 13.
196. "Clean Up and Plant Week is Proclaimed," *Sacramento Bee*, April 8, 1942, 11.
197. "Co-operative Extension Work, 1942," 21.
198. "Victory Garden Intentions Are Signed by 200," *Sacramento Bee*, November 17, 1942, 16.
199. Ibid.
200. "310 War Industry Families Move into New Helvetia," *Sacramento Bee*, August 27, 1942, A3.
201. "15,000 Victory Gardens Are Growing in Sacramento," *Sacramento Bee*, February 17, 1943, 39.
202. "Five Lot Owners Offer Space for Victory Gardens," *Sacramento Bee*, March 28, 1944, 3.
203. "Co-operative Extension Work, 1943," 10.
204. "Victory Vegetable Gardens Command Wide Interest," *Sacramento Bee*, April 8, 1942, 10.
205. "Victory Gardens Call for New Ideas about Vegetables," *Sacramento Bee*, May 26, 1942, 3.
206. "The Nut Season Appears," *Sacramento Bee*, November 10, 1942, 16.
207. "Nautical Denim," *Sacramento Bee*, May 1, 1942, 5.
208. "Victory Garden Awards Are Made," *Sacramento Bee*, June 12, 1942, 12.
209. "Stray Dogs Are to Be Thrown into Pound," *Sacramento Bee*, May 26, 1944, 3.
210. Ibid.
211. "Co-operative Extension Work, 1942," 5.

212. "Governor Makes First Entry in Victory Garden Festival," *Sacramento Bee*, July 10, 1943, 17.
213. "Finishing Touches Are Put on Bee's Garden Festival," *Sacramento Bee*, August 3, 1943, 1.
214. Ibid.
215. "Garden Festival Opens with Record Displays," *Sacramento Bee*, August 3, 1944, 1.
216. Ibid.
217. "Victory Garden Film." Sacramento History Online, accessed September 29, 2017, http://www.sacramentohistory.org/films_victory.html.
218. "Victory Garden Motion Picture Will Be Previewed," *Sacramento Bee*, November 15, 1944, 7.
219. *Gardening for Victory*, 16mm film, directed by Robert Handsaker, 1943, KFBK/Sacramento Bee, Center for Sacramento History, https://archive.org/details/casacsh_000021.
220. "Victory Garden Motion Picture Will Be Previewed," *Sacramento Bee*, November 15, 1944, 7.
221. Stephen Andrew, *The Japanese Army, 1931–45* (Oxford, UK: Osprey Publishing, 2002), 6.
222. "Harvest Festival Presents Exhibits, Entertainment," *Sacramento Bee*, August 4, 1945, 10.
223. Ibid.
224. "Hiram Johnson Dies of Stroke in Navy Hospital," *Sacramento Bee*, August 6, 1945, 1.
225. "McClatchy Radio Group, Papers Get Garden Award," *Sacramento Bee*, December 19, 1945, 4.
226. Ibid.
227. Membership records 1968–1970, California Native Plant Society, accessed September 16, 2016.
228. Rachel Carson, *Silent Spring* (New York: Houghton Mifflin, 2002), 297.

Chapter 6

229. Jack Voss, interview by James Scott, tape recording, Sacramento, California, June 21, 2003.
230. Ibid.
231. Ibid.

232. Ibid.
233. Ibid.
234. Ibid.
235. Ibid.
236. Ibid.
237. Ted Bell, "It Took Him 32 Years to Get a Print," *Sacramento Bee*, January 13, 1978, 24.
238. Philip P. Choy, *Canton Footprints: Sacramento's Chinese Legacy* (Sacramento, CA: Chinese American Council of Sacramento, 2008), 134.
239. Joe Wayne Fong, interview by James Scott, tape recording, Sacramento, California, May 15, 2002.
240. Tom Arden, "For Whom the Bell…," *Sacramento Bee*, May 26, 1972, B2.
241. Voss, interview.

Conclusion

242. "NSGW Protest Against Return of Nipponese," *Sacramento Bee*, April 6, 1945, 5.
243. "Legion Stand on Kohler Draws Ire of WRA Official," *Sacramento Bee*, November 8, 1945, 16.
244. "Bob Fletcher Dies at 101; Saved Farms of Interned Japanese Americans," *Los Angeles Times*, June 3, 2013.
245. "Cheers for a Hero at his 100th Birthday Celebration," *Sacramento Bee*, July 25, 2011, B1.
246. George S. Craft Jr., *CSUS: The First Forty Years, 1947–1987* (Sacramento, CA: Hornet Foundation, 1987), 11.
247. Ibid., 14.
248. "Vital Questions of Post War Era Are Confronting People," *Catholic Herald*, September 1945, 3.
249. *Forecasting a City's Future: Sacramento, California* (Sacramento: California State Reconstruction and Reemployment Commission, 1946), 17–18.
250. Richard S. Peterson, *Growth of Sacramento County, 1940–1970* (San Francisco, CA: Bank of America, 1961), 6.

INDEX

D

E

F

G

H

I

J

K

L

M

N

O

P

R

S

T

U

V

W

Y

ABOUT THE AUTHORS

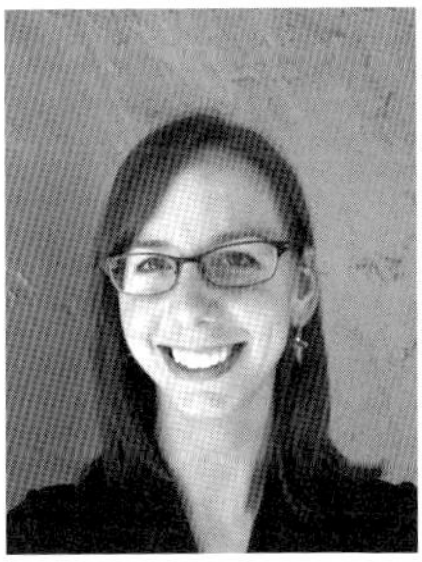

AMANDA G. DEWILDE has served as the archivist for the Special Collections of the Sacramento Public Library since 2010, working in the Sacramento Room of the Central Library. DeWilde earned her bachelor's degree in history from Southern Oregon University and her master's degree in information studies with an emphasis in archival studies from the University of Texas at Austin. She resides in Folsom with her husband and daughter.

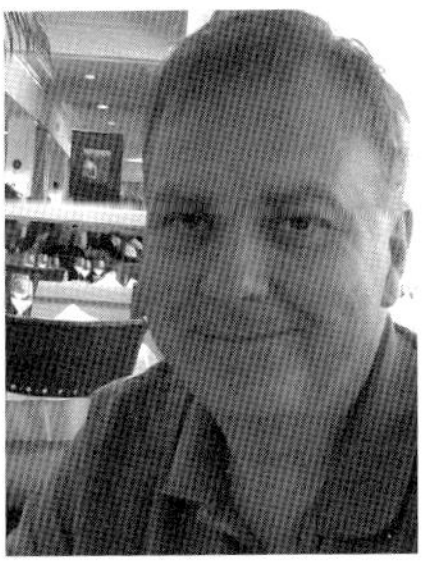

ERIC WEBB has been with the Sacramento Public Library since 2001, and he currently serves as a circulation supervisor. He completed his undergraduate and graduate studies in history and humanities at Sacramento State University. He resides in Sacramento with his wife and beloved native plant garden.

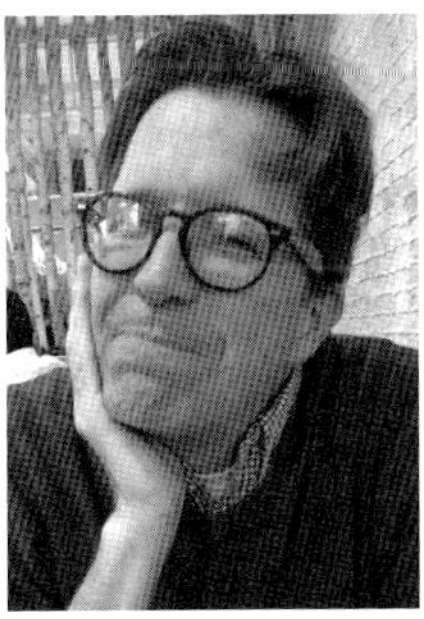

JAMES C. SCOTT has been a reference librarian with the Sacramento Public Library since 2000. For most of that period, he has worked in SPL's Sacramento Room, where he's coauthored five other books on Sacramento history. He holds a bachelor's degree in history and political science from Marquette University, and has master's degrees in European history and information science. He lives in East Sacramento with his wife, son and a black-and-tan dachshund called Schweinsteiger.

Set in the original 1917 Carnegie Foundation–funded section of the Sacramento Public Library, the Sacramento Room was founded in 1995 as an archives and special collections for primary and secondary research materials relative to the history of the Sacramento Region. Its rare book, book art, map, city directory, photograph, digital and manuscript collections make it one of the premier spots for historical research in Northern California. The Sacramento Room can be visited online at www.saclibrary.org/locations/sacramento-room.

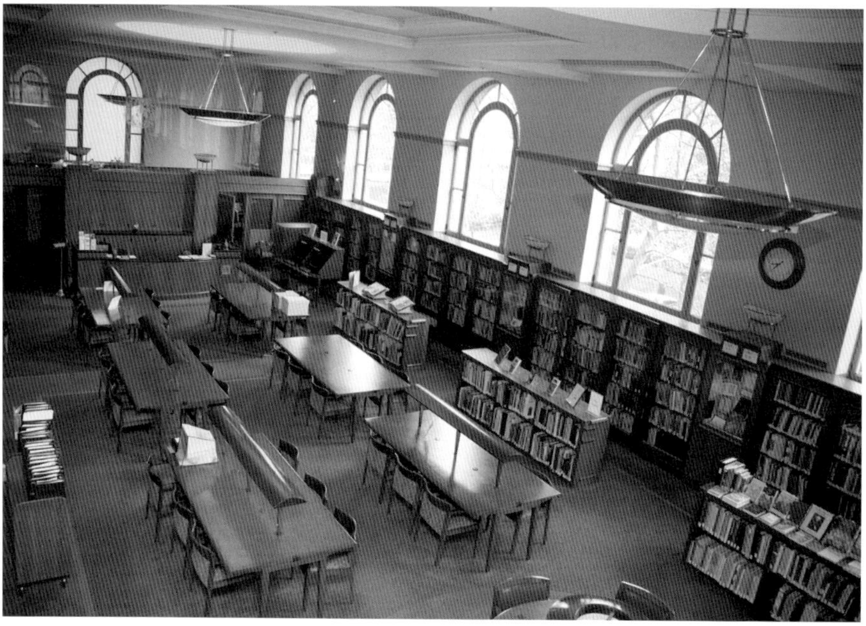